Canada, the United States, and Cuba: An Evolving Relationship

edited by

Sahadeo Basdeo and Heather N. Nicol

North·South Center Press
UNIVERSITY OF MIAMI

The publisher of this book is the North-South Center Press at the University of Miami.

The mission of The Dante B. Fascell North-South Center is to promote better relations and serve as a catalyst for change among the United States, Canada, and the nations of Latin America and the Caribbean by advancing knowledge and understanding of the major political, social, economic, and cultural issues affecting the nations and peoples of the Western Hemisphere.

© 2002 North-South Center Press at the University of Miami. Published by the North-South Center Press at the University of Miami and distributed by Lynne Rienner Publishers, Inc., 1800 30th Street, Suite 314, Boulder, CO 80301-1026. All rights reserved under International and Pan-American Conventions. No portion of the contents may be reproduced or transmitted in any form, or by any means, including photocopying, recording, or any electronic information storage retrieval system, without prior permission in writing from the North-South Center Press.

All copyright inquiries should be addressed to the publisher: North-South Center Press, 1500 Monza Avenue, Coral Gables, Florida 33146-3027, U.S.A., phone 305-284-8912, fax 305-284-5089, or e-mail mmapes@miami.edu.

To order or to return books, contact Lynne Rienner Publishers, Inc., 1800 30th Street, Suite 314, Boulder, CO 80301-1026, 303-444-6684, fax 303-444-0824. Lynne Rienner Publishers is the distributor for books published by the North-South Center Press.

Library of Congress Cataloging-in-Publication Data

Canada, the United States, and Cuba: an evolving relationship/ edited by Sahadeo Basdeo and Heather N. Nicol.

p. cm.

Includes bibliographical references and index.

ISBN 1-57454-103-X (hc:alk.paper)

1. United States—Foreign relations—Cuba. 2. Cuba—Foreign relations—United States. 3. Canada—Foreign relations—Cuba. 4. Cuba—Foreign relations—Canada. 5. United States—Foreign relations—Canada. 6. Canada—Foreign relations—United States. 7. United States—Foreign relations—1989- I. Basdeo, Sahadeo. II. Nicol, Heather N. (Heather Nora), 1953-

E183.8.C9 C28 2002

327.7307291—dc21   2002070324

Printed in the United States of America/TS/6/02

∞ The paper used in this publication meets the requirements of the American National Standards for Information Sciences — Permanence of Paper for Printed Library Materials, ANSI Z39.48.1984.

07 06 05 04 03 02   6 5 4 3 2 1

Contents

Canada, the United States, and Cuba: An Introduction

SAHADEO BASDEO AND HEATHER N. NICOL

With the passing of the Cold War and the recognition of a new world order, it has become increasingly clear that the relationship between Cuba and its North American neighbors will be transformed in the new millennium. In fact, all frames of reference in this relationship have changed considerably — some overnight and some over a more protracted period. These changes are significant not only for U.S. and Canadian citizens, who now must view this neighboring island nation in new ways, but they are also significant for Cubans.

Even though change may be inevitable in the evolving relationship among Canada, Cuba, and the United States, no consensus exists as to what the future holds in store for this three-part connection. The essays in this volume demonstrate just this point, approaching the topic of Cuba-United States and Cuba-Canada relations from very different perspectives and proffering divergent insights into the nature and direction of change. In fact, in the course of writing this book, many of the contributors had to rethink their perspectives. Since we began this project, an important change in political orientation occurred within the United States, with the replacement of the Bill Clinton administration (1993-2001) by the George W. Bush administration. While the Clinton White House was sensitive to general problems in the implementation of Title III of the Cuban Liberty and Democratic Solidarity (LIBERTAD) Act (Helms-Burton), the Bush government, has signaled that it will approach the "Cuba problem" in its own way, leading Cuba-watchers to speculate about what this means for U.S.-Cuba relations.

This era of uncertainty and conflicting viewpoints is, however, by no means unique. Changing times, changing administrations, and changing conditions characterize the new climate of international relations, and in this era of post-modern scholarship, a book such as this can use contradictory analyses to heighten, rather than diminish, our understanding of the evolving relationship among Cuba, Canada, and the United States. While exploring the discordant notes that have developed among the three countries, this volume sees these contradictions as a means of identifying the ongoing political processes that contribute to the evolving relationship, amidst the triangle's tensions and cooperation.

This volume begins by outlining the nature of the evolving relationship and developing an appreciation of its significance. As Hal Klepak observes in Chapter One, the fundamental changes that have occurred in Cuba, particularly those that influence economic, social, and security issues, have catapulted the Cuban state into a new, increasingly international arena. Cubans have been called upon to develop new approaches to their North American relations, as a result of the political, economic, social, and cultural currents that swept the island in the aftermath of the collapse of the Soviet Union and in consequence of the evolution of a new global economy.

In Klepak's analysis, Cubans and their government have had to reinvent responses to an ongoing U.S. political agenda for the island, based upon misunderstandings against a background of U.S. intervention in Cuba. He argues that the ongoing nature of U.S. intervention has created conditions of penury that actually threaten the continuation of the Special Period and suggests that if one examines the Cuban security agenda in detail, it is clear that the new response is a mixture of old and new approaches. The main difference lies in the fact that "during the time of the old challenges, a more united Cuban people were joined to vastly greater resources in order to face the various crises." He is concerned that in addition to the traditional problem of U.S. enmity, new challenges will arise as Cuban armed forces are confronted with an explosive social scene fueled by ongoing economic problems.

What has been or will be the impact of these changes upon Cuba's North American neighbors? In Chapter Two, Sahadeo Basdeo and Ian Hesketh suggest that changes in Canada-Cuba relations at the beginning of the twenty-first century represent less a break with the past and more a reaffirmation that the two countries, despite their differences, continue to have more in common than otherwise. They explain that domestic politics in Canada only recently have created instability and inconsistency in traditional Canadian relations with Cuba, these being the result of actions by Canadian Prime Minister Jean Chrétien, who was anxious to appease political opposition at home. Chrétien pressured Cuban leader Fidel Castro for human rights concessions in Cuba at a time when to do so was disadvantageous to the Cuban government. Still, as Basdeo and Hesketh argue, "constructive engagement" has been a time-honored approach of Canadian parliamentarians to Cuba relations, and the historical record still stands Canada in good stead with Cuba, particularly because Canadians have resisted U.S. pressure to isolate Cuba economically and politically, at least until recently. They conclude, "Nothing has altered the Canada-Cuba relationship radically, . . . the recent human rights wrangle notwithstanding."

This argument is countered by Peter McKenna, John M. Kirk, and Christine Climenhage in Chapter Three. These scholars are much less optimistic. In fact, they suggest that the break over the human rights agenda and the chill in bilateral relations between Canada and Cuba are neither reversible nor inevitable. Some clearly identifiable problem areas exist in the Canada-Cuba relationship, the authors argue, including Cuba's failure to realize Canada as a valuable ally in North America because of Cuba's preoccupation with the United States. The result may well be a protracted chilly relationship, which will see Canada committed to constructive engagement but somewhat ineffective in stimulating movement along the human rights front.

In Chapter Four, Stephen J. Randall discusses the continuing relationship between the United States and Cuba in the context of the post-Cold War transition. Framing his analysis within this broader period, Randall suggests that despite all that is new, the stability that has followed the Cold War has not ended Castro's hold on power, while bilateral relations with the United States "remain only slightly less strained than they were when Castro nationalized foreign property and allied his government with the Soviet Union." The so-called peace dividends provided by the end of the Cold War did little to change the U.S.-Cuba relationship. Improved relations during this period have proved elusive. While the issue of the *balseros* (rafters) has been dealt with, the public controversy surrounding Elián González's return to Cuba in 1999-2000 demonstrated how Cuba remains an emotional as well as a political issue for U.S. citizens, particularly for Cuban-Americans.

Daniel W. Fisk observes in Chapter Five that the situation is not so clear-cut, reflecting as it does the undercurrents of a dynamic U.S. political scene fraught with changes in domestic and international agendas. Fisk suggests that it is fair to ask how much longer the U.S. embargo can persist, given the evolving climate of U.S.-Cuba relations since the Helms-Burton Act was passed. While, prior to fall 2000, it was evident that supporters of the embargo were losing ground, Fisk suggests, "The election of George W. Bush and 'Elián's revenge,' however, did change the political calculus." Moreover, Bush has claimed that his position on Cuba has "less to do with political expediency" and more to do with "moral" certainty, thus reinserting notions of U.S. morality and nationalism into the Cuba debate. This constitutes a "red flag" as far as Cuba is concerned and may only further strain relations between the two nations. As Fisk observes, the Cuba debate in Congress is not going to disappear, but it may play itself out in unexpected ways. Like Klepak and Randall, Fisk sees traditional attitudes, politics, and history as important factors in how the United States will respond to Cuban initiatives during the new millennium.

To Karl B. Koth, the Special Period in Cuba represents more than a temporary pragmatism. It is a longer-term response, as the Cuban state adjusts to sweeping changes in the post-Soviet, post-Cold War era. Synonymous with the concept of socialism via an opening to tourist dollars, this opening highlights the efforts of the government to come to terms with neoliberalism in ways that are distinctly Cuban. In Chapter Six, Koth observes that "the government continually searches for ways to satisfy the people's demands without generating the attendant drawbacks that more capitalism has brought and will bring in its train," indicating that the Special Period in Cuba is probably here to stay.

While the papers in this collection are diverse, often contradictory, and represent very different national and scholarly viewpoints, some observations can be made among all positions. In the concluding chapter, Heather N. Nicol suggests that differing Canadian and U.S. positions on Cuba (many of which are reflected in this volume), as well as the political discourses that support the international agendas of both states, have undergone profound changes since 1996. The end result is that rather than one defining narrative to which all Canadian, U.S., or even Cuban citizens subscribe, remarkably divergent popular and formal political discourses have flowered. Nicol suggests that Canadians have moved to the right on Cuba issues, while the U.S. perspective has become somewhat more liberal. As a result, a new diversity is found in the media and in formal political debates in both countries. Such a shift may or may not prompt new ways of defining relations between Cuba and its North American neighbors, but it does allow for widely differing opinions, perceptions, and actions at all levels. As such, new possibilities for international relations emerge.

In the final analysis, it is difficult to say what the new millennium will bring. Will it bring stability in the face of political, social, and economic development? Will it bring considerable changes in relations among the three countries? The chapters in this volume present the case for both scenarios — a reaffirmation of or a radical break with the past. However, perhaps more important than the presentation of these divergent viewpoints is the hope that we may begin to understand where and how the viewpoints diverge and why one interpretation of events or one set of analyses is no more real than another. This volume represents an effort to begin to address the problems of why the Canada-Cuba-United States relationship is so complex and how it is constantly evolving.

As this book was going to press, former U.S. President Jimmy Carter visited Cuba from May 13 through May 17, 2002. On May 14, Carter delivered a speech in Spanish at the University of Havana; Castro was in attendance. The speech was televised live in Cuba and printed in *Granma* the following day. The English translation was provided by The Carter Center and made available worldwide by the Associated Press on May 15. It is our hope that Carter's diplomacy will reap benefits for the Cuban people and for future relations among Canada, Cuba, and the United States. The following excerpts from Carter's momentous speech set an appropriate tone for this volume:

> . . . The hard truth is that neither the United States nor Cuba has managed to define a positive and beneficial relationship. . . . There are some in Cuba who think the simple answer is for the United States to lift the embargo, and there are some in my country who believe the answer is for your president to step down from power and allow free elections. . . . my hope is that the Congress will soon act to permit unrestricted travel between the United States and Cuba, establish open trading relationships, and repeal the embargo. I should add that these restraints are not the source of Cuba's economic problems.

> . . . Today, almost every country in the Americas is a democracy. I am not using a U.S. definition of 'democracy.' The term is embedded in the Universal Declaration of Human Rights, which Cuba signed in 1948. . . . It is based on some simple premises: all citizens are born with the right to choose their own leaders, to define their own destiny, to speak freely, to organize political parties, trade unions and non-governmental groups, and to have fair and open trials. . . . Your constitution recognizes freedom of speech and association, but other laws deny these freedoms to those who disagree with the government.

> . . . It is gratifying to note that Articles 63 and 88 of your constitution allow citizens to petition the National Assembly to permit a referendum to change laws if 10,000 or more citizens sign it. I am informed that such an effort, called the Varela Project, has gathered sufficient signatures and has presented such a petition to the National Assembly. When Cubans exercise this freedom to change laws peacefully by a direct vote, the world will see that Cubans, and not foreigners, will decide the future of this country.

> . . . After 43 years of animosity, we hope that someday soon, you can reach across the great divide that separates our two countries and say, 'We are ready to join the community of democracies,' and I hope that Americans will soon open our arms to you and say, 'We welcome you as our friends.'

Part I.
Cuba in the Wider World

CHAPTER ONE

Cuba's New Security Agenda: Much New, Much Old

HAL KLEPAK

INTRODUCTION

S oon after the triumph of the Cuban Revolution in early 1959, it became only too
clear to policymakers in the United States that the new government of Fidel
Castro was determined to carry out reforms that were both damaging to U.S.
interests and generally unacceptable to Washington.[1] Although many in the U.S.
Department of State and the Department of Defense called for moderation and
patience, a host of misunderstandings (added to the historical background of U.S.
intervention in Cuba) propelled the two countries along a path that led to the longest-
lasting ostracism of any country in the modern history of the Americas.

The ensuing conflict soon had a security dimension as well, with the United
States determined to unseat what it saw as Castro's communist and pro-Soviet
dictatorship. Meanwhile, Castro found ways to hold on to power despite the fierce
hostility of the greatest power in the world, situated a mere 90 miles away from the
island. For more than 40 years, the new Cuban government would be forced to take
a series of new responses to the various manifestations of U.S. hostility, while the
Cuban armed forces themselves were sent on tasks never before imagined — and
completely out of keeping with Cuba's size, resources, and real or even potential
power.

Facing the mightiest nation in the world, Cuba pursued imaginative and
taxing initiatives (both politically and in terms of military organization and strategy)
in order to deter Washington from attack or, if this failed, to make such an operation
as risky and expensive as possible for the United States. Most dramatically, on the
political front, this involved increasingly close military connections with the Soviet
Union and other Warsaw Pact countries — linkages that would completely reshape
Cuba's defense policy and armed forces. In terms of strategy, tactics, deployments,
and military organization, extraordinary political moves were combined with an
equally dramatic military transformation.

This chapter briefly traces the evolution of Cuban defense policy and military
affairs and then compares the current security agenda and the changes it represents
to those of earlier years. The study will focus on the major shifts in emphasis that
were occasioned by the evolving and sometimes exploding contexts that Cuba's
military leaders were obliged to face, particularly in dealing with their powerful

U.S. neighbor. Of course, no real *war* between the two countries has taken place during the period under review. Only once, in Grenada in 1983, did Cuban and U.S. soldiers actually fire upon one another. At every stage, however, the story has included a security element. That part of the story, especially recent developments, will be explored below.

THE ARMED FORCES OF CUBA BEFORE 1959

Defense issues have been crucial in Cuban politics since Christopher Columbus arrived on the island of Cuba in 1492. For Spain, military conquest was followed quickly by a need to defend the island from pirates and corsairs from France, the Netherlands, and Great Britain. By the eighteenth century, Cuba saw serious military assaults, one of which gave western Cuba and Havana to Great Britain after a short campaign in 1762.

Although restored to Spain in 1763, within a half-century, Cuba was the scene of a number of failed revolts against the mother country. These revolts had as their backdrop the wars of independence in continental Spanish America and the new, independent life of those countries after 1826. Major wars flared in Cuba from 1868 to 1878 and from 1895 to 1898, the year in which the United States temporarily seized the island from Spain, giving it "paper independence" four years later.

Revolutions and coups d'état marked the years after 1902. A half century later, in the years before Castro's victory in January 1959, two armies were in Cuba. The first was the regular army of the Cuban state, which was under the presidency of the former sergeant, then general, commander-in-chief, and dictator Fulgencio Batista y Zaldívar. The other army was that of Castro, the insurgent leader whose 26th of July Movement had both a "field army" essentially located in the mountains of the Sierra Maestra in Oriente Province and an "urban resistance branch" in the towns and cities of virtually the entire island. The regular army was the successor of the small force trained and equipped by the United States when it occupied the island in 1898-1902. The occupation had given the U.S. military an opportunity to shape the organization, doctrine, training, equipment, weapons, and, of course, politics of the Cuban armed forces.[2]

Later training missions ensured that U.S. influence remained even when actual occupation was not undertaken. Indeed, the naval base at Guantánamo acted as the seat of a U.S. military presence on the island long after Cuba's nominal independence. The Cuban army was highly politicized, deeply affected by the instability of the republic in its first five decades, and split by political and racial issues. In addition, it never reached a high degree of military efficiency, although Cuba declared war on the side of the United States in both world wars and is credited with sinking a Nazi submarine during World War II.[3]

This Cuban army, fresh from installing Batista in power in 1952, soon was facing the growth of an insurgent movement under Castro, a young and charismatic lawyer full of reformist zeal. After a series of major reverses, Castro began to build a true insurgent force in the Sierra Maestra, fighting off a number of government attempts to dislodge him. In the final two years before 1959, he was able to increase his attacks and, in the last months of the insurgency, to begin a major campaign moving toward the center of the island and the capture of real power. His army of *barbudos* (bearded ones) proved more than a match for Batista's dispirited army and won victory after victory along the way.[4] Equally important, significant urban terrorist activity ensured that the Cuban people knew a civil war was occurring and that the government was incapable of bringing the insurgents to heel.

From their modest beginning as a force using hit-and-run tactics to obtain arms and munitions and to score small victories against the regular army, the *barbudos* gained strength and confidence, allowing them to sustain the costs of a more open campaign in the last months of the war.[5] This determined little army finally defeated Batista, forced him into exile, and occupied Havana in the early days of January 1959.

THE NEW ARMY

Castro lost little time in getting rid of the old army. By disbanding army and air force units, firing and even shooting a number of commanders, and taking little interest in the integration of old cadres into his own forces, Castro ensured the establishment of an army whose loyalty undoubtedly belonged to the new government and to him personally.[6] While the old navy was to a very slight extent spared the purge, due to its mutiny against Batista during the Revolution and its tiny role in the Batista counterinsurgency campaign, loyalty to the new regime was the benchmark for further service. Relatively few naval officers could meet the test.

At first, the new army was hardly the Castro's regime's main preoccupation. Radical reforms of other kinds took priority. Castro's deeply cutting agrarian reforms and his nationalization of the holdings of pro-Batista Cubans and foreigners created a highly disgruntled upper class and a suspicious international investment community. Furthermore, Castro's political moves, placing all power in the hands of the 26th of July Movement and thus of Castro himself and his collaborators, quickly ensured that this disenchantment found expression in a mass exodus of the upper class and much of the middle class. Added to this was the growing dissatisfaction of the United States, a country long accustomed to calling the tune in Havana but now finding it difficult to do so. Moreover, the United States was also encountering difficulty in convincing Castro that he would have to "toe the line," as all of his predecessors had done.

In the context of mounting, vociferous domestic and foreign opposition, the Castro government began to take the armed forces more seriously. The young revolutionary leader was unsure which way to go to improve Cuban defenses, while Ernesto "Che" Guevara apparently preferred to count on a militia as the main arm of the armed forces. Trying first to arm his military forces with U.S. purchases, Castro was rebuffed by the United States. Attempts to do so through other North Atlantic Treaty Organization (NATO) or Western countries were unsuccessful because these nations were either frightened of the United States or uninterested in supplying arms to Cuba for reasons of their own. Only some members of the Warsaw Pact showed any interest in selling weapons to Castro, and, even there, key circles were reluctant. For the time being, there was to be no such support.[7]

The famous visit to Havana by Soviet leader Anastas Mikoyan,[8] in early 1960, resulted in considerable support on the industrial and agricultural fronts but regarding military equipment, it became clear to Castro that the Soviets were determined to move slowly until they could judge Washington's reactions more clearly. Although no major moves were made toward ideological alignment with Moscow that year, there could be little doubt that the Soviet connection was now to be a real one.

In March 1960, President Dwight D. Eisenhower (1953-1961) accepted the Central Intelligence Agency (CIA) recommendation of a program to arm and train Cuban exiles, signaling, after 15 months of hesitation, U.S. determination to break Castro by whatever means necessary. U.S.-Cuba relations continued to decline for the rest of 1960, with nationalization of private property and companies proceeding at such a pace that Cuba no longer could be ranked as a capitalist country by the end of that year. A series of small but noisy protests, one or two of which were qualified in Miami as uprisings, took place over the next months. Some executions by firing-squad of active armed dissidents followed, most without due process. Castro increasingly talked of anti-revolutionary plots supported by Washington and of the likelihood of a future U.S. invasion. In view of this claim, the Cuban press was silenced in May, and nonessential personnel of the U.S. embassy, along with their dependents, were removed in late September.

A proper Ministry of Defense was established in October 1960 and placed under Castro's brother, Raúl Castro. An early revolutionary militia scheme was instituted, with youth and student corps attached, while the revolutionary army was given more serious training.[9] At the same time, the regular army was reduced in size and reorganized. Clearly, the militia was to grow and expand its influence in order to ensure loyalty in an armed force that was being asked to accept changes at a bewildering rate, changes that often were far from the objectives for which many of its personnel thought the Revolution had been fought.

A volunteer militia some 150,000 strong was the result, training and guarding vital points of the country for variously assigned periods every week. The regular army seemed more and more divided about the future of the Revolution, especially its leftward march. Soon ubiquitous on the island, the militia may have appeared poorly trained, but clearly it was superbly motivated. Castro now had his loyal armed force.[10]

Relations with the United States were broken off in January 1961. In April of that year, the U.S.-backed Bay of Pigs invasion force came ashore on the southerly Playa Girón and met ferocious resistance from the Cuban military. CIA analyses of the political situation in Cuba proved to be entirely off the mark when they predicted that considerable opposition to Castro existed in Cuba and that a landing would spark a serious uprising, which then could be supported by the United States to oust the troublesome leader easily. Instead, following more carefully framed predictions by U.S. armed forces analysts, the Cuban people did not rise up or openly oppose Castro, and the Cuban military made quick work of the exiles who took part in the invasion.[11] The militia, including the least trained elements, performed remarkably well and justified Castro's faith in the existing mobilization system. The Bay of Pigs invasion was an unmitigated disaster that massively reinforced not only the Cuban government but also the message Castro had been giving the Cuban people, namely, that a U.S. invasion was a real possibility and would have to be prepared for on a permanent basis.[12]

In the wake of the fighting, Castro was able to get an even tighter hold on the armed forces and sell them on the need for massive reform of the institution, tighter linkages with the rising Communist Party, and acceptance of Soviet models in most aspects of military life. Officers who resisted these trends either were not favored or simply removed.

His prestige immensely reinforced, Castro in only a few weeks' time declared the Marxist-Leninist nature of his regime and proclaimed the absolute necessity to militarize Cuban society, in order to deter or defeat further inevitable U.S. attempts to unseat him and turn back the tide of the Cuban Revolution.[13] A vast scheme for the expansion of the regular forces, the creation of several levels of reserve troops, and expansion of the size and activities of enormous worker- and student-based militias were undertaken in the post-Bay of Pigs context.

President John F. Kennedy's administration (1961-1964), beginning with the Bay of Pigs invasion, which solidified Castro's hold on the island, were years of continued frozen relations between Washington and Havana. The island's government moved steadily toward full-blown socialism, and further plots were hatched to unseat Castro.

Early in 1962, Cuba faced expulsion from the inter-American system at the Punta del Este meeting of the Organization of American States, a conference that attempted to decide what to do about the Castro regime.[14] Cuba responded with the Second Declaration of Havana, calling on the Latin American people to rise up against their "masters" and join Cuba in the drive to oust the United States from its dominant position in the hemisphere. The "export of revolution" phase of Cuban foreign policy had begun. Castro's thinking was that, as in the cases of the French and Soviet revolutions and in the face of opposition to its existence by virtually all its neighbors, Cuba was obliged to try to overthrow their governments and install others that would be more accepting of the Cuban Revolution — or, even better, would accept the Revolution's goals as common ones for the region. As a result, the armed forces began to play a more active role in training exiles and dissidents from various Latin American countries.[15] Alongside these foreign policy moves, the rest of 1962 saw major efforts to communize the state apparatus, the youth movements, and the armed forces.

The greatest test of Castro's regime came, of course, with the Cuban Missile Crisis in October of 1962. That story is far too complicated for our purposes here, but it reinforced the perception on the island of the need for Cuba to ensure its own defense, in the final analysis, through its own resources. The Soviet Union negotiated the crisis by itself with no real reference to Castro and made its decisions exclusively on the basis of Soviet national interests.[16] Castro was furious but was in no position to do anything about it.

Cuba pressed for a solution that included an end to the embargo and other such pressures by the United States, U.S. withdrawal from Guantánamo, a crackdown on exile raids, and cessation of U.S. military overflights of the island. None of these demands were addressed even remotely in the agreement reached as a result of the

Missile Crisis. Indeed, despite the popular myth, no formal promise to eschew forever an invasion of Cuba was made by the United States.

The lack of significant Cuban military power ensured Havana's role as a mere bystander in the bilateral discussions of those who did have the strength to back up their words.

THE POST-CRISIS ARMED FORCES

The year and a half between the Bay of Pigs invasion and the Cuban Missile Crisis was dominated by security concerns. Exile forces succeeded in establishing elements in the Escambray Mountains of central Cuba, and they were able to maintain them there. As militia forces were not up to the task of dislodging these new rebels, the job fell to the regular Revolutionary Armed Forces (Fuerzas Armadas Revolucionarias — FAR). Moreover, during the Missile Crisis, Cuba's extensive militia system could do nothing to control events. Although it could be argued that the regulars in the army could not have done so either, many Cubans believed that serious conventional forces could have done something useful if only by existing as a "force in being."

At the same time, militia units were proving difficult to control, and much of their activity was not under FAR supervision. As a result, many militia units were disbanded, and a compulsory service law was adopted in 1963 for the regular armed forces. Service for three years was foreseen, and the militia was further weakened Thus, over several years, Castro gave the FAR increased importance, realizing how much he depended on it to solidify the changes brought on by the Revolution.[17] From then on, the FAR would be the government's response to the U.S. challenge, both at home and abroad, and its links with the dominant Communist Party would be strengthened even further.

After Che Guevara's death in 1967 and until 1968, Cuba engaged in widespread support of revolution in Latin America and elsewhere. Largely in response to this exportation of the Revolution, the United States mounted the Alliance for Progress assistance program and launched a series of unparalleled military support arrangements for Latin American countries threatened, or alleg-edly threatened, by leftist insurgency.[18] Counterinsurgency toward Cuban-led activities became the order of the day, and those efforts proved successful. Despite their Cuban training and backing, the insurgents were defeated almost everywhere in the hemisphere. While Cuba's FAR was certainly hurt by these defeats, they also felt considerable pride and achieved significant experience in these operations. In Cuba itself, "internationalism" was praised at the highest levels and rewarded with promotions, privileges, and prestige.

As the 1970s began, Cuba still was making residual efforts in some parts of Central America, and occasionally elsewhere in Latin America, to assist insurgen-cies or guerrilla groups. However, the sting had been taken away from the threat.[19] Nor was the Soviet Union, which was enjoying greater, more significant influence in Cuba at this time, always pleased with such moves. From the Soviet point of view, Cuba's assistance to those movements could annoy the United States without bringing many concrete results otherwise. Later in the 1970s, the Soviet Union was interested in Cuban help in Africa, but the Soviets remained leery of Castro's efforts in Latin America. Curiously however, there were some significant leftist successes in the Western Hemisphere during the period. Most dramatic of these triumphs was the Sandinistas' rise to power in 1979 in Nicaragua.[20] Rather less significant in the military field were further leftist gains in Grenada.

Cuba's successes in the mid-1970s in southern Africa captured the attention of the United States in ways that had not been seen since the early 1960s. The government of President Jimmy Carter (1977-1981) began to make moves toward reestablishing relations with Cuba. U.S. reasoning was as interesting then as it would be today:

> We have been moving to restore communications with Cuba for a very simple reason: None of the many serious problems that concern us in our relations with Cuba have been solved — or can be solved — by isolation. We stand a better chance of achieving these objectives through quiet negotiation and reciprocal moves toward cooperation than through inflexible hostility and a continuing refusal even to talk.[21]

Cuban intervention in Africa, especially in Angola, put an end to this effort. As part of Carter's general toughening of U.S. foreign policy in the late 1970s, the initiative to open relations with Cuba ended at that time. Before that, however, some cooperative gestures had been made by the two countries, the most dramatic of which was the opening of interests sections in each other's capitals.[22]

Tens of thousands of Cuban soldiers served in Africa, primarily in Angola and Ethiopia, over the years. This was no longer the sort of small-scale assistance of a few dozen personnel common during the export-of-revolution phase.[23] Further-more, these complete units and large numbers of troops ensured that the armed forces received what was doubtless the most significant injection of active service experience since Cuba's 1895-1898 war for independence.[24] Praise for the Cuban military was widespread, especially from one of its key enemies, the South African armed forces. Though the FAR suffered some reverses, it generally was considered to be an effective and hard-hitting military.

The costs of such internationalism were significant. Some 2,000 fatalities resulted, according to generally reliable sources.[25] In the United States, the Carter administration found the African interventions too much to handle. Several Euro-pean governments slowed or stopped a variety of assistance programs to Cuba, and even the usually understanding Canadian government ended its assistance to the island.[26] Thus, the African activity had severe political and economic costs that soon became too much for Cuba, not to mention for its Soviet protector and partner, which was increasingly keen not to annoy the United States in matters considered vital to U.S. interests.

THE 1980s AND THE "WAR OF ALL THE PEOPLE"

Thus, the end of the 1970s came with the Soviet Union feeling more unsure than it had been in many years about the success of its foreign policy. Cuba, in turn, also felt uncertain as to what degree it could count on Moscow if things became difficult again. The Carter government's shift to the right; the generalized growth of conservative sentiment in the United States, which was to lead to the election of President Ronald Reagan (1981-1989) a few months later; and, doubtless, the perceived internal security needs of the Castro government all led in 1980 to a new strategic posture and new military structures for Cuba.

The "War of All the People," as Defense Minister Raúl Castro called it, was an attempt to ensure social mobilization in the event of enemy attack or even actions short of it. The strategic picture faced by Cuba in the early part of the 1980s appeared to justify such a change. During the Reagan administration, the United States appeared more bellicose toward Cuba than for many years, and the Soviet Union was less supportive of the island. Among other factors, the defeat of national liberation movements in much of the Third World, the beginning of the Soviet intervention in Afghanistan, the end of Soviet influence in Egypt and much of the Middle East, and lessened Soviet influence in sub-Saharan Africa gave Cuba the context for serious planning of national defense against invasion or other lesser aggression. Clearly, in light of circumstances like those created by Castro's forward foreign policy, real dangers might lie ahead.

Despite Cuba's generally heightened confidence in the FAR, it was clear that these forces alone could not answer national defense needs. Based on the model of what he regarded as the Vietnamese experience, Raúl Castro proposed the "War of All the People" as the best strategic basis for Cuban defense. This plan was founded on a program of national mobilization for defense, with an improved FAR and a new body, the Territorial Militia Troops (Milicia de Tropas Territoriales — MTT), as its pillars.

Although previous attempts at joining the efforts of Cuban regular and reserve elements had been half-hearted, in many ways this effort was effective. Good officers were posted to the headquarters and charged with organizing and running the MTT. Resources provided by the Ministry of the Armed Forces (Ministerio de las Fuerzás Armadas — (MINFAR) were also serious. New urgency was given in response to the endeavor by the U.S. invasion of Grenada in the autumn of 1983, an operation that took 13 Cuban lives, and to the increasing anti-revolutionary military involvement of the United States in Central America. In retaliation against these U.S. initiatives, Raúl Castro delivered a public speech in which he referred to the vital necessity of waging total war against invaders as the only means to deter an attempted attack.

The plan was for the FAR to have the central role of maneuvering and attempting to defeat the U.S. main attack, while MTT resources would be deployed in delaying actions, defeating rear area airborne and amphibious landings and defending vital points, towns, and roads. The MTT's job would be to inflict as many casualties as possible and yield ground in exchange for time and enemy lives; it would also cover the flanks of the FAR.[27] As with reserve commitments in the past and on a constant basis, even in peacetime, the MTT would supplement the work of the Committees for the Defense of the Revolution (Comités de Defensa de la Revolución — CDR), the neighborhood vigilance and organizational structures located throughout the island. The CDR also would provide replacements for the regular forces as needed.

Moreover, the size of the MTT, now in the hundreds of thousands, would eventually allow it to turn from providing Cuba with guerrilla resistance instead of conventional defense. This shift would be based almost completely on the MTT, although, logically, its members would be supported by those FAR units and individuals who were not already *hors de combat*. This system of guerrilla resistance remained virtually unchanged until the Special Period (Período Especial).

THE SPECIAL PERIOD AND CUBAN DEFENSE

R ecent years have witnessed massive changes in Cuba's security picture. No single event has so shaken the Cuban Revolution as the collapse of communism in Eastern Europe and the Soviet Union, followed by the dismantling of the Soviet Union itself. Castro had seen the change coming and had been very critical from the outset of *perestroika* and *glasnost*. Especially worrying to him in defense terms were moves to make Cuba's purchases from the Soviet Union and Eastern Europe become "cash-and-carry" transactions.

In July 1990, Castro made a major speech referring to the present time for Cuba as a Special Period or, in its more formal phrasing, a "special period in time of peace" (*período especial en tiempo de paz*). As the Cuban leader explained it, Cubans would have to show their willingness to undergo great sacrifices in order to maintain the Revolution in the face of massive and negative changes of an unparalleled kind. The shocks were massive at this time — over the next three to four years in particular. The Cuban economy, as a whole, shrank in horrendous fashion: by a variety of accounts, anywhere between 35 and 50 percent. Before 1991, the Soviet Union took 63 percent of Cuba's sugar, 73 percent of its nickel, 95 percent of its citrus, and 100 percent of its electrical exports. Moreover, the Soviet Union exported to the island 90 percent of its machinery and other equipment and 98 percent of its fuel. This situation changed dramatically over a matter of months. In less than four years, Cuba lost 80 percent of its purchasing power abroad.[28]

As if this were not enough, the United States moved with speed to reinforce its embargo. Early in the decade, the 1992 Cuban Democracy Act (CDA, also known as the Torricelli Act) added greater stringency to the policy and aimed to make such U.S. laws impede foreigners' trade with Cuba as well. In 1996, the Cuban Liberty and Democratic Solidarity (LIBERTAD) Act (Helms-Burton) did even more in this regard.

Cuba's armed forces could not escape the impact of this series of blows. While some room was left for nuance where military equipment and weapons were concerned, in general, arms purchases soon became part of the cash-and-carry policy of the Soviet Union, as mentioned earlier. Additionally, neither Moscow nor the other East European capitals had the slightest interest in annoying the United States, the sole remaining world superpower, by appearing to be helping its Cuban "enemy."

Consequently, the siege mentality of the island grew apace, but the means to counter any threat soon began to decline in other ways than access to weapons and equipment. Cuba simply could not afford to maintain so many personnel in uniform.

The armed forces were cut repeatedly and left at perhaps half of their pre-1989 strength. Ammunition for training or for stocks was virtually unavailable except for cash, and no cash was at hand. While stocks were quite good in 1990, they were not inexhaustible.

Spare parts for the Cuban army's equipment and weapons, especially for more sophisticated systems, suffered from the same problem. Thus, cannibalization of military vehicles and other equipment began early and has continued to this day. Successes such as the last-minute delivery of new MiG-29 fighters were minor when compared with the shattering losses in everyday military life as a result of the fall of the Soviet Union.

All defense training previously done in the Soviet Union or other Warsaw Pact countries, especially sophisticated courses for high seas navigation, high command, senior tactics, handling of armored forces, and jet flying, was curtailed drastically or simply abandoned as impossible in the 1990s. Since that time, fuel has also been an especially thorny problem, and this shortages impeded greatly all manner of training. Many other negative impacts have also added to the readiness problems of the FAR.[29]

Cuba's long-standing and proud military intelligence system, probably the best in the Third World, also has been particularly hard hit. With its links to the Soviet system almost gone and with its representation abroad massively cut back, the FAR's eyes and ears on the world are reduced to a shadow of their former efficacy. Cuban embassies are working on a shoestring budget in most parts of the world, adding to the relative blindness on things international that the armed forces now are forced to face but from which they had been immune in the heyday of Cuba-Warsaw Pact cooperation.

The armed forces have responded, however, with great alacrity and originality to the challenges posed by Cuba's loss of Soviet cooperation. Desperate, they have sought solutions undreamed of before. With governmental blessing, the FAR has moved into industry, both institutionally and through assignment of individual officers to selected state or mixed enterprises. In today's Cuba, the term *military industry* does not mean a defense industry or even an industry owned by the armed forces, as in much of Central America. Rather, it signifies that commercial and related activities are run by the military or by armed forces officers so that these enterprises may benefit from the military's superior hierarchy, discipline, organizational skills, and the like.

In addition, military personnel have been tasked with a major role in agricultural production, especially sugar, and in growth and dollar-earning industries such as tourism. The army runs tours for tourists, a taxi agency, an internal air service, language training facilities, and hotels. This unprecedented series of moves has made the armed forces virtually self-sufficient in fuel, food, and many other fields in which their access to dollars helps them face challenges that otherwise they could not possibly sustain.

The cost in military efficiency of all this, of course, has been significant. The FAR has had to accept that only a limited number of major combat units could be kept on a basis of full readiness for meeting an invasion. Likewise, the MTT, dependent on major levels of regular assistance and resources, has taken a beating as its relative priority waned. While the most vital ships and aircraft are maintained at high readiness and, indeed, are used on a regular basis in antinarcotics and related activities, less high-priority vessels and air force resources, as mentioned previously, often are cannibalized or maintained insufficiently to keep up their fighting potential. This is often true of human as well as of other material resources in Cuba. For example, many conscripts see virtually no military training after their basic recruit course. Instead, they are sent to the sugar fields or, if they speak a foreign language or have other attributes useful to the tourism industry, to tourist industry jobs. Little wonder, then, that the U.S. Department of Defense has seen fit to reduce its threat perception virtually to zero where Cuba is concerned.[30] While the Cuban government considers invasion or other military pressure as more likely in the near future than at any time since late 1962, the gap between threat perception and the means to deal with it appears never to have been wider.

A last reflection on Cuba's present security situation may be useful here. The evolution of U.S. military thinking on the Cuban issue is interesting in more than one sense. Not only has the Cuban threat become rather more a source of humor than concern in the Pentagon, but, in addition, a grudging respect for the FAR has grown among U.S. military analysts and simple working officers. The Cubans have been effective collaborators with the U.S. defense establishment (including the Coast Guard) in the handling of the highly sensitive illegal immigration issue, especially during and after the rafter (*balsero*) crisis of 1994. In addition, the Pentagon acknowledges the helpfulness of the Cuban government — and the FAR, in particular — where new arrangements for Guantánamo are concerned and where the United States has benefited from Cuban receptiveness to its proposals. Havana has also been welcoming to U.S. overflight requests when recent natural disaster assistance to Central America and Caribbean destinations has been needed.

Perhaps most indicative of the changed U.S. military perception of Cuba security, however, is the following. Recently, the U.S. military and, indeed, the Drug Enforcement Agency (DEA) itself have dramatically praised the seriousness and importance of Cuban antinarcotics efforts and have gone as far as to call for a major joint effort against the drug scourge. Despite the negative reaction to this by conservative members of Congress and some sectors of the Miami exile community, the Department of Defense and the DEA have stood by their guns on the issue. Thus, a kind of confidence-building process is going on, not between the two governments, but between key elements of each country's security apparatus. The Cuban military is remarkably well-informed about trends in U.S. military thinking, despite reduced access to strategic intelligence on the world stage. Considerable respect for the U.S. armed forces also exists within the FAR. How this might play out in any transition is, of course, a matter of conjecture at this time.[31]

CONCLUSION

The Cuban Revolution has been under siege from the early years of its history. Challenging the United States, arguably the greatest power of the era, has resulted in extremely high costs for the Cuban people. Nowhere has the impact of this been clearer than in Cuba's armed forces, which have been tasked with deterring a U.S. attack and defeating it, should these actions become necessary.

The FAR has shown great skill in providing such a deterrent force for over 40 years. They have defeated small-scale insurgency and plotting at home and have added deterrent elements to any decisionmaking about Cuba in the United States. The U.S. Pentagon never has taken Cuba lightly, differing on this point with the CIA since 1961. In fact, the U.S. Pentagon has continued to see Cuba and its people's willingness to defend the Revolution at all costs as serious issues.

What long-term effect the Special Period will have on Cuba and the Cuban people is more difficult to assess. The links between the Communist Party and the army, the privileges both sectors enjoy even now when compared with those of rank-and-file Cubans and the entire self-perception of the armed forces as the armed shield of the Revolution all work together to ensure the loyalty of the officer corps. However, growing charges of corruption have shaken the cohesion of the military force to some extent. Concern is widespread in Cuba regarding when the Special Period actually will end. Difficulties of training and equipment cannot be left unaddressed forever. Popular dissatisfaction, as expressed in the Havana's extraordinary 1994 *Habanazo* riots,[32] is problematic for an army accustomed to a firm tradition of "the army not firing on the people" (*El ejército no tira contra el pueblo* — a phrase often repeated by Castro and others).[33] Unless the vast economic problems of the economy are addressed successfully, it is debatable how long the lid can be kept on the explosive Cuban social scene.

If the combination of negative effects of the continuing and tightened U.S. blockade continue to be added to those of the socialist mismanagement Cuba has seen over so many years, the FAR may be obliged to abandon its closeness and rapport with the Cuban people. Such a trend would almost certainly mean that the 40 years of "war" with the United States would end in victory for the larger of the two combatants.

Cuba's new security agenda thus reflects both domestic and foreign concerns. Many issues, such as internal security against subversion and the threat from the United States, are virtually traditional after so many years. Others are new — or at least *nuanced*.

The armed forces must remain the bulwark of the Cuban state, or the state's existence as currently conformed surely will be in the greatest jeopardy. While the powerful Ministry of the Interior (Ministerio del Interior — MININT) remains formally the lead agency in this role, the links between it and the FAR are growing apace. This is merely logical in the context of the very visible strains the Cuban people are facing as the supposedly Special Period enters its second decade.

The FAR also must continue, with greatly reduced resources, to ensure the deterrence of enemy invasion or even its own defeat if such an invasion comes. For all the reasons explained in this chapter, the FAR's ability to defend Cuba's sovereignty is much less credible now, after so many years of penury, than it was during the island's better times.

Cuba's security agenda, therefore, is a mix of the old and the new. The main difference is that, during the time of the old challenges, a more united Cuban people were joined to vastly greater resources in order to face the various crises. However, the agenda has expanded considerably, and the means to address it have contracted massively. Only time will tell whether Cuba's new and often imaginative answers will suffice.

Notes

1. After all, Fidel Castro had warned as much in his *La historia me absolverá* (Havana: Prensa de Radio Habana), the published text of his 1972 speech in defense of his first armed attack in 1953.

2. Ramón Eduardo Ruiz, 1968, *Cuba: The Making of a Revolution* (New York: Norton), 36-54.

3. Hugh Thomas, 1971, *Cuba: The Pursuit of Freedom* (London: Eyre and Spottiswoode), 838-852.

4. Thomas 1971, 997-998.

5. Some debate continues about the strength of Castro's forces in the last months of the insurgency. See Neill Macaulay, 1978, "The Cuban Rebel Army: A Numerical Survey," *Hispanic American Historical Review* (May): 284-295.

6. Jaime Suchlicki, 1989, *The Cuban Military Under Castro* (Coral Gables, Fla.: The North-South Center at the University of Miami), 4-9.

7. See the chapter on Cuba in Adrian English, 1984, "The Armed Forces of Latin America" (London: *Jane's Defense Weekly*), 195-220.

8. A highly influential Soviet statesman in charge of foreign and domestic trade during the administrations of Joseph Stalin and Nikita Khrushchev.

9. This ministry's name later was changed to Ministry of the Armed Forces (Ministerio de las Fuerzas Armadas Revolucionarias), with its Spanish acronym MINFAR ubiquitously used to describe it, even in other languages.

10. Thomas 1971, 1321.

11. Interviews by the author in 1997 in Miami, Florida, with U.S. naval personnel stationed at the embassy in the early 1960s; interview by the author in January 1999 in Havana with Carlos Alzugaray, security expert on U.S.-Cuban relations during that period, at the Institute of International Studies (Instituto Superior de Estudios Internacionales).

12. Meanwhile, the U.S. embargo had been strengthened steadily, to the point that Cubans spoke of it with the more military term "blockade." After that, officials in Washington and Havana engaged in a semantics battle on this issue, with Washington saying its embargo was not military and did not close off Cuban harbors and thus could not be considered a blockade. Meanwhile, Cuba argued that the level and nature of the impositions, their application outside the United States to non-U.S. citizens, and their coming from a power of the size of the United States meant that, in effect, this constituted a real blockade. The U.S. argument is fairly straightforward, if far from airtight. The Cuban argument is elaborated in Olga Miranda Bravo, 1996, *Cuba/USA: Nationalizations and Blockade* (Havana: Editorial de Ciencias Sociales), 40-46; and Carlos Batista Odio, 1998, "Bloqueo, no embargo," in *El conflicto Estados Unidos-Cuba,* ed. Francisco López Cibeira (Havana: Editorial Félix Varela), 38-48.

13. Ernesto "Che" Guevara had described the Revolution as Marxist months before.

14. For this story, see Francisco V. García-Amador, 1987, *La cuestión Cubana en la OEA y la crisis del sistema interamericano* (Coral Gables, Fla.: University of Miami North-South Center).

15. Earlier moves had been made toward this end. See Demetrio Boersner, 1990, *Relaciones internacionales de América Latina* (Caracas: Nueva Sociedad), 258-268.

16. See Rafael Hernández, 1999, *La otra guerra* (Havana: Editorial Ciencias Sociales).

17. Suchlicki 1989, 9-10.

18. See Lars Schoultz, 1987, *National Security and United States Policy Toward Latin America* (Princeton, N.J.: Princeton University Press), 19-22.

19. Cuban support for urban guerrilla movements was also a reality in many cases. This resulted in little other than the smashing of such movements and, frequently enough, the establishment of military regimes promising to deal more effectively with the threat they posed.

20. It is important to keep in mind, however, that the Cuban role in the Sandinista Revolution, at least in terms of Havana's direct help to the Sandinista National Liberation Front (Frente Sandinista de Liberación Nacional – FSLN), is easily exaggerated. Indeed, Venezuela and Mexico, and even Costa Rica, may in the end have been more helpful than the supposedly more active Cubans. See Jiri Valenta and Virginia Valenta, 1986, "The FSLN in Power," in *Conflict in Nicaragua: A Multidimensional Perspective*, eds. Jiri Valenta and Esperanza Durán (Coral Gables, Fla.: Soviet and East European Studies Program, Graduate School of International Studies, University of Miami).

21. United States Department of State, 1977, *Department of State Bulletin* 77 (December 5), 2006. 20.

22. This story is told in Wayne Smith, 1987, *The Closest of Enemies* (New York: Norton).

23. Smaller-scale, but still significant, Cuban assistance had been given earlier to other African countries. However, the Cuban expeditionary force in Angola seems to have reached the exceptional figure of more than 20,000 troops, and the personnel sent to the Ogaden War appear to have numbered about 17,000. Figures differ for these operations. The ones considered most accurate are found in Suchlicki 1989, 40-41, although recent work by other authors may provide more details.

24. Indeed, it is likely that this effort was the greatest military operation mounted by a Latin American country overseas in the independent history of the region. See, for comparison, the only real competition in Brazil's World War II initiatives, recounted in Ricardo Bonalume Neto, 1995, *A nossa segunda guerra: Os brasileiros al combate 1942-1945* (Rio de Janeiro: Expressão e Cultura).

25. See the various references to these conflicts and Cuba's role in them in Luis Suárez Salazar, 1997, *Cuba: ¿aislamiento o reinserción en el mundo cambiado?* (Havana: Editorial de Ciencias Sociales).

26. John Kirk and Peter McKenna, 1997, *Canada-Cuba Relations: The Other Good Neighbor Policy* (Gainesville, Fla.: University of Florida Press), 113-115.

27. Interviews by the author with senior Cuban military officers in Montreal, spring 1990; and in Havana, February 1996.

28. For purposes of comparison, before 1991, only 6.7 percent of Cuban trade was with Western Europe, and a mere 5.7 percent was with the nearby Americas. All these figures come from one of the best works on this period, Homero Campo and Orlando Pérez's 1997 book, *Cuba: Los años duros* (Mexico, Plaza y Janés), 14-15.

29. These matters were discussed earlier, and in more detail, in this author's 1991 article, "Hard Times Ahead for Havana," *Jane's Defense Weekly* 12 (October 12).

30. Bryan Bender, 1998, "Report Confirms Cuba Is No Longer a Threat," *Jane's Defense Weekly* (April 15).

31. Interviews by the author in May 1998 in Havana with senior FAR officers of the Center for Studies of Defense and International Security (Centro de Estudios de Defensa y Seguridad Internacional — CEDSI).

32. On August 5, 1994, thousands of Cubans gathered to protest the Revolution's Special Period along Havana's seawall and other sections of the old city. According to reports, some 23 "dollarized" businesses were looted, and 375 persons were arrested during the riots, 75 of them receiving anywhere from two- to four-year jail sentences. On the following day, August 6, 1994, thousands of Cubans began heading to Florida on fragile boats and homemade rafts. This mass exodus became known as the rafter (*balsero*) crisis. See Freedom House (Washington, D.C.) web site at <http://www.freedomhouse.org/index.htm> and Cubanet News, Incorporated (Coral Gables, Fla.) web site at <http://cubanet.org/search.html>.

33. Literally, "The army does not fire on the people."

References

Batista Odio, Carlos. 1998. "Bloqueo, no embargo." In *El conflicto Estados Unidos-Cuba,* ed. Francisco López Cibeira. Havana: Editorial Félix Varela

Bender, Bryan. 1998. "Report Confirms Cuba Is No Longer a Threat." London: *Jane's Defense Weekly,* April 15.

Boersner, Demetrio. 1990. *Relaciones internacionales de América Latina* (Caracas: Nueva Sociedad).

Bonalume Neto, Ricardo. 1995. *A nossa segunda guerra: Os brasileiros al combate 1942-1945.* Rio de Janeiro: Expressão e Cultura.

Campo, Homero, and Orlando Pérez. 1997. *Cuba: Los años duros.* Mexico: Plaza y Janés.

Castro, Fidel. 1972. *La historia me absolverá.* Havana: Prensa de Radio Habana.

CubaNet News, Incorporated, Coral Gables, Fla., website at <http://cubanet.org/search.html>.

English, Adrian. 1984. *The Armed Forces of Latin America.* London: *Jane's Defense Weekly.*

Freedom House, Washington, D.C., website at <http://www.freedomhouse.org/index.htm>.

García-Amador, Francisco V. 1987. *La cuestión cubana en la OEA y la crisis del sistema interamericano.* Coral Gables, Fla.: University of Miami North-South Center.

Hernández, Rafael. 1999. *La otra guerra.* Havana: Editorial Ciencias Sociales.

Kirk, John, and Peter McKenna. 1997. *Canada-Cuba Relations: The Other Good Neighbor Policy.* Gainesville, Fla.: The University Press of Florida.

Klepak, Hal P. 1991. "Hard Times Ahead for Havana." London: *Jane's Defense Weekly* 12: October 12.

López Cibeira, Francisco, ed. 1998. *Conflicto Estados Unidos-Cuba.* Havana: Editorial Félix Varela.

Macaulay, Neill. 1978. "The Cuban Rebel Army: A Numerical Survey." *Hispanic American Historical Review,* May: 284-295.

Miranda Bravo, Olga. 1996. *Cuba/USA: Nationalizations and Blockade.* Havana: Editorial de Ciencias Sociales.

Ruiz, Ramón Eduardo. 1968. *Cuba: The Making of a Revolution.* New York: Norton.

Schoultz, Lars. 1987. *National Security and United States Policy Toward Latin America.* Princeton, N.J.: Princeton University Press.

Smith, Wayne. 1987. *The Closest of Enemies.* New York: Norton.

Suárez Salazar, Luis. 1997. *Cuba: ¿Aislamiento o reinserción en el mundo cambiado?* Havana: Editorial de Ciencias Sociales.

Suchlicki, Jaime. 1989. *The Cuban Military Under Castro.* Coral Gables, Fla.: The North-South Center at the University of Miami.

Thomas, Hugh. 1971. *Cuba: The Pursuit of Freedom.* London: Eyre and Spottiswoode.

U.S. Department of State. 1977. *Department of State Bulletin* 77, December 5: 2006.20.

Valenta, Jiri, and Virginia Valenta. 1986. "The FSLN in Power." In *Conflict in Nicaragua: A Multidimensional Perspective,* eds. Jiri Valenta and Esperanza Durán. Coral

Gables, Fla.: Soviet and East European Studies Program, Graduate School of International Studies, University of Miami.

Valenta, Jiri, and Esperanza Durán, eds. 1986. *Conflict in Nicaragua: A Multidimensional Perspective*. Coral Gables, Fla.: Soviet and East European Studies Program, Graduate School of International Studies, University of Miami.

Part II.
Canada and Cuba in
the Twenty-First Century

CHAPTER TWO

Canada, Cuba, and Constructive Engagement: Political Dissidents and Human Rights

SAHADEO BASDEO AND IAN HESKETH

S ince the end of the Cold War and Canada's entry into the Organization of
American States (OAS) in 1989, much scholarly interest has been devoted to the
study of Canadian-Latin American relations.[1] The interest and publicity given to
this topic is understandable. Since World War II, Canada's foreign policy has been
influenced heavily by the United States, to the extent that Canadian foreign
policymakers have placed Canada's relationship with the United States ahead of all
others. This is hardly surprising, given the Cold War reality and Canada's geopolitical location in North America. In addition, Canada's economic vulnerability and
dependence on the United States for military security help to explain the bond
between the two countries. While understandably constrained in making foreign
policy decisions that the United States may find objectionable, Canada has taken
independent decisions, particularly concerning Fidel Castro's Cuba.

From the time that Castro's Revolution began in 1959, Canada and the United
States have not seen eye to eye on Cuba. Their foreign policy perspectives have
differed mainly because Canada has been more tolerant of ideological pluralism in
other countries. As George Schuyler so convincingly argues, the United States "has
tended to see its security threatened when political and ideological pluralism crop
up in the Western Hemisphere. Canada, on the other hand, has been more prepared
to accept ideological diversity while seeking to negotiate . . . political differences."[2]
Precisely this approach has characterized Canadian foreign policy toward Cuba
since 1959. From the John Diefenbaker administration (1957-1963) to that of Jean
Chrétien, Canada has refused to buckle completely under U.S. pressure to treat
Cuba as a pariah nation in the Western Hemisphere.[3] Indeed, despite efforts by 10
successive Republican and Democrat administrations in the United States to
remove Castro from power "by isolating Cuba economically and politically from
hemispheric affairs, engaging in constant anti-Castro media propaganda, supporting anti-Castro Cuban nationalist groups in the United States, and provoking
internal subversion of Castro's government,"[4] Canada has maintained continuous
diplomatic relations with Cuba. This fact is remarkable, considering that it was
largely due to U.S. persuasion that Cuba was booted out of the OAS and the majority
of countries in the Americas have isolated themselves from Cuba diplomatically,
economically, and politically at least for some brief period during the last 40 years.

Canada has not fully endorsed all aspects of Castro's rule, however, and it has often disapproved of Cuban policies. For example, Canada has been vocal in denouncing human rights abuses in Cuba and Castro's intolerance of political dissent. Canada also did not mince words in its criticisms of "Castro's large-scale intervention seemingly as a Soviet surrogate on the side of socialist forces in the Angolan War of 1975."[5] In fact, the government of Prime Minister Pierre Trudeau (1968-1979; 1980-1984), reputedly more sympathetic to the Castro Revolution than were other Canadian administrations, suspended development aid in 1978 because of Cuba's mercenary role in Angola.

Moreover, at a conference in Halifax, Nova Scotia, in November 1989, Richard Gorham, Canada's roving ambassador to Latin America, condemned Cuba for instigating and supporting what "we [Canada] consider disruptive activities in Central America."[6] In April 1995, Canada was among the first countries to express concern at the severe sentence handed down against human rights activist Francisco Chaviano.[7] In February 1996, Canada denounced the harassment of an official opposition group, the Concilio Cubano, an emerging coalition of human rights activists. On Februrary 24, 1996, when the Cuban Air Force shot down two civilian aircraft operated by Brothers to the Rescue, a U.S.-based organization of anti-communist Cuban exiles,[8] Canada condemned Cuba's action as a violation of internationally accepted rules prohibiting military attacks on civilian aircraft.[9] In 1997, Canada again criticized the Cuban government for the arrest of four political activists who spoke out against the policies of Cuba's Communist Party. The dissidents were Marta Beatriz Roque Cabello, Vladimiro Roca Antúnez, René Gómez Manzano, and Félix Bonne Carcassés. In May 2000, Roque Cabello, Gómez Manzano, and Bonne Carcassés were released. On May 5, 2002, Roca Antúnez was finally released, one week prior to former President Jimmy Carter's visit with President Castro in Havana.[10] When the four were tried and sentenced to lengthy jail terms, the Chrétien administration took severe measures, putting on hold any aid that was not directly used for humanitarian purposes and calling for a review of future relations with Cuba.

These issues aside, however, Canada has not isolated Cuba as the United States has done since the Castro Revolution. In fact, Canada has pursued a policy of engaging Cuba since the 1960s, though not without moments of difficulty. Part of this difficulty has arisen because of the geographic positions of Canada and Cuba. During the Cold War, relations between the two countries could not be divorced from the interests of their much larger neighbor, the United States. Indeed, U.S. domestic politics continued to be a critical factor in the Canada-Cuba-United States triangle. As James Guy reminds us, the United States' "attitudes and actions toward Cuba are important influences affecting Canada's relations with Cuba."[11] Partly in response to this external reality, the Chrétien administration has developed a policy of "constructive engagement" toward Cuba since the mid-1990s. This policy has combined increased trade and investment with quiet but insistent diplomatic pressure on the Castro administration over such issues as human rights, with the expectation that Cuba will conform slowly to the rules of the hemisphere. This chapter will focus on the policy of constructive engagement pursued by the Chrétien administration since 1993, but more particularly since the historic visit by Pope John Paul II in 1998. It will examine the nature of constructive engagement with respect to human rights in particular, assess the extent of its success in this area to date, and outline some likely directions for Canada-Cuba relations in the new millennium. In essence, the chapter will argue that, notwithstanding the differences that developed between the Chrétien administration and the Castro regime in the late 1990s over the issue of human rights, constructive engagement still remains the most viable policy option for Canada as Ottawa attempts to influence the rise of democratic institutions in Cuba.

BACKGROUND TO CONSTRUCTIVE ENGAGEMENT

Canadian administrations before that of Chrétien had contributed to the establishment of cordial diplomatic ties with Cuba. The Trudeau administrations, for example, showed considerable sympathy for the aspirations of the Cuban Revolution by maintaining diplomatic relations with Cuba at all times. Trudeau even visited Havana in 1976. This visit formed the basis of a lasting friendship between Trudeau and Castro, as well as between Canada and Cuba.[12] The Conservative administration of Brian Mulroney (1984-1993) built upon this friendship in the decade of the 1990s. The Mulroney government took a number of interesting initiatives between 1989 and 1991 to reintegrate Cuba into the hemispheric fold, notwithstanding Mulroney's close relationship with Presidents Ronald Reagan (1981-1988) and George H.W. Bush (1989-1993).[13]

For instance, Mulroney took Canada into the OAS in 1989, thereby legitimizing its voice in the multilateral forum where Latin American issues are of foremost importance. In 1990, his Conservative government signaled its position on Cuba when Secretary of State for External Affairs Joe Clark acknowledged in a speech at the University of Calgary that some of the "current problems in Latin America could become more manageable if Cuba were brought back into the family of hemispheric nations."[14] This view was endorsed one year later by Clark's successor, Barbara McDougall, when she addressed the OAS General Assembly in Chile: "We look forward to the time when the vision of the founders of the OAS for a universal hemispheric forum can be realized and Cuba will retake its place in the Organization as a full member of the hemispheric family."[15]

In fact, from 1990, under both Conservative and Liberal administrations, Canada has been forthright in its position, denouncing at the United Nations (UN) the continuation of the long-standing U.S. embargo, the Mack Amendment (1989), and the Cuban Democracy Act (1992). Indeed, over the past 10 years at the UN, Canada has made it an annual ritual to condemn the embargo and has repeatedly voted against this measure.[16] By 1994, André Ouellet, then Canada's Liberal secretary of state for external affairs, said that, with the Cold War over, it was time "to turn the page" with Cuba. As he explained, given the dramatic termination of trade and aid relations with the former Soviet Union, Castro's Cuba needed hemispheric assistance to avert the rise of social tensions. This idea expressed a new Canadian concern. In this regard, Ouellet promised to provide developmental aid to Havana and called upon the United States to follow the Canadian example.[17] Secretary of State Ouellet's call was a clear manifestation of the humane internationalism that has become a vital ingredient of Canada's foreign policy in the hemisphere and has shaped the Chrétien administration's approach to Cuba.

By the mid-1990s, then, Canada's official policy toward Cuba was evident. In Canada's view, Cuba was no longer a security threat to anyone. The Cold War was over, and with it, the security and ideological threat that Cuba had posed. In this context, Canadian policymakers believed that Cuba should be reintegrated into the world economy and that multinational assistance should be provided to revive its ailing economy. Again, by the mid-1990s, Canada was prepared to play a leading role in the effort to help Cuba. Indeed, Peter McKenna and John M. Kirk have argued that Canada's development assistance to Cuba took on a renewed vigor after June 1994. As they explain,

> [after a] . . . protracted series of negotiations, both countries agreed, in March of 1996, to establish a formal government-to-government bilateral aid program, which amounted to some $30 million over a five-year period. As a result, Canada became one of the largest donor countries in Cuba today, and thus [is] in a position to influence Cuban policy-making, if only marginally. Some of the funding was to be earmarked for strengthening "civil society" in Cuba — including funding for Cuban NGOs, human rights institutions, and various ministries within the Cuban government.[18]

As of this bilateral aid program, official backing was given to the Canadian private sector already investing in Cuba; humanitarian support in the form of food and medical supplies was provided by Ottawa; and the industrial cooperation arm of the Canadian International Development Agency (CIDA) funded many Canadian companies considering investment in Cuba.[19]

Other initiatives were taken by the Chrétien government to enhance official bilateral relations. These included senior-level contacts, beginning with the visit to Cuba in 1995 of Christine Stewart, secretary of state for Latin America and Africa. Cuba's Foreign Minister, Roberto Robaina, reciprocated in 1995, followed during the same year by the Cuban minister of foreign investment and economic cooperation, the president of the Cuban National Assembly, and the president of the National Bank of Cuba.[20] In all cases, discussions centered upon economic and commercial cooperation and investment opportunities in Cuba. Other Canadian initiatives included strong support for parliamentary exchanges and encouragement for the work of non-governmental organizations (NGOs) such as Oxfam-Canada, CUSO (Canadian University Students Overseas, a Canadian organization that supports global justice alliances), the Anglican and United churches, the Canadian Foodgrains Bank, the Ottawa-Cuba Connection, the Jesuit Centre for Social Faith and Justice, and Carleton University of Canada.[21]

At the multilateral level as well, Canada spoke out in favor of a new hemispheric outlook toward Cuba. In December 1994, for instance, at the Summit of the Americas in Miami, Prime Minister Chrétien was openly critical of the U.S. position on Cuba. He asserted that the best way to cultivate democracy in Cuba was through constructive engagement rather than isolation.[22] This position was repeated at the meetings of the General Assembly of the OAS held in Haiti, in June 1995, and Panama, in June 1996. On both occasions, Canada's position of constructive engagement was reiterated when Secretary of State Christine Stewart emphasized,

"Political and economic advances can [only] be encouraged by maintaining a dialogue with the Cuban people and government." While acknowledging that much work was still outstanding in Cuba in the areas of democratic development and human rights, Stewart called upon member states of the OAS "to examine ways of opening up a similar dialogue with Cuba."[23] So adamant was Canada's position that, even when world opinion turned against Cuba, following the February 1996 downing of the two Brothers to the Rescue aircraft, Canada remained unconvinced about ostracizing Cuba. Isolation, Stewart countered, would not "prevent such tragedies; indeed, [isolation] only give[s] rise to the hardening of militant policies and reinforce[s] the wrong kind of nationalism and political rigidity."[24]

When President Bill Clinton (1993-2001) signed the Helms-Burton Act into law in March 1996, amid domestic pressure following the shooting down of the two civilian aircraft, Canada, which considered the legislation an intrusion upon its own sovereignty, joined an international campaign against the bill. Canada has maintained that the legal provisions of the act violate international law and unlawfully impose domestic U.S. legislation extraterritorially on non-U.S. citizens and companies. Most important, the act establishes a dangerous precedent for U.S. foreign policy in the hemisphere by unilaterally imposing U.S. action to force other countries to comply with its wishes. Canada also opposes the act as a violation of the principles governing international trade and as a direct attack against a number of the provisions of the North American Free Trade Agreement (NAFTA).[25] In essence, Canada regards Helms-Burton as a violation of the principles governing international coexistence, an obstacle to the process of multilateralism, and contrary to the spirit of international cooperation.

Likewise, Canada has condemned the objective of Helms-Burton to starve Cuba of hard currency by dissuading foreign investment. This measure, in Canada's view, can only exacerbate the suffering of the Cuban people. Hence, the act is seen as morally unjust, politically unsound, and, consequently, unacceptable. Canada also has been reluctant to accept the U.S. argument that Helms-Burton has the potential of forcing Castro out of office through public disenchantment with a collapsing economy. If anything, that policy mind-set has strengthened Castro's grip on power. In May 1996, Secretary of State Stewart explained that Canada's approach is more realistic and pragmatic than that of the United States. In May 1996, in Ottawa, at a symposium on the Helms-Burton Law, hosted by the Canadian Foundation for the Americas (Fundación Canadiense para las Américas — FOCAL) and the Washington-based Center for International Policy, Stewart stated that, while Canada and the United States share many of the same goals with respect to Cuba,

> ... our aim is a peaceful transition to a genuinely representative government ... that fully respects internationally agreed human rights standards. And we look forward to Cuba becoming an open economy. However, we differ from the United States on how to reach these objectives. We have chosen the path of engagement and dialogue; the United States has picked isolation.[26]

Indeed, the Canadian profile of engagement had risen considerably since 1994.

AXWORTHY, CONSTRUCTIVE ENGAGEMENT, AND THE HUMAN RIGHTS DEBATE

The profile of engagement was further enhanced when Lloyd Axworthy became Canada's secretary of state for external affairs in early 1996. Certain events threw Axworthy into the vortex of the Canada-Cuba-United States triangular debate. The passage of the Helms-Burton Act, with its international consequences, made him a major player in the debate on the subject. By mid-1996, Canada not only had spoken out forcefully against Helms-Burton but also had built a coalition of forces with its allies in the World Trade Organization (WTO), the Organisation for Economic Cooperation and Development (OECD), the European Union (EU), the OAS, and the Group of Seven (G-7).[27] As 1996 was also an election year in the United States, unusual pressure emanated from Washington to force Canada to conform to U.S. wishes. In this context, Axworthy's profile rose considerably as a major spokesman on the issue.

After the outcome of the 1996 U.S. presidential elections was known, Clinton had more room to maneuver. His administration became less bellicose and more sensitive to the wishes of Canada and other major U.S. trading allies. The Clinton administration then sought to counteract the impact of the legislation on its allies by exercising power delegated under Title III of Helms-Burton, permitting the president to suspend the effective date of the section for a period not to exceed six months. Clinton consistently extended the application of Title III[28] until his departure from office in January 2001. In part, Canada's unrelenting position — coupled with international support provided by Mexico, the 15-member EU, and others — forced Clinton to act.

Another factor weighed against the United States. Canada had become equally vehement in its condemnation of the unilateral decision taken by the U.S. administration to enact the Iran and Libya Sanctions Act (ILSA) of 1996 (see also Fisk, Chapter Five, this volume). ILSA was designed to punish Iran and Libya, countries described by the U.S. president as "two of the most dangerous supporters of terrorism in the world."[29] This legislation imposed sanctions on foreign companies undertaking new investments worth more than US$40 million in oil or gas projects in either Libya or Iran. These firms would be barred from doing business with the U.S. government and from borrowing more than US$110 million from U.S. financial houses.[30] Already outraged by Helms-Burton, Canada, like the EU, saw this as a U.S. attempt to impose its hegemony on the Islamic world. Axworthy spoke out against ILSA largely on principle. He stated that, while Canada shares "the concerns of the United States and other countries on international terrorism and places a high priority on finding ways to combat it, this is not the way to proceed."[31] Axworthy received support from his cabinet colleague Art Eggleton, minister of international trade, who saw the Iran and Libya Sanctions Act as another "attempt by the United States to dictate trade policy to its allies" and vowed that Canada "will continue to defend its interests against the extraterritorial application of such legislation."[32]

Under pressure, the United States retreated, which amounted to an admission that other options needed to be explored to avoid a disruption of good relations with its major trading allies.[33] President Clinton then appointed Ambassador Stuart Eizenstat, his special envoy on Cuba, who traveled to Ottawa and other world capitals to make the case for a real multilateral effort at promoting democracy in Cuba.[34] Clinton's new agenda advocated international pressure on Cuba to accelerate the democratic process. To this end, Eizenstat was mandated to persuade Canada, Mexico, the EU, and others to adopt five key principles to overthrow Castro: 1) to make public statements calling for democracy in Cuba, 2) to funnel government aid through Cuban NGOs, 3) to increase support for independent journalists, 4) to end government subsidies to Cuba, and 5) to pledge not to help Cuba develop a nuclear reactor.[35]

Eizenstat made additional demands when he visited Canada in August 1996. He called for Canadian companies investing in Cuba to adopt new standards for trade and investment as well as more stringent business practices through the introduction of The Sullivan Principles.[36] These regulations would force Canadian companies to pay workers directly, rather than through a government agency, and would recognize the formation of trade unions. Canada's Business Council on National Issues (BCNI), representing some 150 large corporations, rejected the position that Canadian companies should reform their hiring and payment policies and other aspects of doing business in Cuba to satisfy the Clinton administration. BCNI President Thomas D'Aquino asserted that large Canadian companies generally behave responsibly around the world and said that "there were limitations of operating in countries, from Cuba to China, with repressive government[s]. Just being in such countries helps bring about political change."[37]

The BCNI's support of the official Canadian policy of engagement met with similar support from the Canadian Labour Congress (CLC), representing some 60 percent of all trade unions in Canada. As early as February 1995, the CLC had opposed Helms-Burton (passed by the U.S. House in September 1995, passed as amended by the Senate in October 1995, and signed into law by President Clinton in March 1996) on the grounds that it would "destroy Cuba's successful trading relations with the world and penalize Canadian companies lawfully engaged in business," leading to "the loss of significant government revenues and employment for several thousand Canadian workers."[38] What was particularly galling was the intent of the Helms-Burton Act with respect to Canada itself. As CLC President Bob White explained,

> [Helms Burton] is intended to "punish" Canada for its continued, independent policy towards Cuba. I would reiterate that the Canadian Labour Congress supports Canada's policy of promoting the reintegration of Cuba in the international community as has been previously communicated to Canadian officials. Canada cannot have its international relations determined by another country.[39]

White restated this position while on a visit to Cuba in April 1995, but he went further:

> [The] CLC is in Cuba to strengthen our relationship with Cuban workers' organizations. . . . We want to engage constructively with Central de Trabajadores Cubanos (CTC) and Cuban NGOs to explore ways to promote peaceful change. . . . Canada has an important role to play in the hemisphere in supporting Cuban workers and in counteracting the destructive role the United States plays through its embargo and recent investment laws.[40]

By the end of 1996, neither the Helms-Burton Act nor U.S. diplomatic pressure had derailed Canada from its policy of engagement. With the backing of the Canadian public, Axworthy, who had a personal interest in the Cuba file, stayed the course and proceeded to explore ways and means of accelerating political liberalization in Cuba within the context of constructive engagement. No doubt sensitive to the challenge issued by Eizenstat, Axworthy set about to prove that the Canadian approach to Cuba was more likely to bring about positive change than the more confrontational U.S. approach.

Human rights constituted an important item on Canada's post-1996 agenda, as a result of Eizenstat's mandate. However, while Axworthy placed a new emphasis on the issue of human rights and liberal democratic reforms in Cuba, respect for human rights was never lost to the architects of engagement in Ottawa. Canadian officials have been proud to identify with the progress made in improving Cuba's human rights image in the first half of the 1990s, asserting that the change was in part a product of constructive engagement and ongoing dialogue. In fact, in November 1994, Cuba invited UN High Commissioner José Ayala Lasso to visit Havana, and Canada arranged for Cuban Foreign Minister Roberto Robaina to meet with Ayala Lasso in Ottawa in March 1995.[41] Cuba signed the UN Convention on Torture in May 1996 and has since claimed to be favorably disposed to visits from the UN and other human rights organizations.[42] However, since Cuba's signing of the Convention on Torture, there is no evidence that the UN High Commissioner for Human Rights has visited Cuba. Nevertheless, in the opinion of these authors, there have been improvements in Cuba's human rights record as of Pope John Paul II's 1998 visit. Indeed, Cuba's record is much better than that of some other Latin American countries. As figures provided by Elizardo Sanchez, director of the Commission for Human Rights and Reconciliation (Comisión de Derechos Humanos y Reconciliación) in Havana suggest, the number of political prisoners in Cuba has decreased dramatically in recent years: from more than 1,000 in early 1997 to approximately 381 in mid-1998.[43] This is not a justification of any human rights violations that may have taken place in the past in Cuba or that are still taking place. According to an Amnesty International report on Cuba in 2001, there is still cause for concern:

> Individuals and groups peacefully exercising their rights to freedom of expression, association and assembly continued to face repression. Some conditional releases of prisoners of conscience gave rise to hopes that the attitude of the Cuban government towards dissidents might be thawing, but new sentences and a serious escalation in repression during the closing months of 2000 discouraged such optimism. Journalists, political opponents and human rights defenders were subjected to severe harassment. . . .[44]

Cuba has publicly confirmed its willingness to broach the subject of human rights. And why not? The Castro government is obviously conscious of its own human rights shortcomings and equally conscious that its record can stand up against those of many Latin American and Asian countries that continue to enjoy strong commercial relations with the United States. China and Vietnam, both communist states, have abominable human rights records, yet they continue to receive most favored nation treatment.[45] This double standard led Peter Schwab to argue that ever since "the presidency of Jimmy Carter, the polemic surrounding human rights has reached a new crescendo that tends to overwhelm any rational discourse of the subject." Schwab went on to argue,

> [T]he very support given by Washington to Third World leaders who blatantly violate the political rights of their citizens calls into question both the honesty and seriousness of the United States when it condemns human rights violations in Cuba. . . . The double standard indicates that the U.S. position is based less on the issue of human rights and more on its fury in seeing Fidel Castro retaining power in a communist state 90 miles away and in the heart of America's special interest, while being frustrated that its 37-year-long embargo has been unable to alter Cuba's political dynamic.[46]

Indeed, Fisk suggests (in Chapter Five of this volume) that such arguments have begun to turn the tide of popular opinion in the United States and to renew dialogue on the whole concept of the embargo. It has not gone unnoticed that in the Latin American context, Amnesty International (AI) reported in 1996 that Cuba — when compared with such countries as Brazil, Chile, Colombia, Mexico, Nicaragua, and Guatemala — had a better human rights rating.[47] The same AI report noted extrajudicial executions by police and death squads in those countries. Likewise, it pointed out torture and the annual disappearance of hundreds of people, many of whom, in the case of Guatemala and Colombia, were "activists, former refugees, religious personnel, street children, and trade unionists."[48] In most cases, the perpetrators of the violations in these two countries were security forces and government-backed armed groups. According to the AI report, torture, extrajudicial execution, and disappearance of individuals were absent in Cuba's case, though reference was made in the report to the presence of some prisoners of conscience and several political prisoners in Cuban jails.

More than U.S. decisionmakers, Canadian officials who visited Cuba in the mid-1990s shared the views of the AI report and went out of their way to praise Cuba's strengths. These officials maintained that Cuba is not a frightening police state and that its record pales in comparison with the violent repression in nearby countries with which the United States encourages business. Mark Entwistle, Canada's ambassador to Cuba, argued in 1996 that Cuba has made major advances in health care and education and has provided a minimum standard of life. "There are cases of violations of human rights, but the kind of abuses of the individual that you see in many other countries doesn't exist in Cuba. There are no patterns of torture. People don't disappear in the middle of the night." Entwistle continued, "Canada would like to see greater freedom in Cuba but is not about to lecture or harangue Havana."[49] Even Max Yalden, a retired human rights commissioner appointed by Ottawa to help make its citizen complaint system more transparent and independent, agrees with Entwistle: "I don't have the impression Cuba is a boiling cauldron of anti-Castroism or that a lid is being kept on." He argues that many of the civil and political rights Canadians take for granted — a free press and multiparty elections — are not the only measures of progress. His view is that Cuba should be given credit for "significant achievements in the rights of the population to health care, education, social safety, and equality for women, children, and the disabled." As for other rights, he has noted, "It will take patient work with Cuban authorities — we realize you're not going to change them overnight."[50]

Yalden's pronouncements mirrored Canada's official position that it is better to coax civil and political freedoms out of Cuba by constructive engagement, that is, increased investment and trade combined with diplomacy, rather than by adopting the more combative U.S. approach. This is why Axworthy made his historic visit to Cuba in January 1997, the first time that a senior member of the cabinet had visited Cuba since Trudeau's visit in 1976. Groundwork for this meeting had been laid in the latter part of 1996, when Ottawa hosted Cuban Foreign Minister Robaina and Cuban Vice President Carlos Lage for discussion of important bilateral issues, including human rights. Axworthy met in Havana with Castro, Robaina, and other senior Cuban officials.[51] Discussions covered a wide range of issues, including foreign investment, economic cooperation, drug interdiction, terrorism, and human rights. The eventual result was the signing of a 14-point Canada-Cuba Joint Declaration on Bilateral Cooperation. The contents of the communiqué issued at the end of the meeting became the cornerstone of Canadian policy toward Cuba and spelled out the principles of constructive engagement.[52]

The communiqué stressed joint cooperation and continuing dialogue between both states in the administration of justice, including exchanges of judges; parliamentary exchanges; broadening and deepening of cooperation and consultation on human rights through exchanges among officials, academics, professionals, and experts; support for the activities of Cuban and Canadian NGOs; technical support for Cuba's policy of economic reform; collaboration on narcotics interdiction; prevention of international terrorism; provision of food aid to Cuba; and exploration of joint research and development projects in the health and environment sectors.[53]

Axworthy's meeting in Havana predictably generated strong reaction in the United States. Nicholas Burns from the U.S. Department of State was blunt; he dismissed Axworthy's initiatives in this way: "There is no reason to believe that... the tiger is going to change its stripes."[54] Clinton also was critical: "While I am gratified that the Canadians ... are now talking more to the Cubans about human rights and democratic reforms ..., I am skeptical, frankly, that the discussions ... will lead to advances." However, Clinton was pleased that "the Canadians are trying to make something happen in Cuba."[55] U.S. Senator Jesse Helms (Republican, North Carolina) was less sanguine, drawing the analogy between Axworthy's visit to Cuba and Neville Chamberlain's appeasement of Hitler in 1938:

> You had someone named Neville Chamberlain, he went over and sat down with [Hitler] and came back and said, 'We can do [b]usiness with this guy,' and you saw what happened. One guy stood up and said, 'No, no,' [and his] name was [Winston Churchill]. Now if we're going to forget all principle and let Fidel Castro get by with all his atrocities, then we [had] better look at the status of our policy, and [Canada] certainly should look at the status of hers.[56]

Partly because of U.S. pressure and Canada's attempt to prove its southern neighbor wrong, Canada gave a higher profile to the human rights issue on the Canada-Cuba agenda. In this regard, a spate of activities followed Axworthy's January 1997 meeting. A Canada-Cuba Joint Committee on Human Rights was formed. Its mandate included the holding of joint seminars in Canada and Cuba on human rights and the promotion of reciprocal visits by legislators, academics, judges, and others. In May 1997, Havana hosted a seminar on children's rights in which Canada participated.[57] In that same month, as a result of Axworthy's intervention during his January meeting with the Cuban president, Castro released imprisoned dissident poet and author Cecilio Ismael Sambra Habar.[58] In June, Ottawa convened a conference on women's rights in which a high-powered Cuban delegation participated. Four months later, a delegation of legislators from the Cuban National Assembly met with Canadian parliamentarians in Ottawa as part of the Canada-Cuba parliamentary exchange program. In December 1997 and February 1998, Canadian and Cuban officials met to review the progress of the 14-point Joint Declaration. At the February encounter, both countries even signed an Air Transport Agreement and an Anti-hijacking Treaty.[59] No doubt influenced by U.S. pressure, Axworthy not only had put the human rights debate in Cuba on the front burner by 1998, but also had demonstrated the merits of constructive engagement.

THE POPE AND CASTRO

A historic event occurred in Cuba in January 1998, which contributed to the prominence that Canada had been giving to the policy of constructive engagement and the issue of human rights: the five-day visit by Pope John Paul II to the island. Castro welcomed the pope to Cuba, extremely mindful of the advantage he would gain from this visit through mobilization of world opinion against the U.S. trade embargo. In some respects, the Cuban leader had been preparing for the pastoral visit for some time. He had initiated political and economic reforms from the beginning of the 1990s and had made certain religious concessions. Proclaiming itself an atheist state since the 1959 Revolution, Cuba officially became a "secular" state in 1991, and practicing Catholics were allowed to join the Communist Party.[60] Christmas was declared an official holiday in 1997, outdoor masses and processions were encouraged, and more than 100 foreign priests and nuns were allowed to immigrate to Cuba.[61] Castro allowed an additional 28 priests and 29 nuns to enter Cuba from Colombia, Haiti, and Spain a few months before the pope's arrival, bringing the total number of clergy in the country to 754.[62] Indeed, a number of the concessions that the Vatican hoped to elicit from Castro had already been made by the time the pope arrived.

The pope not unexpectedly stressed the spiritual and religious nature of his visit. He praised those who maintained their "loyalty to Christ, the Church, and the pope" during Cuba's era of atheism and exhorted Cubans to rededicate themselves to Christianity. [63] His message had a common and simple theme: Faithfully following Christ must be the first step in solving many of Cuba's social ills. But the pope went further. In a subtle, yet obvious, tone, he criticized Cuba's human rights record, particularly in the realm of political dissent. While addressing a huge rally in Santiago de Cuba, the pope made a dramatic appeal for freedoms that extended beyond the religious sphere. He stated that there is much "suffering of the soul" in Cuba,

> . . . such as we see in those who are isolated, persecuted, imprisoned for various offenses or for reasons of conscience, for ideas which though dissident are nonetheless peaceful. These prisoners of conscience suffer an isolation and a penalty for which their own conscience does not condemn them. What they want

is to participate actively in life with the opportunity to speak their mind with respect and tolerance. I encourage efforts to reinsert prisoners into society.[64]

The pope's address was certainly a compassionate appeal for political dissidents in Cuba. Indeed, at the end of his Santiago de Cuba address, he submitted a list of 302 political prisoners the Vatican wanted released.

The category of human rights raised by the pope is interesting. No mention was made of social rights enjoyed by Cubans in such areas as health and education or of race and gender equality. The central issue for the Vatican was the lack of progress in political freedom. While the pope may have felt strongly about the lack of press freedom and the absence of a multiparty political system in Cuba, he gave prominence to the restrictions placed upon political dissidents by the Castro regime. In the eyes of the Vatican, as in those of the United States and Canada, Cuba stood accused of political abuse.

In one respect, however, the pope also stood on the side of Castro. He castigated economic embargoes, criticized unbridled capitalism, and attacked neoliberalism for subordinating "the human person to blind market forces" and conditioning "the development of peoples to those forces."[65] He echoed much of what Castro had been arguing for years. The pope's attack on economic embargoes culminated his visit. No doubt targeting the U.S. embargo on Cuba, Pope John Paul II said,

> In our day, no nation can live in isolation. The Cuban people, therefore, cannot be denied the contacts with other peoples necessary for economic, social, and cultural development, especially when the imposed isolation strikes the population indiscriminately, making it ever more difficult for the weakest to enjoy the bare essentials of decent living — things such as food, health, and education.[66]

This denunciation allowed Castro to take the moral high ground. In the presence of the pope, at José Martí International Airport, he launched a scathing attack on Washington for continuing the embargo. Using tDe biblical comparison of David and Goliath, Castro stated,

> Cuba, like a new and a thousand times smaller David, is currently confronting the greatest power in history, and, with the same sling of biblical times, is fighting for its survival against a mammoth Goliath of the nuclear age who is trying to prevent our development and bring us to our knees through hunger and through disease. If history had not been written then, we would have to write it now. This monstrous crime cannot be overlooked or excused.[67]

The pope's visit, while highlighting Cuba's democratic shortcomings, provided Castro with the perfect opportunity to plead his case against the United States and win international sympathy. By the end of the visit, it was clear, whether it was the intended purpose of the pope's visit or not, that this sympathy had been won and the real hindrance to Cuba's reintegration into the international community was neither Castro nor communism but the "Goliath of the nuclear age." The Cuban leader transmitted this message effectively to the world community through the electronic media and the 2,000 journalists from 56 countries who covered the papal visit.[68]

The positive atmosphere generated by the pope's visit did not end with his departure. Castro exploited the prevailing mood by implementing some of the pope's requests and, in so doing, maintained a perpetual glow of benevolence. By mid-February 1998, only a few weeks after the pope's departure, the Cuban government released 299 prisoners, of whom 70 were political dissidents. Alejandro González, a Cuban Foreign Ministry spokesman, announced that 75 of those released had been requested by the pope, while 106 of those on his list had been released prior to the pope's arrival in Cuba. González pointed out, however, that between 60 and 70 of those on the list could not be released because of the severity of their crimes.[69] To many observers, Castro's actions signaled that the papal visit was the beginning of a new era in Cuba. His actions were seen as a genuine gesture for Cuba's inclusion in the new world order. International optimism and expectations rose to new heights. Castro was expected to make further concessions, but this he was reluctant to do — at least for the time being.

CONSTRUCTIVE ENGAGEMENT AFTER THE POPE'S VISIT

The pope's visit gained credibility for Canada's policy of constructive engagement. The presence of the pope in Cuba reflected the importance that the Vatican attached to dialogue; on that score alone, Canadian foreign policymakers had to be elated. Equally significant was the pope's criticism of economic embargoes as "unjust and ethically unacceptable,"[70] which mirrored Canada's position. The pope's visit certainly was a boon for the architects of constructive engagement.

Buoyed by a supportive climate in the afterglow of the pope's visit, Canada continued its activist role in the field of human rights in Cuba. In the context of Castro's concession-making following the departure of the pope, Canada agreed to accept some 19 Cuban prisoners of conscience who had been included on the list presented by the pope to the Cuban government. Canada eventually accepted 14 of these after routine medical and security checks.[71] While Ottawa would have preferred that the dissidents remain in Cuba, its decision to allow them into Canada must be seen as a credible expression of its commitment to the policy of constructive engagement.

Three months after the pope's visit, Prime Minister Chrétien decided to make an official trip to Havana to cement relations further between the two countries. Chrétien's plan for the visit was leaked at the OAS Summit in Santiago, Chile, by the U.S. delegation, which expressed its usual misgivings about the Canadian initiative. Other countries at the summit, however, were quite supportive. In fact, the international criticism that had accompanied Axworthy's trip 15 months earlier was missing on this occasion. Obviously, this was no coincidence. For one thing, the trip was made in the wake of the euphoria created by the pope's visit; for another, it was planned in consultation with the Vatican.[72] In addition, by March 1998, the United States had responded to the pope's visit by taking steps to ease restrictions on Cuba. U.S. Secretary of State Madeleine Albright met with the pontiff in early March at the Vatican, where she was persuaded that Castro had made significant concessions to the Cuban Catholic Church to the extent that priests could now deliver uncensored sermons. It was time, therefore, for the United States to respond accordingly.

Consequently, President Clinton announced in mid-March 1998 that the United States would ease restrictions on food and medical supplies to Cuba, restore daily charter flights from Miami to Havana, and streamline the legal procedure for "nonprofit organizations to sell pharmaceuticals to Cuba." Ten months later, in January 1999, additional restrictions were relaxed. U.S. firms were allowed to sell food and agricultural supplies to private farms and restaurants in Cuba, U.S. citizens could send up to $1,200 in gifts to Cubans annually, and "the Baltimore Orioles were allowed to play two exhibition games against Cuba's national baseball team."[73] (See Chapter Five in this volume.)

While these relaxations theoretically allowed for some limited medical and food sales to Cuba, they were circumscribed by politically driven provisos that made them somewhat ineffective.[74] In any event, the pope's attack on the embargo led to this accomplishment. It was, therefore, not surprising for Chrétien to say at the Group of Eight (G-8) meeting in England, in May 1998, shortly after meeting with Clinton, that his trip to Cuba did not meet with the usual hostility expected from the United States.[75] The United States, it would seem, was prepared at that time to encourage further moves toward democratization in Cuba. Therefore, Chrétien's visit scheduled for April 1998 was strategically opportune. More important, it revealed the leadership role that Canada was prepared to take in the affairs of the Americas less than one decade after joining the OAS.

Chrétien's visit to Cuba, however, did not please his political critics at home. In the House of Commons, the Reform Party, Canada's main opposition force, called for a firm stance against human rights abuses in Cuba. In the Reform Party's view, "soft diplomacy" with Castro should give way to political and diplomatic rigidity. As Preston Manning, leader of the Reform Party, stressed in the Commons, if the pope was able to raise the issue of human rights publicly in Cuba, so should Chrétien. In fact, Manning was more direct when he sarcastically asked whether Canadians were likely to see the prime minister "not grandstanding with Castro" on television "to satisfy the anti-American component of his own caucus, but publicly raising human rights abuses in this harsh political dictatorship."[76]

The Reform Party's call for firm action and quick results in Cuba was partly the product of heightened expectations generated by the papal visit and partly the product of political expediency. Should Castro make additional human rights concessions because of Chrétien's intervention, the Reform Party wanted to share in the credit. Just as important, Reform's stance was reminiscent of the position that had been plaguing the U.S. relationship with Cuba for some 40 years. As hard-liners, the critics of constructive engagement were not prepared to entertain political or diplomatic flexibility on the issue of human rights. What Manning and his cohorts did not fully appreciate was that rigidity was incompatible with constructive engagement. In addition, it was foolhardy and even naïve to expect Chrétien to raise the sensitive issue of additional human rights concessions in the public sphere and thereby jeopardize constructive engagement. Additionally, the unwritten rules of diplomacy would not allow it.

Prime Minister Chrétien, however, seemed overwhelmed by Reform's trucu-lence and decided to gamble for high stakes. Given the concession-making mood in Cuba, Chrétien was somewhat optimistic about the possibility of managing some concessions from Castro. With this achieved, he would be able to remove the sting from Reform's tail. The misfortune, however, was that by trying to appease Manning, Chrétien gave himself little room to maneuver, especially when he committed himself to raising human rights issues and promised that the visit would "create some positive results just as the pope's visit did a few weeks ago."[77]

When Chrétien's televised public speech at José Martí International Airport on April 26, 1998, made little or no mention of human rights at the conclusion of his meeting with Castro, the Canadian prime minister played into the hands of his critics. They were waiting for this moment, and not even the stoic defense put up by Axworthy the following day during Question Period in the Commons would prevent a deluge of queries about the nature of the private discussions held between the heads of government in Cuba. To Reform Party critics especially, Axworthy's explanation that the prime minister's trip was not intended to start a confrontation but to build "effective bridges" to facilitate and reinforce positive changes taking place in Cuba rang hollow.[78] Even the media spoke out against the value of the visit. For instance, Marcus Gee wrote in *The Globe and Mail:* "Mr. Castro gave Mr. Chrétien almost nothing for the trouble of coming to Havana."[79] Like other critics, Gee felt that the prime minister should have demanded the unconditional release of political prisoners. A diplomatically sensitive issue, rightly discussed in private, unfortunately had now been forced into the public domain and blown out of proportion (for details, see Nicol, Chapter Seven in this volume.)

When Chrétien returned to Canada, he felt compelled to disprove the failure of his trip. In the midst of perceived public pressure,[80] he contributed to making the issue larger than it ought to have been. In an ill-advised act of political brinkmanship, he claimed that during his first meeting with Castro he demanded the release of four political prisoners whose names were included on the list earlier submitted by the pope (Marta Beatriz Roque Cabello, Vladimiro Roca Antúnez, René Gómez Manzano, and Félix Bonne Carcassés).[81] What was not publicized was Castro's reluctance to act. As Chrétien later admitted, Castro himself "would have preferred [me] not to raise [the issue of political dissenters]. . . . He defended his legal system, but took the list and said he would consider it."[82] Chrétien clearly did not appear confident that Castro would accede to his demands. Castro's reluctance became obvious when in response to the debate in Canada, he refused to get involved. Questioned about the possibility of changes in Cuba following Chrétien's visit, Castro quipped: "[T]he Revolution is the biggest change in history, and we aren't about to give it up." He also refused to discuss the fate of the political prisoners, basically stating that what transpired in his discussion with Chrétien was a private matter.[83] In fact, by the summer of 1998, Chrétien's hype, pressure by the right-wing media and the opposition parties, and Castro's refusal to release the four political prisoners as requested by Chrétien all contributed to a new urgency in Canada-Cuba relations that some critics felt would test the viability of constructive engagement.

To prove that constructive engagement was alive, Axworthy visited Cuba in January 1999 and made another plea for the release of the four dissidents. Since they were about to be put on trial, he requested that they be tried in an open court, where "claims against them could be made."[84] However, on this occasion, Axworthy, unlike Chrétien, was quick to point out that his trip was not exclusively designed to gain human rights concessions, but rather, intended to further dialogue and cooperation. To support that claim, he signed bilateral agreements on narcotics trafficking with his Cuban counterpart, Roberto Robaina.[85] Ottawa's main objective, undoubtedly, was for Castro to release the dissidents and allow the Liberal government to save face in Canada. This did not occur at that time.

The dissidents were not given an open trial and eventually were sentenced to several years in prison. Obviously, the Canadian government was disappointed. Chrétien commented that the judicial outcome in Cuba "sends an unfortunate signal to her friends in the international community when people are jailed for peaceful protest."[86] Castro's action, however, forced Chrétien to do something to save face because of the embarrassment he had brought upon himself. As Christina Warren of FOCAL argued, the Canadian prime minister had "staked himself out" on one issue — the release of four political prisoners — and when that did not materialize, he had nothing to fall back on.[87] In the meantime, criticisms mounted. Brian Mulroney, Canada's former prime minister, denounced the failure of the "soft diplomacy" of the Liberals,[88] and Bob Mills, the Reform Party's foreign affairs critic, asked, "How can the government deny that its 20 years of soft power policy toward Cuba has been anything but a total failure?"[89]

Chrétien found a solution. He argued that, while a minor setback had occurred in Canada-Cuba relations, constructive engagement was still working and provided the medium through which continuing pressure could be applied to the Castro regime: "If you have no relations with them," he said, "you cannot react, you cannot put pressure."[90] Axworthy expanded this explanation: "Constructive engagement and dialogue have produced major changes in helping broaden the area of religious freedom in Cuba. Last year, a number of political prisoners were released. We have had agreements signed on anti-terrorism and anti-drug matters. We have been able to improve the political space for civil groups. We have been able to help build the capacity in that country to deal with the problems of legislation and human rights. We are making some progress. There is a setback. It is a long road, but this government continues to be committed to try to bring about democratic change in that country."[91] In fact, Roque Cabello, Gómez Manzano, and Bonne Carcassés were released in May 2000. Roca Antúnez was released in May 2002. (See Koth, Chapter Six in this volume, Note 58.)

The Liberal government then agreed to undertake a review of Canada-Cuba relations. This action was intended to appease those at home who felt Canada was not tough enough with Castro. To that extent, the review was an act of political gamesmanship. The review did not challenge the tenets of constructive engagement, nor did it challenge engagement with Cuba. Economic sanctions definitely were not considered, but many bilateral programs were frozen until Castro showed signs of moving human rights issues forward. As Chrétien explained, Canada was still engaged with Cuba, but it was necessary "to put some northern ice in the middle of it."[92] The review concluded that Canada, a major supporter of Cuba's reentry into the OAS, would no longer encourage other OAS members to push for Cuba's reintegration. In fact, Canada would refrain from endorsing Cuba's invitation to the OAS Summit in Quebec City in April 2001. Foreign aid, although not entirely frozen, was to be reviewed on a case-by-case basis, while many projects were put on hold.[93]

The right-wing media and politicians were pleased with the results of the review. Such captions as "Canada Cooling on Cuba" and "Canada Gets Tough with Cuba" were prominent. It seemed as though Chrétien and Axworthy had brought the media to their side and had made a shift in policy toward Cuba. Perhaps they wanted to show that the Liberal government was not a victim of soft diplomacy but could act effectively.

Unfortunately, this shift in policy was unnecessary and unwarranted and was taken for the wrong reasons. Having committed an error in political and diplomatic judgment, the Liberal government fell victim to media hype and criticisms leveled by right-wing politicians. Under these circumstances, the Chrétien administration felt it politically expedient to take a firm stance against Castro in order to dispel any sign of alleged weakness on the part of the government. However, this decision was misguided, since it undermined the policy of constructive engagement and its potential for the resolution of differences through dialogue and negotiation, a strategy that had worked very well during the Chrétien years. Equally unfortunate was the fact that this step was taken to placate a small right-wing element in Canada that traditionally had been hostile to Castro's Cuba. By taking this route, the Liberals placed in jeopardy the strong record of good relations with Cuba established throughout the Chrétien years and culminating in the high point reached around the time of the pope's visit.

Canadian media hostility toward Cuba continued into the summer of 1999. During the Pan American Games, held in Winnipeg between July and September, news coverage focused more on the politics of defection by some Cuban athletes than on the outcome of the games. This was true of the *National Post, The Globe and Mail,* and *The Winnipeg Sun.*[94] Cuba was portrayed as a land of repression, where young athletes were denied freedom of mobility and freedom of choice, leaving defection as their only option. In a sense, what transpired in the media during the Pan American Games was a continuation of the campaign begun a few months earlier, which led Canada to undertake a review of Canada-Cuba relations. What was not adequately addressed in the media during the games was the alleged unethical and deliberate planting of agents in Winnipeg to encourage and facilitate defection. It appeared that the media was trying to undermine good relations between Canada and Cuba until Castro would agree to accelerate the process of democracy in Cuba (see Chapter Seven, this volume).

Castro was understandably incensed that the games had become a political arena. He also contended that in Winnipeg there were "scouts seeking athletes, advertising in the press — either subtly or openly, directly or indirectly, on television and other media — exhorting people to defect. . . . It is in such an adverse and hostile environment that our teams are competing."[95] Castro went to extremes by calling Canada "enemy territory" on account of this development, but the fact is that by the end of the 1990s, a substantial element in the Canadian media was not prepared to be flexible regarding Castro.

CONCLUSION

Constructive engagement evolved as a viable and fruitful policy in Canada's relations with Cuba during the Chrétien years. Although the roots of engagement go back to earlier administrations, Canada-Cuba relations received renewed vigor after the Liberal government came to power in the early 1990s. Canada has helped in the resuscitation of the Cuban economy; Canada's trade and investment in Cuba have grown exponentially; Canadian NGOs have played an important, constructive role in the development of present-day Cuba; and Canadians, who constitute the largest national grouping to visit Cuba annually, contribute substantially to the success of Cuba's tourism industry. Constructive engagement also has led to the rise of a market-based economy in Cuba through the emergence of farmers' markets, the "dollarization" of the economy, and the creation of family economic enterprises.

In addition, Canada has condemned Cuba's isolation and has openly criticized U.S. policy toward Cuba. During the Chrétien years, Canada has consistently called for Cuba's reintegration into the world economy and has joined others in the international community in condemning the U.S. trade embargo of the island. For Cuba, Canada represents an economic lifeline at a time of considerable economic and financial need. Indeed, since Prime Minister Chrétien took office, the profile of Canada-Cuba relations has risen. Beyond doubt, Canada's policy of constructive engagement continues to remain internationally acceptable and morally defensible.

For this reason, the decision of Chrétien's Liberal government not to invite Castro to the Summit of the Americas in Quebec City in April 2001 was unfortunate. Even though the decision had to be based on consensus and was not the exclusive prerogative of the Canadian government, the fact that John Manley, Axworthy's successor as foreign affairs minister, endorsed the decision not to invite Cuba because it "lacks a commitment to democratic principles" demonstrated inconsistency and digression from previous Canadian policy.[96] Some critics of the Liberal government in Canada even have been led to conclude that the Canadian decision may have been the product of U.S. pressure. Nonetheless, the absence of Cuba at the Summit of the Americas in 2001 made Canadian policy toward Cuba vulnerable to accusations of inconsistency, and it undermined the sincerity of the call made in 1998 by Chrétien at the second Summit of the Americas in Santiago, Chile, to bring Cuba into the *gran familia* (big family) of the Americas — particularly as nothing had changed fundamentally in Cuban society since then.

As of mid-2002, Canada-Cuba relations remain somewhat strained, but tremendous goodwill still exists between the countries. Constructive engagement continues as the cornerstone of Canada's policy toward Cuba, and both countries agree upon far more issues than they disagree. However, since Pope John Paul II's visit to Cuba, Canada has displayed an element of unnecessary impatience by pushing for quick changes in the human rights sector, in hopes of winning political kudos at home. The rush to push Castro failed. Canada's style was both uncharacteristic and not in conformity with constructive engagement, contradicting what Canadians themselves had been saying for years: "Change in Cuba is not going to happen overnight."[97] It also was contrary to the view articulated by Secretary of State Stewart a few years earlier — that such an approach could only reinforce "the wrong kind of nationalism and political rigidity" in Cuba. Canadian leaders have acknowledged that their impatience backfired. Constructive engagement, by its very nature, entails a long-term process of dialogue and negotiation.

To Castro's credit, some 299 out of a total of approximately 600 political prisoners were released after the papal visit, a positive gesture of movement and progress. However, expecting Castro to bend in the face of pressure tactics was a gross miscalculation of Castro's personality and the history of his regime. What Chrétien failed to appreciate was that Castro "is unlikely to implement reforms in the face of pressure tactics, as nine U.S. presidents have witnessed personally."[98] Moreover, the parameters of the agenda set by Chrétien were far too limited to achieve positive results. As author John M. Kirk has commented, "To expect immediate results following four decades of U.S. hostility would be dreaming in technicolor."[99] Moreover, as Kirk later said, Chrétien was "foolishly optimistic and naïve."[100]

Now in 2002, Canada, for its part, must ensure that nothing untoward is done to undermine or derail the policy of constructive engagement. Certainly, the circumstances and dynamics that have produced the debacle over human rights do not justify putting foreign aid assistance to Cuba on hold nor isolating it from multilateral hemispheric discussions. These restrictions should be reviewed, and constructive engagement should be put back on track. Canada's liberal and progressive outlook as well as its diplomatic culture of compromise and understanding, for which it has become well-known, must not be jeopardized. Experience has shown that Castro is not one to buckle under pressure, and nothing that he did after the visit of the pope with respect to human rights justified Canada's negative actions. In recent years, Cuba has embarked upon a policy of economic liberalization. However, although signs of political liberalization can be seen in the island, Castro is not going to rush headlong into that process. No doubt, he found the Tiananmen Square experience in China instructive, as was the Soviet experience with *glasnost* and *perestroika*.[101]

Canada must continue to demonstrate patience, prudence, and flexibility in its dealings with Cuba if it is to offer an alternative to U.S. policy. After all, Canada also has vital economic and entrepreneurial interests to protect and must be politically pragmatic. Castro is not likely to continue as head of government for too much longer. Change is inevitable after his passing, and Canada needs to position itself to assist in the liberal democratic transition that will ensue in the new millennium. Canada is well placed to influence the direction that Cuba takes, despite the aforementioned outburst by Castro that Canada is "enemy territory." A better barometer of Canada-Cuba relations is the statement Castro made about Canada in 1994, when he said the following about Canada and Canadians:

> [Canadians have been] . . . our best friends — the most firm and loyal, the most independent. . . . I have always [referred to] Canada-Cuba relations as an example to follow. What a pity that, instead of having the United States so close by, and Canada so far away, it wasn't the other way around . . . and I often ask myself, just what are these Canadians? Are they English? Or Europeans? Are they French? Or Indians or Inuit? What are they, anyway? And I can find only one answer: they are good people.

In this world in which there have been so many colonialists — the Canadians have colonized nobody. In this world where rich nations have intervened everywhere — especially in Africa and Latin America — the Canadians have not intervened anywhere. So what are Canadians? And I say that they are good people, wonderful people. And for all these reasons, we Cubans are proud to be their friends.[102]

Nothing has altered the Canada-Cuba relationship radically since the time of Castro's statement above, the recent human rights wrangle notwithstanding. In this political context, constructive engagement, whatever its weaknesses, is more likely to contribute to positive change in Cuba than a policy of estrangement. Canada is well placed to influence this change. Cuban soil is fertile. The opportunity for Canada to make a significant difference during Cuba's transition to a new administration in the future must not be missed because of political or diplomatic miscalculation.

Notes

1. A number of scholars have contributed to the literature on this subject, including Peter McKenna and John M. Kirk, 1999, "Canada, Cuba and 'Constructive Engagement' in the 1990s," in *Canada, the US, and Cuba: Helms-Burton and Its Aftermath,* ed. Heather N. Nicol (Kingston, Ontario: Centre for International Relations, Queen's University); Sahadeo Basdeo, 1999, "Helms-Burton Controversy: An Issue in Canada-U.S. Foreign Relations," in *Canada, the US and Cuba: Helms-Burton and Its Aftermath,* ed. Heather N. Nicol (Kingston, Ontario: Centre for International Relations, Queen's University); Stephen J. Randall, 1998, *A Not So Magnificent Obsession: The United States, Cuba, and Canada from Revolution to the Helms-Burton Law* (Orono, Maine: University of Maine); Edgar J. Dosman, 1985, "Hemispheric Relations in the 1980s: A Canadian Perspective," *Journal of Canadian Studies* 19 (Winter): 42-60; James Rochlin, 1994, *Discovering the Americas: The Evolution of Canadian Foreign Policy Towards Latin America* (Vancouver, B.C.: University of British Colombia Press); George W. Schuyler, 1991, "Perspectives on Canada and Latin America: Changing Context . . . Changing Policy," *Journal of Interamerican Studies and World Affairs* 33 (Spring):19-59; Peter McKenna, 1993, "How is Canada Doing in the OAS?" *Canadian Foreign Policy* (Spring).

2. Schuyler 1991, 2.

3. Basdeo 1999, 10.

4. Randall 1998, 9.

5. Randall 1998, 3.

6. Canadian Association for Latin American and Caribbean Studies (CALACS) (Atlantic Chapter), 1989, "Thirty Years of the Cuban Revolution: An Assessment," a conference held at St. Mary's University, November 1-4, Halifax, Nova Scotia, Canada.

7. In 1984, Francisco Chaviano González lost his position as a high school mathematics teacher in Havana for his open criticism of Cuba's educational system. While working for several years in the Ministry of the Interior (Ministerio del Interior — MININT), he continued to denounce the Castro government and was eventually fired from his job. In 1989, he was caught by Cuban police as he tried to leave the island on a raft and sent to police headquarters' prison at Villa Maristas. While in jail, he formed the Cuban Rafters Council (Consejos de Lancheros de Cuba), a support group for Cuban prisoners serving time for trying to leave the island clandestinely. Chaviano's organization later became the National Council for Civil Rights in Cuba (Consejo Nacional por los Derechos Civiles en Cuba), a group whose research on the Cuban rafter problem attracted international attention to this migration issue. In 1994, Cuban authorities broke into Chaviano's home and arrested him, sentencing the civil rights activist to 15 years in Havana's Combinado del Este prison. See "Brief Biography of Francisco Chaviano González," at <http://www.fiu.edu/~fcf/chaviano 102797.html>.

8. See note 5 in Chapter Seven, by Heather N. Nicol, this volume.

9. *Maclean's,* 1996, March 11.

10. See note 58 in Chapter Six, by Karl B. Koth, this volume.

11. James J. Guy, 1990, "The Caribbean: A Canadian Perspective," in *Canadian-Caribbean Relations: Aspects of a Relationship,* ed. Brian Tennyson (Sydney, Nova Scotia: Centre for International Studies, University College of Cape Breton), 293.

12. *Ottawa Citizen,* 1996, December 7.

13. For an extensive discussion of these initiatives, see John M. Kirk and Peter McKenna, 1997, *Canada-Cuba Foreign Relations: The Other Good Neighbor Policy* (Gainesville, Fla.: The University Press of Florida), 133-135.

14. Cited in Schuyler 1991, 6.

15. Cited in Rochlin 1994, 119.

16. Basdeo 1999, 10.

17. *Ottawa Citizen,* 1996, December 7.

18. McKenna and Kirk 1999, 59.

19. Basdeo 1999, 11.

20. Canada, Department of Foreign Affairs and International Trade, 1995, "Robaina Visit to Mark 50 Years of Diplomatic Ties between Canada and Cuba," News Release No. 56 (March 17), 1. See also McKenna and Kirk 1999, 60.

21. Basdeo 1999, 11.

22. "Cuba's Absence at America's Summit Skirts Formal Agenda," 1996, *Cuba INFO* 6 (16): 3.

23. Canada, Department of Foreign Affairs and International Trade, 1995, "Notes for an Address by the Honourable Christine Stewart, Secretary of State (Latin America and Africa), to the 25th General Assembly of the Organization of American States," Statement (June 6), 3.

24. Canada, Department of Foreign Affairs and International Trade, 1996, "Notes for an Address by the Honourable Christine Stewart, Secretary of State (Latin America and Africa), to the 26th General Assembly of the Organization of American States," Statement (June 3), 7.

25. Christine Stewart, 1996, "Keynote Address," in *Helms-Burton and International Business: Legal and Commercial Implications,* ed. Wendy Drukier (Ottawa: FOCAL), 4-5.

26. Stewart 1996, 3.

27. For a discussion of the international responses to the Helms-Burton Act, see Donna Rich Kaplowitz, 1998, *Anatomy of a Failed Embargo: U.S. Sanctions Against Cuba* (Boulder, Colo.: Lynne Rienner Publishers), 184-186.

28. For a discussion on this subject, see Basdeo 1999, 19-21; see also Randall 1998, 18.

29. *Maclean's,* 1996, August 19.

30. *Maclean's,* 1996, August 19.

31. Cited in *Maclean's,* 1996, August 19.

32. Cited in *Maclean's,* 1996, August 19.

33. The reasons President Clinton was forced to back down are discussed in Basdeo 1999, 19.

34. *Financial Post Daily,* 1996, December 3.

35. *Financial Post Daily,* 1996, August 29.

36. Leon Sullivan was a black American Baptist minister who died on April 25, 2001. He was a strong defender of human rights and contributed considerably to the U.S. fight against apartheid in South Africa. He was best known for developing The Sullivan Principles, drafted in 1977, which called for social desegregation in the workplace, equal pay for equal work, and the promotion of nonwhites to better positions, among others. These ethical guidelines were later accepted by some 125 U.S. corporations conducting business in South Africa. See "Leon Sullivan Dies at 78," May 3, 2001, *Christianity Today,* at <http://www.christianitytoday.com/ct/2001/118/44.0.html>.

37. *Financial Post Daily,* 1996, August 31.

38. Cited in Kirk and McKenna 1997, 158.

39. Cited in Kirk and McKenna 1997, 158.

40. Cited in Kirk and McKenna 1997, 158.

41. Kirk and McKenna 1997, 179.

42. Stewart 1996, 4.

43. Elizardo Sanchez, director of the Comisión de Derechos Humanos y Reconciliación in Havana, cited in John Rice, 1998, "Urgen a EEUU que afloje el cerco a Cuba," *El Nuevo Dia Interactivo* (San Juan, Puerto Rico), July 12.

44. Amnesty International, 2001, "Cuba," *Amnesty International Report 2001,* <http://www.web.amnesty.org/web/ar2001.nsf/webamrcountries/cuba>.

45. Peter Schwab, 1999, *Cuba: Confronting the U.S. Embargo* (New York: St. Martin's Press), 1.

46. Schwab 1999, 7.

47. *Ottawa Citizen,* 1996, December 9.

48. *Ottawa Citizen,* 1996, December 9.

49. *Ottawa Citizen,* 1996, December 9.

50. *Ottawa Citizen,* 1996, December 9.

51. *Globe and Mail,* 1997, January 24.

52. Department of Foreign Affairs and International Trade, 1998, *Joint Declaration of the Ministers of Foreign Affairs of Canada and Cuba* (Havana, January 22, 1997), available at <http://www.dfait-maeci.gc.ca/english/foreignp/jd_w_cba.htm>; this site also contains a link for the document in Spanish.

53. *Ottawa Citizen,* 1997, January 24.

54. *Ottawa Citizen,* 1997, January 24.

55. *Ottawa Citizen,* 1997, January 24.

56. *The Economist,* 1997, February 8.

57. McKenna and Kirk 1999, 68.

58. *Maclean's,* 1998, January 19.

59. McKenna and Kirk 1999, 69.

60. *Maclean's,* 1998, January 19; see also Alma Guillermoprieto, 1998, "A Visit to Havana," *New York Review of Books* 45 (5) (March 26): 19-20.

61. *U.S. News & World Report,* 1998, January 26.

62. Schwab 1999, 129.

63. Cited in *Granma International Digital Edition,* 1998, January 21.

64. Cited in *New York Times,* 1998, January 25.

65. *New York Times,* 1998, January 26.

66. *New York Times,* 1998, January 26.

67. Fidel Castro, 1998, January 25, cited in *Granma International Digital Edition.*

68. *Cnews (Associated Press),* 1998, January 21.

69. *Catholic World News,* 1998, February 20.

70. Cited in Schwab 1999, 128.

71. *Catholic World News,* 1998, February 27; see also McKenna and Kirk 1999, 74.

72. *Globe and Mail,* 1998, April 20.

73. *The Economist,* 1999, January 9, 29.

74. Schwab 1999, 130-131. The slight easing of U.S. regulations could scarcely improve the island's health or nutritional conditions. For one thing, each transaction must receive prior approval from U.S. officials to validate that the sale would not benefit the Cuban government and that such supplies will be handled only by independent, non-governmental agencies. Furthermore, with supplies issued only to NGOs, most medical resources tend to end up being dispersed to wealthier Cubans and foreigners who can afford private clinics. The majority of Cubans use government clinics that do not qualify under U.S. regulations.

75. McKenna and Kirk 1999, 70.

76. Preston Manning, 1998, Oral Question Period in the House of Commons, April 21.

77. Jean Chrétien, 1998, Oral Question Period in the House of Commons, April 21.

78. Lloyd Axworthy, 1998, Oral Question Period in the House of Commons, April 27.

79. Marcus Gee, 1998, "Chrétien's Cuban Folly," *Globe and Mail,* April 29.

80. *The Globe and Mail,* 1998, April 28.

81. *Maclean's,* 1998, May 11.

82. Cited in *Globe and Mail,* 1998, April 28.

83. Cited in *Globe and Mail,* 1998, April 29.

84. *Ottawa Citizen,* 1999, January 11.

85. *Globe and Mail*, 1999, January 8.

86. Cited in *Globe and Mail*, 1999, March 16; see also Canadian Press Newswire, 1999, March 15.

87. Cited in Canadian Press Newswire, 1999, March 16. See <http://www.ap.org/is/canpress.html>.

88. Cited in *National Post*, 1999, April 24.

89. Bob Mills, 1999, Oral Question Period in the House of Commons, March 16.

90. Cited in Canadian Press Newswire, 1999, March 16.

91. Lloyd Axworthy, 1999, Oral Question Period in the House of Commons, March 16.

92. Cited in *New York Times*, 1999, June 30.

93. For terms of the bilateral review, see *Globe and Mail*, 1999, June 29.

94. *National Post*, 1999, July 19; *Globe and Mail*, 1999, September 4; and *Winnipeg SUN*, 1999, July 21 and July 26.

95. Cited in *Washington Post*, 1999, August 4.

96. Canadian Press Newswire, 2001, "Canada Changed Position on Cuba's Participation in Summit, Minister Reveals," March 15.

97. McKenna and Kirk 1999, 70.

98. McKenna and Kirk 1999, 70

99. Cited in *Toronto Star*, 1999, March 17.

100. Cited in *Human Events*, 1999, July 30.

101. Basdeo 1999, 5.

102. President Fidel Castro, cited in Kirk and McKenna 1997, 182.

References

Amnesty International. 2001. "Cuba." *Amnesty International Report 2001.* <http://www.web.amnesty.org/web/ar2001.nsf/webamrcountries/cuba>.

Axworthy, Lloyd. 1998. Oral Question Period in Canada's House of Commons. April 27.

Basdeo, Sahadeo. 1999. "Helms-Burton Controversy: An Issue in Canada-U.S. Foreign Relations." In *Canada, the US and Cuba: Helms-Burton and Its Aftermath,* ed. Heather N. Nicol. Kingston, Ontario: Centre for International Relations, Queen's University.

Boehm, Peter H. 1998. "Notes for a Speech to the Annual Meeting of the Cuban Committee for Democracy." *Statements and Speeches.* September 12.

"Brief Biography of Francisco Chaviano González." See <http://www.fiu.edu/~fcf/chaviano102797.html>.

Burnside, Scott. 1999. "Cubans Carping about All That's Evil." *National Post,* July 30.

Canada, Department of Foreign Affairs and International Trade. 1995. "Notes for an Address by the Honourable Christine Stewart, Secretary of State (Latin America and Africa), to the 25th General Assembly of the Organization of American States." Statement. June 6.

Canada, Department of Foreign Affairs and International Trade. 1995. "Robaina Visit to Mark 50 Years of Diplomatic Ties between Canada and Cuba." News Release No. 56, March 17.

Canada, Department of Foreign Affairs and International Trade. 1996. "Notes for an Address by the Honourable Christine Stewart, Secretary of State (Latin America and Africa), to the 26th General Assembly of the Organization of American States." Statement. June 3.

Canadian Association for Latin American and Caribbean Studies (CALACS), Atlantic Chapter. 1989. "Thirty Years of the Cuban Revolution: An Assessment." A conference held at St. Mary's University, November 1-4, Halifax, Nova Scotia.

Canadian Press Newswire. 1999. March 15. See <http://www.ap.org/is/canpress.html>.

Canadian Press Newswire. 1999. March 16. See <http://www.ap.org/is/canpress.html>.

Canadian Press Newswire. 2001. "Canada Changed Position on Cuba's Participation in Summit, Minister Reveals." March 15.

Catholic World News. 1998. February 20.

Catholic World News. 1998. February 27.

Chrétien, Jean. 1998. Oral Question Period in Canada's House of Commons. April 21.

Cnews (Associated Press). 1998. January 21.

"Cuba's Absence at America's Summit Skirts Formal Agenda." 1996. *Cuba INFO* 6 (16): 3.

Department of Foreign Affairs and International Trade. 1998. *Joint Declaration of the Ministers of Foreign Affairs of Canada and Cuba.* Havana, January 22, 1997. Available at <http://www.dfait-maeci.gc.ca/english/foreignp/jd_w_cba.htm>; this site contains a link for the document in Spanish.

Dosman, Edgar J. 1985. "Hemispheric Relations in the 1980s: A Canadian Perspective." *Journal of Canadian Studies* 19: Winter.

Drukier, Wendy, ed. 1996. *Helms-Burton and International Business: Legal and Commercial Implications.* Ottawa: Canadian Foundation for the Americas (FOCAL).

Economist, The. 1997. February 8.

Economist, The. 1999. January 9.

Fife, Robert. 1999. "Chrétien Stung by Castro's Vitriol Over Pan Am Games." *National Post,* July 28.

Financial Post Daily. 1996. August 29.

Financial Post Daily. 1996. August 31.

Financial Post Daily. 1996. December 3.

Gee, Marcus. 1998. "Chrétien's Cuban Folly." *Globe and Mail,* April 29.

Globe and Mail. 1997. January 24.

Globe and Mail. 1998. April 20.

Globe and Mail. 1998. April 28

Globe and Mail. 1998. April 29.

Globe and Mail. 1999. January 8.

Globe and Mail. 1999. March 16.

Globe and Mail. 1999. June 29.

Globe and Mail. 1999. September 4.

Granma International Digital Edition. 1998. January 21.

Green, Graham N. 1999. "No More Mr. Nice Guy." *National Post,* August 4.

Guillermoprieto, Alma. 1998. "A Visit to Havana." *New York Review of Books* 45 (5) March 26: 19-24.

Guy, James J. 1990. "The Caribbean: A Canadian Perspective." In *Canadian-Caribbean Relations: Aspects of a Relationship,* ed. Brian Tennyson. Sydney, Nova Scotia: Centre for International Studies, University College of Cape Breton.

Hoy, Claire. 1999. "Right Stand on Cuba." *Toronto Star,* March 17.

Human Events. 1999. July 30.

Jiménez, Marina. 1999. "PM's Favour to Pope Unravels as 4 Cubans are Left in Limbo." *National Post,* September 30.

Kaplowitz, Donna Rich. 1998. *Anatomy of a Failed Embargo: U.S. Sanctions Against Cuba.* Boulder, Colo.: Lynne Rienner Publishers.

Kirk, John M., and Peter McKenna. 1997. *Canada-Cuba Foreign Relations: The Other Good Neighbor Policy.* Gainesville, Fla.: The University Press of Florida.

"Leon Sullivan Dies at 78." 2001. *Christianity Today,* May 3, at <http://www.christianitytoday.com/ct/2001/118/44.0.html>.

Maclean's. 1996. March 11.

Maclean's. 1996. August 19.

Maclean's. 1998. January 19.

Maclean's. 1998. "Jean and Fidel: How a Pragmatist Tried to Sway an Ideologue," May 11.

Maclean's. 1999. "A Deepening Chill on Cuba," July 12.

Manning, Preston. 1998. Oral Question Period in Canada's House of Commons. April 21.

McKenna, Peter. 1993. "How Is Canada Doing in the OAS?" *Canadian Foreign Policy* 1(2) Spring: 81-98.

McKenna, Peter, and John Kirk. 1999. "Canada, Cuba and 'Constructive Engagement' in the 1990s." In *Canada, the US and Cuba: Helms-Burton and Its Aftermath*, ed. Heather N. Nicol. Kingston: Centre for International Relations, Queen's University.

Morris, Nomi. 1998. "Cooling on Cuba: Many Canadians May Detest It, but Helms-Burton Is Having an Impact." *Maclean's* March 9.

National Post. 1999. April 24.

National Post. 1999. July 19.

New York Times. 1998. January 25.

New York Times. 1998. January 26.

New York Times. 1999. June 30.

Nicol, Heather N., ed. 1999. *Canada, the US, and Cuba: Helms-Burton and Its Aftermath*. Kingston, Ontario: Centre for International Relations, Queen's University.

Ottawa Citizen. 1996. December 7.

Ottawa Citizen. 1996. December 9.

Ottawa Citizen. 1997. January 24.

Ottawa Citizen. 1999. January 11.

Phillips, Andrew. 1998. "Preparing for the Pope." *Maclean's,* January 19: 40-44.

Powell, Camille. 1999. "Cubans Angry at Coverage of Defections at Games." *Washington Post*, August 4.

Randall, Stephen J. 1998. *A Not So Magnificent Obsession: The United States, Cuba, and Canada from Revolution to the Helms-Burton Law*. Orono, Maine: University of Maine.

Robinson, Linda. 1999. "Catholics, Cuban Style: Castro Stands to Gain, Not Lose, from the Pope's Visit." *U.S. News & World Report,* January 26.

Rochlin, James. 1994. *Discovering the Americas: The Evolution of Canadian Foreign Policy Towards Latin America*. Vancouver, B.C.: University of British Columbia Press.

Sanchez, Elizardo. 1998. Cited in John Rice, "Urgen a EEUU que afloje el cerco a Cuba." *El Nuevo Dia Interactivo* (San Juan, Puerto Rico), July 12.

Schuyler, George W. 1991. "Perspectives on Canada and Latin America: Changing Context . . . Changing Policy." *Journal of Interamerican Studies and World Affairs* 33: Spring.

Schwab, Peter. 1999. *Cuba: Confronting the U.S. Embargo*. New York: St. Martin's Press.

Scoffield, Heather. 1999. "End Cuban Embargo, U.S. Business Leader Says." *Globe and Mail*, November 3.

Stewart, Christine. 1996. "Keynote Address." In *Helms-Burton and International Business: Legal and Commercial Implications*, ed. Wendy Drukier. Ottawa, Ontario: FOCAL.

Tennyson, Brian, ed. 1990. *Canadian-Caribbean Relations: Aspect of a Relationship*. Sydney, Nova Scotia: Centre for International Studies, University College of Cape Breton.

Toronto Star. 1999. March 17.

Trickey, Mike. 1999. "PM's Cuba Stance Criticized: Human Rights Report." *National Post*, July 24.

U.S. News & World Report. 1998. January 26.

Wallace, Bruce. 1999. "Cuba's Sweet, Uneven Beat." *Maclean's*, July 19: 28-29.

Washington Post. 1999. August 4.

Winnipeg SUN. 1999. July 21.
Winnipeg SUN. 1999. July 26.

CHAPTER THREE

Canada-Cuba Relations: "Northern Ice" or *Nada Nuevo?*[1]

PETER MCKENNA, JOHN M. KIRK, AND CHRISTINE CLIMENHAGE

C anadians are often considered easygoing people. In contrast, Cubans frequently appear inflexible. When the two groups meet, their bilateral relationship can be awkward. The Canada-Cuba relationship is undergoing a rough period, described by Prime Minister Jean Chrétien as experiencing some "northern ice."[2] As this chapter will show, several problem areas have influenced the relationship over the past few years. From a long-term perspective, there is nothing particularly new about short-term disruptions in Canada-Cuba relations. In 2000, a senior Canadian official in Washington remarked, "It's basically a bizarre vignette in the overall relationship."[3]

In fact, every Canadian government, regardless of political stripe, has experienced difficulties with the government of Fidel Castro. Prime Minister John Diefenbaker (1957-1963) refused to meet with Castro in Montreal and had to endure the 1961 Cuban Missile Crisis; Lester Pearson (1963-1968) adopted a "coldly correct" approach to Cuba and dreaded the thought of Castro's making a grand appearance at Montreal's Expo '67 celebrations; and Pierre Trudeau (1968-1979, 1980-1984) saw the relationship sour over Cuban involvement in the Angolan War in the late 1970s. By focusing on closer relations with the United States, Brian Mulroney (1983-1993) allowed Canada's relationship with Cuba to deteriorate. Although the Jean Chrétien administration (1993-) has developed a more open, positive relationship with Cuba, there have been a few low points.[4]

This chapter examines the most recent phase in Canada-Cuba bilateralism in a larger historical context. Various problems and difficulties afflicting the two countries' relations over the past several years are outlined, beginning with Chrétien's April 1998 visit to Cuba. Explanations of this recent period in light of the overall relationship and the principal driving forces behind this bond are given. The chapter concludes with an overview of the likely future of the Canada-Cuba relationship.

CANADA AND CUBA HIT A ROUGH PATCH

I n what might be termed "moderately successful" official meetings in Cuba early in 1998, both Chrétien and Castro left the table with some tangible benefits.

Chrétien was able to strengthen the Canada-Cuba relationship politically, an issue important to the U.S. government, which at that time was quietly positioning itself for a post-blockade Cuba. Canada also signed a perfunctory trade and investment agreement with Cuba and met with representatives of its nascent civil society. Castro, for his part, was able to use Chrétien's visit to embarrass and condemn the United States, secure some international political respectability, and bolster a solid commercial and technological relationship with a leading industrialized country. On the thorny issue of human rights, however, very little meaningful progress was made.

Clearly, a good deal of what underscores the current freeze in Canada-Cuba relations can be explained by the question of human rights.[5] The July 1997 incarceration of four political dissidents — Marta Beatriz Roque Cabello, Vladimiro Roca Antúnez, Félix Bonne Carcassés, and René Gómez Manzano — was a critical breaking point in the relationship. These dissidents were dubbed the Group of Four or the Dissidence Working Group (Grupo de Trabajo de la Disidencia Interna).[6] Indeed, during his high-profile visit, Chrétien pushed very hard to have these cases reviewed and reexamined by Cuban authorities (see also Basdeo and Hesketh in Chapter Two of this volume). Some speculation has it that Chrétien actually linked Canada's willingness to champion Cuba's re-inclusion in the Organization of American States (OAS) to the release of the Group of Four.[7] Chrétien's prestige was on the line, along with his desire to disarm criticism from the United States with demonstrable evidence of success on the human rights front, following Foreign Affairs Minister Lloyd Axworthy's January 1997 Canada-Cuba Joint Declaration. The subsequent prison sentences meted out to the Group of Four were interpreted by officials in Ottawa as an insult to the bilateral relationship.

Setting aside the merits of Chrétien's plea, his efforts in this instance amounted to a blatant misreading of the Cuban modus operandi. Highly sensitive to human rights issues, Cubans do not respond well to implied pressure or questionable side deals. The Cuban government was not about to release what it viewed as four criminals (who had challenged Cuba's socialist Constitution) merely because the Canadian government was trying to play hardball while staking some credibility on its request. To Castro and his government, yielding to the request would have sent the wrong message internally, while establishing a bad precedent internationally. Although Canadian diplomats may have believed that some conces-sions could be wrested from the Cuban government, they learned the hard way that the Castro regime was not prepared to budge on this matter. Moreover, Canadian foreign policy mandarins miscalculated, believing that the Cuban government was far more interested in a seat at the OAS Permanent Council table than it actually was.

In June 1998, senior Canadian officials returned to Havana to explore with their Cuban counterparts the possibility of easing Cuba back into the inter-American fold. Although complete reintegration into the OAS was at issue, the question of closer cooperation was on the table in a number of functional areas — for example, the drug trade, confidence and security-building measures, the OAS Inter-American Drug Abuse Control Commission, and the Pan American Health Organization (PAHO). Any enthusiasm at the official level evidently dissipated as these initiatives made their way to the top.[8] In the main, the Castro government had been consistently cold toward the OAS and obviously was content with the existing inter-American status quo. If officialdom in Ottawa needed reminding, the message now was made clear: The Cuban government operates in its own world and definitely marches to the beat of a different drummer.

Three months after Chrétien's visit to Cuba, Canada's permanent representative to the OAS, Peter Boehm, waded into the Canada-Cuba dynamic. In an excellent speech before Miami's Cuban Committee for Democracy,[9] Boehm noted, "We should face the fact that the Cold War is over; it is time to get on with things and for the largest country in the Caribbean region to be part of the new order."[10] He also said that Canada's policy of "constructive engagement" was intended to promote peaceful change in Cuba, economic reforms, and Cuba's reintegration into the inter-American family.[11] In arguing that Canada's approach was more "results-oriented" than the "confrontational" policy of the United States, he was careful to say that Ottawa did have sharp differences with Havana in many key areas. However, on the question of Cuba's re-inclusion in the OAS, Boehm echoed the call of Minister Axworthy about the need to undertake exploratory efforts to have the Cubans return as full-fledged members of the hemispheric body.

In December 1998, senior officials from Axworthy's office met with Cuban officials in Havana to prepare for a second visit by Canada's foreign minister. Early in January 1999, Axworthy held a brief meeting with his Cuban counterpart, who at that time was Roberto Robaina, and with Vice President Carlos Lage to review the 14-point Joint Declaration of 1997, to sign a handful of minor bilateral accords, and to seek the release of the Group of Four. As Axworthy was unable to secure any movement on these human rights cases after three hours of talks with Castro, the likelihood of a cooling-off in the bilateral relationship appeared very real.[12]

When Havana announced the prison sentences for the leaders of the Group of Four some two months later, the Chrétien government responded quickly. Canada expressed its displeasure with Cuba in a tersely worded statement from the Prime Minister's Office that read: "Cuba sends an unfortunate signal to her friends in the international community when people are jailed for peaceful protest."[13] Accordingly, the prime minister ordered a full review of bilateral relations, effectively halting Canadian efforts to reintegrate Cuba in the hemisphere and canceling any planned ministerial visits — but stopping well short of imposing economic sanctions or canceling initiatives designed to foster political liberalization[14]

It is instructive to note that the review of the Cuba file was purely a political decision and not something that percolated upward from the Foreign Affairs bureaucracy. It was obvious that both Chrétien and Axworthy were bitterly disappointed over Cuba's actions, especially as they had expended a good deal of personal and political capital on the Group of Four. In addition, cross-pressures always have come from the United States, ever skeptical of Axworthy's 1997 Joint Declaration with the Cubans, for Canada to demonstrate some concrete results on the human rights front. Having failed to do so, Ottawa most likely undertook a program review to send diplomatic messages to Washington and Havana.

Interestingly, although Ottawa publicly professed its deep displeasure with the Cuban government, a month had passed without a single departmental meeting on the program review of bilateral relations with Cuba. In fact, members of

Canada's Standing Committee on Foreign Affairs and International Trade were demanding a full and prompt explanation from Axworthy. One government official was quoted as saying, "We don't have anything to announce yet. But the intention is still to continue our policy of constructive dialogue."[15] Thus, with the exception of scaling back the number of ministerial exchanges between the two countries, thereby denying the Castro government some international legitimacy, little had changed in the overall relationship.

The results of the Cuba review were articulated by Chrétien in the last week of June 1999, three months after the review was announced. One Canadian official characterized Ottawa's response in the following manner: "Continued engagement, curtailed activity."[16] The freeze on high-level visits to the island would continue, including those by International Trade Minister Sergio Marchi and International Cooperation Minister Diane Marleau, and Ottawa informed the Cuban government that it would not undertake efforts to have Cuba reintegrated into the OAS or pave the way for its attendance at the April 2001 Summit of the Americas in Quebec City. In addition, some bilateral aid projects were put on hold, and Canada used its vote at the UN Human Rights Commission to support a resolution condemning Cuba's record on human rights. According to a Department of Foreign Affairs and International Trade official, "Cuba suffered a diplomatic setback that hopefully will require them to kind of think about why this is happening."[17] Curiously, all of this took place at around the same time that Governor-General Roméo LeBlanc was swearing in Cuba's new ambassador to Canada, Carlos Fernández de Cossío, who received an uncharacteristically cold shoulder from the Canadians.

The already strained relationship took another turn for the worse in late July 1999, during the Pan American Games in Winnipeg. In the course of a strongly worded July 26 speech to the Cuban people and after several Cuban athletes had sought political asylum in Canada (while other Cuban athletes had failed their drug tests), Castro referred to "so many tricks, so much filth" at the Games. He even said Cuban athletes were, in words he often reserved for the United States, "competing in enemy territory."[18] The best statement a spokesperson for Chrétien could muster was, "We are disappointed at the harsh and accusatory tone of President Castro's remarks in which he accused Canada of rigging the Pan American Games to its own advantage."[19] Obviously, Castro's ill-conceived comment did nothing to reverse the downward slide in Canadian-Cuban relations.

Similarly, a diplomatic brouhaha between Canada and Cuba in March 2000 was symptomatic of a bilateral relationship experiencing some difficulty. An action intended as a favor to the Castro government — namely, an agreement to provide a 48-hour transit visa for Cuban diplomat José Imperatori (deemed persona non grata by the U.S. government) in order to facilitate his return to Havana — became a minor embarrassment for Canadian authorities.[20] In a typically Cuban twist, Imperatori refused to leave the grounds of the Cuban Embassy in Ottawa when his visa expired. After high-level discussions between the governments, Imperatori finally agreed to return to Cuba,[21] leaving Canadian officials miffed about being caught in the middle of the U.S.-Cuba propaganda war and being exploited by the Cubans. The officials wondered out loud what exactly the Cuban government had been thinking about besides making things a little more difficult for Washington.[22]

Although the media blew the Imperatori incident out of proportion, no lasting damage was done to the overall relationship. However, a number of Canadian officials were left frustrated and annoyed with the Cubans, who burned more than a few bridges to Ottawa in the process. The Cubans had given a solemn undertaking that Imperatori would depart from Canada before the 48-hour visa had expired; indeed, Cuban diplomats had done so in the past. As one Canadian official commented, "It was like getting a finger stuck in your eye when you reach down to help someone get up after they've fallen."[23]

Even the release in May 2000 of three members of the Group of Four did not warm the still frosty bilateral relationship. However, the release did warrant a short meeting when senior Foreign Affairs officials in Ottawa called in Cuba's ambassador to Canada. Although Canadian officials pointed out that they were pleased with the release of three of the dissidents, they promptly urged the attending Cuban officials to free the fourth (Vladimiro Roca).[24] Foreign Affairs officials wanted to put Canada's views on the record, including their concerns about increased clampdowns and the numbers of prisoners of conscience, and, in fairly strong diplomatic language, to indicate that improvement in bilateral relations at the political level would require greater freedom of expression in Cuba.

The Cubans asserted that the release of the dissidents was not intended to send a political message to Ottawa; instead, they explained that the measure was undertaken because the three qualified for conditional release under normal judicial procedures in Cuba.[25] The Canadians indicated that the timing was simply not right for approval of the opening of a new consulate in Vancouver, as requested by Havana. At the June 2000 OAS General Assembly in Canada, the issue of Cuba was not on the official agenda, and the Cubans failed to attend, even as observers.

No sign of improvement in the bilateral relationship was apparent in the appointment, just prior to the November 2000 general election, of John Manley as Canada's new foreign affairs minister. From the beginning, it was clear that this former industry minister would not replicate his predecessor's interest in and commitment to Canadian-Cuban relations.

In mid-March 2001, Foreign Affairs Minister Manley confirmed what most people had already suspected — Cuba would not be invited by host country Canada to attend the Third Summit of the Americas in Quebec City.[26] Speaking before Canada's Foreign Affairs and International Trade parliamentary committee, Manley was unequivocal: "Canada agrees that Cuba is not ready to participate in the summit because it lacks a commitment to democratic principles."[27] Then he said, "There hasn't been any demonstration of an acceptance of democratic standards."[28]

For their part, the Cubans were understandably perturbed by these developments. Moreover, since then, they have seen Canadian foreign policy under Manley-Chrétien clearly veering to the right and adopting a stronger pro-Washington line, as was evident in Canadian deference to the bombing of Iraq and reticence to comment critically upon several controversial topics. These topics include the sale of Canadian water and energy to the United States and Canada's favorable view of President George W. Bush's cherished national missile defense (NMD) scheme. All of these are matters of serious concern to Havana.

Perhaps it is still too early to tell whether Manley's stamp on Canadian foreign policy will have a lasting positive impact or signal a sharp and irretrievable shift in Canada's long-standing Cuba policy of constructive engagement. However, recent developments seem to suggest that Manley will adopt a tougher line on human rights with the Cubans, instead of adhering to Axworthy's approach of holding dialogues without pressing the Cuban government too hard on this issue. Indeed, in a speech to the Canadian Society in New York, Manley was unusually blunt regarding Cuba's human rights record: "To be frank, we haven't seen a lot of results from that."[29]

At the conclusion of the April 20-22, 2001 Summit of the Americas, the frostiness of the Canadian-Cuban relationship was evident in Chrétien's closing comments about Cuba's absence from the table. Basically, he intimated that the Cubans had no one to blame but themselves, and he stressed that future acceptance would require changes in the areas of democratization and human rights. Chrétien also said that he had tried to assist the Cuban government during his April 1998 visit to Havana, pleading with Castro to improve his country's human rights record in exchange for easing Cuba back into the hemispheric fold. According to Chrétien, he told Castro: "Let us help you to help yourself," and Castro said, "No."[30]

The Cubans not only protested their exclusion but also rejected Chrétien's concluding remarks at the 2001 Summit. Castro issued a statement criticizing "the brutal manner with which the authorities of Canada [were] repressing the peaceful demonstrations of those that protest against the [attempted] crimes against the political and economic rights of the peoples of Latin America and the Caribbean in Quebec."[31] As a slight aimed at what it saw as Canada's repression of the demonstrations, the official Cuban statement concluded: "Governments that deceive the world by calling themselves defenders of human rights treat their own people in such a way."[32]

Six days later, Castro continued to show irritation regarding Chrétien's Summit comments (and Ottawa's earlier decision to back out of a joint Canada-Cuba aid project to assist impoverished Haiti), voicing his displeasure at a televised roundtable discussion. Using words like "fanatic" and "a tool of U.S. foreign policy" to describe Chrétien and his statements about Cuba, Castro maintained that former Prime Minister Trudeau never would have excluded Cuba from the Summit of the Americas, nor would he have said publicly that he spent four hours lecturing the Cubans on human rights when they had not requested the advice in the first place.[33]

In sum, the Canada-Cuba dynamic went from a high point during Chrétien's controversial visit to Cuba in 1998 to its current cooler status. As of this writing, neither side has undertaken any substantive initiative to improve what clearly is a frosty bilateral relationship at the political and official levels, and, in the short run, no such initiative is expected. While the overall relationship has been bent out of shape, it most assuredly is not broken. Although Cuban ministers are free to visit Canada as they please, ministerial exchanges have been put on hold. Canadian efforts to reintegrate Cuba into the OAS also have ceased, and three development projects of the Canadian International Development Agency (CIDA) have been suspended, including the joint medical project in Haiti, a program that would have been beneficial for all three countries concerned. At present, the bilateral relationship is in a political holding pattern, and the atmosphere is noticeably chilly.

EXPLAINING THE CANADIAN-CUBAN DYNAMIC

While bilateral relations between Canada and Cuba are strained at the political level (exclusively over human rights issues), the overall relationship continues to function in other areas. Indeed, diplomatic linkages have not been severed, commercial relations are still moving forward (although a slight reduction in two-way trade has occurred over the last few years), and CIDA funds continue to flow to Cuba. Granted, the relationship now is more "correct" than friendly or cordial. According to one Canadian official, "We've essentially had to compartmentalize a bit," as the core of the relationship proceeds on a normal basis.[34] In other words, beyond the tensions resulting from the disagreements on human rights, the proximate underpinnings or driving forces of Canada-Cuba relations still remain firmly in place.

The advent of the new millennium and some palpable friction at the political and official levels have not interrupted the relatively normal nature of Canada-Cuba relations.[35] Significantly, even in previous periods when the bilateral relationship was chilly, Canada consistently indicated its commitment to maintain diplomatic relations with what it considered a popular, established Cuban government and continued to oppose the U.S. economic embargo on the island. Never a strong supporter of economic sanctions or any measure that would detract from an open international trading regime, Canada has kept its sights squarely on the monetary aspect of the relationship.

In this context, one should not easily dismiss the impact of the Canadian business community in endorsing a policy of dialogue and exchange with the Cuban government and people. Closer political relations hold the key to opening up Cuba's trade and investment doors, and corporations in Canada know full well that the U.S. embargo gives them a significant competitive advantage and, in some ways, a captive market for their products. By supplying high-tech equipment, spare parts, and machinery, Canadian businesses are able to fill the void left by U.S. companies and carve out a niche for themselves.

Indeed, when one arrives in Cuba, it is impossible not to be aware of Canada's growing trade and investment presence. The airport at Varadero and the new terminal at José Martí International's expanded airport facility, inaugurated by Chrétien during his April 1998 visit, both were constructed with the assistance of Canadian companies. Sophisticated landing equipment at Cuban airports, hotel reservation systems, McCain's french fries, President's Choice cola, auto parts, and compact discs all are being provided by Canadian suppliers throughout the country. The mining company Sherritt International Inc. is one of the largest foreign investors in Cuba. A large number of other Canadian-based companies are selling everything from foodstuffs to paper products, engineering equipment, paint, medical technology, and a bevy of items for the tourism industry. Additionally, the number of joint ventures has increased dramatically since the early 1990s, particularly in the mining sector.

Clearly, the finer points of Canada's Cuba policy are essentially economic and trade-driven. With some U.S. business sectors pushing hard for lifting of the embargo, this thrust is not likely to change in the near future. Even so, Canada's policy response toward revolutionary Cuba cannot be explained solely in commercial or investment terms. It must also take into account important historical, external, and domestic political factors.

Events in the past with respect to Canada-Cuba relations have inevitably shaped the texture of the current relationship. Friction during the second term of the Chrétien government has not weakened Ottawa's positions *against* the following: any severing of diplomatic linkages with Havana, a tightening of the U.S. embargo, and further isolation of Cuba in the hemisphere. In fact, the essence of the policy has not changed since the sentencing of the Group of Four and the program review. Stated differently, Canada's present Cuba policy is largely a function of a government position adopted more than 40 years ago. The Chrétien government has added its own particularly crafted brick and mortar to a preexisting historical foundation.

In some ways, Canada's approach has always reflected a desire by successive governments to carve out a unique, independent international role regarding revolutionary Cuba. As exemplified by Canada's role in banning anti-personnel landmines,[36] the Canadian government has consistently sought to be an "honest broker" and bridge builder on the international stage. This aspiration has become even more noticeable with Ottawa's growing engagement in the hemisphere through its membership in the OAS, negotiation of the North American Free Trade Agreement (NAFTA), and key role in the Summit of the Americas process. It has become quite clear since the late 1980s that Canada's future rests more and more with the Americas — as Europe coalesces around the European Union (EU), the Asia-Pacific region continues to experience financial difficulties, and Africa has all but fallen off the commercial radar screen. Cultivating stronger relations with Cuba has become one component of Ottawa's larger Latin America/Caribbean strategy or policy focus. By courting the Cubans and perhaps even leading the charge to ease Cuba back into the inter-American fold, Canada would not only send a potent message to a host of Latin American countries (which could increase Canada's reputation and influence in the region) but also deliver a pointed message to Washington policymakers.

Needless to say, Canadian governments in the past have not hesitated to invoke or play the proverbial "Cuba card" in the larger context of Canada-U.S.-Cuba relations. Political leaders in Ottawa have rarely missed an opportunity to contrast Canada's Cuba policy with the isolationist and hostile tendencies of successive U.S. administrations. By identifying this sharp difference in policy direction, Canadian governments can argue that Canada does indeed have a truly independent foreign policy, not one crafted by Washington. Ottawa's "Made-in-Canada" Cuba policy, especially when it serves to tweak the United States on occasion, not only reassures Canadians about their political sovereignty and independence, but also plays to their sense of pride and national identity.[37]

For a variety of reasons, then, Canada's policy of engaging the Cubans on many fronts clearly has manifest domestic political import. Symbolically, it makes Canadians feel less dependent upon and dominated by the United States and enables them to differentiate themselves from their U.S. cousins. It is not surprising that public opinion surveys have established repeatedly that Canada's continued relationship with Cuba is a political winner.

For any Canadian government to consider severing relations with revolutionary Cuba would be extremely shortsighted. Indeed, while Canada's approach to Cuba is not based entirely on electoral considerations, the knowledge that a cordial relationship with Havana is politically popular at home has not been lost on Canadian governments. In that regard, the fact that some 380,000 Canadians vacationed in Cuba during the 2000-2001 season is very important politically and in terms of trade and investment.

As for the Cuban government's motivations governing its role in the bilateral relationship, the explanatory variables are similar to Canada's in some respects and different in others. Clearly, however, the bilateral relationship is a win-win situation for the Cubans — with very few risks or costs involved. Understandably, the Castro government is keenly interested in enhancing trade relations with western, industrialized countries such as Canada. Only recently has the Cuban economy exhibited signs of improvement, after several painful years of incredible hardship, power blackouts, high unemployment, and food shortages. While the country has not completely turned the corner economically, two-way trade with Canada has been especially important during most of the 1990s. Furthermore, Canada has become not only a key supplier of high-tech and consumer goods, which have been in short supply in Cuba, but also a crucial source of much-needed foreign investment in the island.

Of course, Cuba's relations with Canada also provide the Cuban government with political and symbolic benefits. It is valuable for Havana to showcase its relationship with a member of the exclusive Group of Eight (G-8) industrialized countries, especially a country that is willing to work cooperatively with Cuba. The high-profile manner in which the Canadian prime minister and senior members of his cabinet have been received, with widespread media coverage and much fanfare, reflects the symbolic importance that the Cuban government attaches to the bilateral relationship and to the message it sends to the rest of the world. In an international community in which the United States stands out as the primary legitimate superpower and makes no effort to hide its disdain for the Castro government, Canada stands out as Cuba's number-one tourism market, with hundreds of thousands of Canadian visitors yearly. Cuba's solid relations with Canada, then, codify a certain degree of international respectability that can be repackaged for domestic as well as external consumption. Chrétien's 1998 visit, for instance, was a propaganda coup for Castro, since it underscored the outmoded nature of U.S. policy toward Cuba.

Cuban authorities are interested in strengthening political and economic relations with Canada for clearly pragmatic reasons. Together with a small but growing number of other so-called friends of Cuba, Canada, through its partnership with Cuba, sends out all the correct signals from the Cuban perspective. As mentioned earlier, some 380,000 Canadians travel to Cuba each year, bringing badly needed currency into the country. In addition, Canada supplies important investment support and valuable development assistance, including CIDA's many excellent programs and technical expertise. Canadian officials are involved, for example, in the improvement of Cuba's banking system, economic planning procedures, tax regime, and tourism sector.

With respect to the Helms-Burton law, the Cuban government has been a beneficiary of Canada's steadfast opposition to the anti-Cuba measure.[38] As the Cubans recognize, Ottawa's criticism of Helms-Burton and its successful effort to have the law impugned by the OAS in 1996 raised contentious issues in Canada-United States relations. Canada has been prepared to expend a certain amount of political capital to defend its prerogative of maintaining a wide range of linkages with Castro's Cuba. Although both Canada and Cuba have been able to derive tangible benefits from their attacks on Helms-Burton, Canada and Europe undoubtedly have done the most to temper the full brunt of the law's effects on Cuba.

In sum, close relations with Canada offer a significant number of benefits to Cuba without onerous preconditions. Cuban authorities know that the Canadian government does not do Washington's bidding and does not intend to do anything to destabilize the Castro regime or punish the Cuban people; instead, it aims to work constructively with Cuba. Down the road, a strong and healthy relationship with Ottawa could be useful to Havana, should it wish to normalize relations with Washington, seek re-inclusion in the OAS, or secure some form of associate status with any future FTAA initiative.

CONCLUSION

At the heart of the most recent chill in the bilateral relationship of Canada and Cuba is the thorny issue of human rights, particularly the restrictions on freedom of expression in Cuba. In diplomatic parlance, the Canadian government is in the process of sending strong signals to Cuban authorities and arguably to the United States as well. All of Canada's actions to date, from undertaking a program review to withholding approval for a Cuban consulate in Vancouver, are intended to send a pointed measure of disapproval to Havana. First, Ottawa wants the Castro government to understand its displeasure with Cuba's actions in jailing dissidents, toughening sentences, and increasing the number of clampdowns. In addition, in private conversations with their Cuban counterparts, Canadian ministers and officials have signaled what is needed for the Cubans to get the relationship back on track, namely, improvement of its human rights climate.

Part of the problem stems simply from a misreading or misunderstanding not of the political signaling or messaging, but of how officials from each country conduct themselves diplomatically. The Cubans, for their part, would do well to remember that Canada is a valuable ally in the Americas and should be treated as such (the Imperatori incident, for instance, still rankles among Canadians). The Cuban government needs to move away from a mindset that only the United States matters, especially when well-intentioned countries such as Canada are willing to expend political and moral capital on Cuba's behalf.[39]

Cuba also should be cognizant of the fact that diplomacy often is based on personal relationships, and if bridges are burned, as they were over efforts by Canadian officials to reintegrate Cuba into the OAS, they may be hard to rebuild.

In light of his aforementioned "filth" and "enemy territory" remarks, Castro himself should give some thought to courting the Canadian media — as well as tone down his harsh rhetoric — perhaps by inviting a high level Canadian Broadcasting Corporation news anchor, such as Peter Mansbridge, to Havana for a one-on-one session. It might also be appropriate for the Cuban president to publish an explanation of his "enemy territory" remark, in much the same way as he did in Mexico, following his observation that Mexican children knew more about Mickey Mouse than about their own national heroes. Finally, both Cuban and Canadian authorities must be prepared to talk openly and critically about their differing interpretations of human rights, while recognizing that the Canadian government does not seek to isolate Cuba hemispherically, overthrow the regime, or demand immediate free and fair elections in Cuba. Cubans should stop camouflaging the human rights issue by hiding behind their continuing obsession with the blockade and their isolation from the United States.

Canadians, in turn, need to understand that the Cubans operate in a unique fashion, on their own terms, and at a pace with which they are comfortable. Moreover, it is worth remembering that Cubans have followed their course for four decades, during which they have overcome enormous political obstacles, and they are not about to change course now. Having survived terrorist acts, the U.S. embargo, and the demise of the Soviet Union, Cubans can easily withstand Canada's diplomatic disgruntlement. Playing hardball by pushing the Cubans, who are well accustomed to hard times and a siege mentality, will only work against Canada's intended policy objectives. Furthermore, by linking issues, for example, reintegration into the OAS and the release of political prisoners, and by withholding positive inducements, for example, approval of Cuba's request to open a consulate in Vancouver, Canada displays a complete lack of appreciation for the way Cubans operate in the diplomatic arena. Indeed, Castro and those in his administration are not prepared to deal with the human rights question because they do not see the issue of human rights from a western, liberal vantagepoint or fully accept Canada's interpretation of it. Nor has Castro's regime really put that much stock in Axworthy's 14-point Joint Declaration or in Canada's professed commitment to human rights — viewing these more in symbolic than in substantive terms. (If they were so inclined, Cuban politicians could emphasize growing poverty indices in Canada and the Third World-like socioeconomic condition of Canada's First Peoples.) Canadians would be better served by working quietly behind the scenes, skillfully prodding the Cubans in the direction of reform and constraining their rhetorical flourishes at the UN Commission on Human Rights in Geneva.

Of course, not one of these suggestions can substitute for sufficient political will and commitment from each government's respective political leadership. The Canadian administration seems destined to hang tough on Cuba, with no obvious costs in doing so, until it witnesses some appreciable progress on the human rights side. Likewise, the Cuban regime is perfectly content to let Canadian policymakers languish in their cooling-off period. Taken together, this is a recipe for preventing any thaw in what is, on some levels at least, a frosty political relationship.

That said, it does seem clear that any bumps along the Canada-Cuba road are not likely to shake the relationship's foundations. Even when relations at the political level are strained and exchanges between officials are curt, as they have been since 1998, the relationship still functions reasonably well. For the most part, Canada remains committed to constructive engagement and people-to-people contact, while hoping to see a greater commitment to reforms, for example, through allowing its people more political space, on the part of the Cuban government.[40]

Both Canada and Cuba derive too many benefits and advantages from their relations to allow a chill in the relationship to freeze or sever ties altogether. However, as long as the area of human rights remains bilaterally compartmentalized, the Canada-Cuba relationship is likely to continue, at least in the short to mid-term, in its current mode. Nonetheless, if a gradual opening were to take place again in Cuba and if a noticeable change in the political climate were evident, as was the case during the mid-1990s, a reassessment by Canadian officials no doubt would be undertaken. Meanwhile, as long as the general human rights climate remains the same in Cuba and both Chrétien and Manley remain in their respective positions, little is likely to change in the two countries' relationship in the foreseeable future.

Notes

1. In Spanish, *nada nuevo* means "nothing new."

2. See Gordon Barthos, 1999, "Canada's Cold Snap Frosts Castro," *The Toronto Star*, November 26.

3. Confidential interview by one of the authors with a senior Canadian official in Washington, D.C., on June 13, 2000.

4. For a thorough treatment of each of the respective periods, see John M. Kirk and Peter McKenna, 1997, *Canada-Cuba Relations: The Other Good Neighbor Policy* (Gainesville, Fla.: The University Press of Florida).

5. See Paul Knox, 1999, "Canada Gets Tough on Cuba," *The Globe and Mail*, June 29.

6. See Chapter Six, Note 58, in this volume. On May 5, 2002, Vladimiro Roca Atúnez was released from prison.

7. Confidential interview with a senior Canadian official on June 6, 2000.

8. Confidential interview with a senior Canadian official in Washington, D.C., on June 13, 2000. It was also suggested that Cuba not only was content with the current status quo, but also was interested in developing a more pan-Caribbean focus in its international relations.

9. Founded in 1993, the Miami-based Cuban Committee for Democracy (Comité Cubano por la Democracia — CCD) is dedicated to finding a peaceful transition to democracy in Cuba and a diplomatic resolution of the long-standing conflict between Cuba and the United States. The CCD emphasizes the importance of dialogue and mutual respect both in its work in Cuba as well as within the Cuban-American community in the United States.

10. Peter M. Boehm, 1998, "Notes for a Speech to the Annual Meeting of the Cuban Committee for Democracy," Statements and Speeches, September 12, 2.

11. Boehm 1998, 2.

12. Canada's dissatisfaction with the Castro government had worsened during the spring 1999 period. As far as Ottawa was concerned, the general climate in Cuba was not auspicious, with critical comments by Castro over the North Atlantic Treaty Organization's bombing campaign in Kosovo and the "scourge" of globalization and market capitalism. Also included in the topics were an apparent increase in the number of Cuban dissidents recently being detained and the announcement of new and tougher national security legislation in Cuba. Moreover, there was alleged Cuban mischief-making at United Nations Commission on Human Rights sessions in Geneva and attempts by Cuba to block the commission's resolutions on indigenous peoples. (Confidential interview with a senior Canadian official on June 10, 2000.)

13. See Canada, Office of the Prime Minister, 1999, "Statement by the Prime Minister," March 15.

14. See Joel-Denis Bellavance, 1999, "PM Orders Review of Cuban Relations After Critics Jailed," *The National Post*, March 16. Minister Axworthy was especially perplexed by the maximum sentences meted out by Cuban authorities, the failure of the Cuban government to grant Canadian officials observer status at the trials, and a subsequent toughening of Cuba's criminal code. In addition, Axworthy was particularly blunt about the question of Cuba's reintegration into the OAS, which, as he explained, meant "accepting rules, accepting the rule of law, and clearly the sentencing of the dissidents indicates there's not much willingness there. . . ." The minister warned further, "We've indicated that if you're going to be a member of the hemispheric community, you have to play by those rules." Cited in Allan Thompson, 1999, "Canada's Diplomatic Aid for Cuba Put on Hold," *The Toronto Star*, March 17.

15. See Joel-Denis Bellavance, 1999, "Axworthy Ordered to Explain Delay of Cuba Review," *The National Post*, April 24.

16. Confidential interview by the author with a Canadian official on June 8, 2000.

17. See Allan Thompson, 1999, "Ottawa Chills Relationship with Castro," *The Toronto Star*, June 30.

18. See Robert Fife, 1999, "Castro Calls Canada 'Enemy Territory,' Talks Pan Am 'filth,'" *The National Post*, July 28.

19. Fife 1999.

20. See Jennifer Ditchburn, 2000, "Foreign Affairs Minister Lloyd Axworthy Has Tough Words, but No Action, on Illegal Cuban at Embassy," *Montreal Gazette*, March 1.

21. See Joel-Denis Bellavance and Campbell Clark, 2000, "Cuban Envoy Flies Home after Ending Hunger Strike," *The National Post*, March 3.

22. Confidential interview with a senior Canadian official on March 2, 2000.

23. Confidential interview with a senior Canadian official on June 6, 2000.

24. Confidential interview with a senior Canadian official on June 10, 2000. [See Chapter Six, Note 58, this volume. — Ed.]

25. Confidential interview with a Canadian official on June 8, 2000.

26. Cubans were not pleased with the decisions, describing the non-invitation as "arbitrary" and "second-level" treatment. (Correspondence from Camilo García, Second Secretary of Cuba's Embassy in Ottawa, on March 19, 2001.) However, a senior Canadian official indicated that the Cubans were not invited because they would not have attended if asked and would not have been able, even though they were consulted, to sign onto the Summit's final Declaration and Action Plan, which placed considerable emphasis on defending and strengthening representative democracy. (Confidential interview with a senior Canadian official on March 21, 2001.)

27. See McKenna, 2001, "Manley Courting Bush with his Cold Shoulder to Cuba," *The Hamilton Spectator*, March 29.

28. Quoted in Ian Jack, 2001, "Ottawa Shifts Policy on Cuba, Supports Bush," *The National Post*, March 16.

29. See Steven Edwards, 2001 "Cuba Keeps Itself on Sidelines: Manley," *The National Post*, March 16.

30. Jean Chrétien, 2001, Closing Press Conference of the Summit of the Americas, CBC Television, April 22.

31. See Embassy of Cuba in Canada, 2001, "Message from Fidel Castro to the Demonstrators in Quebec, April 20.

32. See Embassy of Cuba in Canada, 2001, "Message from Fidel Castro to the Demonstrators in Quebec, April 20.

33. Apparently, Canada has slightly shifted emphasis away from engaging the Cuban government and more toward seeking linkages with Cuban non-governmental organizations, the Cuban people, Canadian NGOs operating in Cuba, and Cuban civil society in general. (Confidential interview with a Canadian official on June 8, 2000.)

34 Confidential interview with a senior Canadian official, June 10, 2000.

35. For a fuller discussion of the relationship's core determinants, see Peter McKenna and John M. Kirk, 1998, "Canadian-Cuban Relations: A Model for the New Millennium?" *Global Development Studies* 1:3-4 (Winter 1998-Spring 1999): 386-409.

36. The 1997 "Convention on the Prohibition of the Use, Stockpiling, Production, and Transfer of Anti-Personnel Mines and on Their Destruction" has been ratified by more than 120 countries. Although most of Africa, Europe, and Latin America and some countries in Asia have joined the treaty, Cuba and the United States are the only two nations in Latin America that have not signed the convention.

37. During a NATO conference in Madrid, Chrétien was heard speaking into an open microphone about Canada's Cuba policy: "It's popular...[,] people like that...[, but] you have to do it carefully because they're friends." (Jeet Heer, 2000, "The PM Is Both Accident-prone and Indestructible...," *The National Post,* June 17.

38. For more on this point, see Peter McKenna, 1997, "Canada and Helms-Burton: Up Close and Personal," *Canadian Foreign Policy* 4:3 (Winter): 7-20.

39. This point was made by a senior Canadian official in Washington. Confidential interview, June 13, 2000.

40. While Ottawa has been reluctant to punish the Cuban government severely and thus acknowledge the ineffectiveness of constructive engagement, actions by the Cubans have brought into question the efficacy of Canada's engagement policy.

References

Barthos, Gordon. 1999. "Canada's Cold Snap Frosts Castro." *The Toronto Star,* November 26.

Bellavance, Joel-Denis. 1999. "PM Orders Review of Cuban Relations After Critics Jailed." *The National Post*, March 16, A1.

Bellavance, Joel-Denis. 1999. "Axworthy Ordered to Explain Delay of Cuba Review." *The National Post*, April 24, A.8.

Bellavance, Joel-Denis, and Campbell Clark. 2000. "Cuban Envoy Flies Home After Ending Hunger Strike." *The National Post*, March 3, A10.

Boehm, Peter M. 1998. "Notes for a Speech to the Annual Meeting of the Cuban Committee for Democracy." Statements and Speeches, September 12.

Canada. Office of the Prime Minister. 1999. "Statement by the Prime Minister." March 15.

Chrétien, Jean. 2001. Closing Press Conference of the Summit of the Americas. CBC Television, April 22.

Ditchburn, Jennifer. 2000. "Foreign Affairs Minister Lloyd Axworthy Has Tough Words, but No Action, on Illegal Cuban at Embassy." *Montreal Gazette*, March 1.

Edwards, Steven. 2001. "Cuba Keeps Itself on Sidelines: Manley." *The National Post,* April, 10, A6.

Embassy of Cuba in Canada. 2001. "Message from Fidel Castro to the Demonstrators in Quebec." April 20.

Fife, Robert. 2000. "Castro Calls Canada 'Enemy Territory,' Talks Pan Am 'filth.'" *The National Post,* July 28, A10.

García, Camilo. 2001. Correspondence with Foreign Affairs Minister John Manley by Camilo García, Second Secretary of Cuba's Embassy in Ottawa, March 19.

Heer, Jeet. 2000. "The PM Is Both Accident-Prone and Indestructible...." *The National Post*, June 17, B4.

Jack, Ian. 2001. "Ottawa Shifts Policy on Cuba, Supports Bush." *The National Post,* March 16, A6.

Kirk, John M., and Peter McKenna. 1997. *Canada-Cuba Relations: The Other Good Neighbor Policy.* Gainesville, Fla.: The University Press of Florida.

Knox, Paul. 1999. "Canada Gets Tough on Cuba." *The Globe and Mail,* June 29, A1.

McKenna, Peter. 2001. "Manley Courting Bush with his Cold Shoulder to Cuba." *The Hamilton Spectator,* March 29, A11.

McKenna, Peter. 1997. "Canada and Helms-Burton: Up Close and Personal." *Canadian Foreign Policy* 4:3 (Winter).

McKenna, Peter, and John M. Kirk. 1998-1999. "Canadian-Cuban Relations: A Model for the New Millennium?" *Global Development Studies* 1:3-4 (Winter 1998-Spring 1999): 386-409.

Thompson, Allan. 1999. "Canada's Diplomatic Aid for Cuba Put on Hold." *The Toronto Star,* March 17.

Thompson, Allan. 1999. "Ottawa Chills Relationship with Castro." *The Toronto Star,* June 30.

Part III.
The United States and Cuba in the Twenty-First Century

CHAPTER FOUR

Cuba-United States Relations in the Post-Cold War Transition

STEPHEN J. RANDALL

In the past two decades, Cuba-United States relations have remained highly strained, despite the potential for accommodation one might have expected as one of the "peace dividends" provided by the end of the Cold War and the effective termination of the Soviet-Cuban threat in the Western Hemisphere. The stability expected after the Cold War has yielded to widespread global conflicts that are local, national, and regional in nature and often fueled by centuries-old antagonisms, racial and ethnic animosities, and struggles for national self-determination, territory, or access to water. To some extent, these conflicts also are triggered by traditional great-power rivalries.

This chapter provides an overview of the bilateral relationship between Cuba and the United States over the past 20 years, from the dying days of the Democratic administration of President Jimmy Carter (1977-1981) to the twilight of the Bill Clinton presidency (1993-2001), with an emphasis on the post-Cold War years. The chapter begins with a review of the impact of the 1980 Mariel exodus, which brought approximately 120,000 Cubans to the United States. It examines the debate over the Cuban Democracy Act (CDA or Torricelli Act) of 1992; the Cuban-U.S. negotiation of accords on Cuban emigration; the role of the Cuban-American community; the crisis that led to the passage of the Cuban Liberty and Democratic Solidarity Act (Helms-Burton); and the implications of that legislation not only for bilateral relations, but also for the relationship of the United States with its neighbors and allies. The chapter touches on sensitive bilateral and hemispheric issues, such as human rights and narcotics trafficking as well as the ongoing debate on the U.S. economic embargo on trade with Cuba.

THE MARIEL EXODUS

Cuban emigration to the United States has been a persistent issue in the bilateral relationship, from the large-scale emigrations that took place in the early 1960s, through the Mariel exodus in 1980, the peak of the *balseros* ("boat people") emigration in 1994, and continuing with the 1999-2000 highly volatile and public controversy that swirled around six-year-old Elián González. The child was plucked from the sea after his boat capsized on the way to Florida, resulting in the death of his mother. The legal and political battle that took place around the efforts of Cuban-Americans to prevent Elián's return to his father in Cuba, the equally determined efforts of Cuban authorities to have him returned, and the indecisiveness of the Clinton administration symbolized the emotional and political volatility of the emigration issue as well as the major political influence of Cuban-Americans.[1]

By the late 1970s, pressure from Cubans seeking to emigrate or attain refugee status outside Cuba had become intense. Between May 1979 and approximately April 1980, several dozen Cuban nationals sought asylum in various Latin American embassies in Havana, beginning with that of Venezuela. Their efforts were dramatic, from driving a bus through embassy gates to crashing a family car through the entrance to the Peruvian embassy in early 1980. The initial response of the foreign embassies was to return those seeking refugee status to Cuban authorities, but in the course of the year, pressure mounted on the international community, and the tensions between embassy officials and Cuban authorities intensified. In late January 1980, the Cuban government announced that it would not grant exit permits to those forcing their way into foreign embassies, except to those who were deemed to be in imminent danger of losing their lives or freedom. In April, the government altered its stance and announced that those seeking asylum in the Peruvian embassy would be allowed to leave Cuba. Within 48 hours, more than 10,000 Cubans crowded into the Peruvian embassy and sent messages to President Carter, Pope John Paul II, and other heads of state, requesting assistance in leaving Cuba. Within a few days, the U.S. government announced that it was going to conduct military exercises at the Guantánamo naval base. Over the next few days, the emigration pressures intensified, with refugees being airlifted by the United States to a variety of destinations, including Costa Rica, Peru, Spain, and the United States. (The United States accepted more than 6,200 refugees in this first wave). Then the situation took a dramatic turn, with President Fidel Castro announcing on April 20, 1980, that all Cubans wishing to emigrate to the United States were free to do so. The reaction of the Cuban populace was immediate, with what came to be known as the "Freedom Flotilla" of boats plying the short distance between Florida and Cuba to bring Cuban refugees to U.S. ports. Although the enthusiasm of U.S. officials for this exodus diminished as the nature and magnitude of the migration became known, President Carter captured the propaganda value of the movement by announcing that the United States would "continue to provide an open heart and open arms to refugees seeking freedom from Communist domination."[2]

On May 6, 1980, the Cuban government announced that the port of Mariel would be used by former political prisoners and their relatives who wished to leave Cuba, thus throwing into the mix of genuine refugees Cubans with questionable backgrounds and motivations. By the end of May, more than 94,000 Cubans and several thousand Haitians had reached the United States and were registered and provided with temporary accommodations under emergency federal measures (those of the new arrivals who were suspected of criminal involvement fared less well)[3] before being relocated to various parts of the United States, mainly Dade County, Florida, and New York, New Jersey, and California. The final tally of those reaching the United States exceeded 125,000. Of the first 62,000 Cubans processed, a rough balance existed between males (55.2 percent) and females (44.8 percent). Many of the refugees (28.5 percent) had relatives in the United States, and the majority were young adults, from 23 to 25 years of age (29.2 percent).[4]

CUBA, THE CARIBBEAN, AND CENTRAL AMERICA

For the balance of the 1980s, the administrations of Ronald Reagan (1981-1989) and George Bush (1989-1993) were preoccupied with crises in Central America. Cuba was central to U.S. policy concerns in Nicaragua and El Salvador, especially because of the perception that Cuba was the main conduit for weapons from the Soviet Bloc to the Sandinista government in Nicaragua and the Farabundo Martí National Liberation Front (Frente Farabundo Martí de Liberación Nacional — FMLN) insurgency in El Salvador. The electoral defeat of the Sandinistas in Nicaragua in February 1990 and the installation of the coalition government led by Violeta Chamorro (1990-1996), combined with the gradual resolution of the conflict in El Salvador and the withdrawal of the Soviet Union from Cuba, served to defuse the Central American situation and largely to neutralize Cuba's international role in the area. For the following decade, however, U.S. attention, both congressional and executive, still focused on Cuba, but primarily on efforts to undermine the Castro government, encourage dissident groups within Cuba, promote human rights and political freedoms, and further isolate Cuba from the international community. Pressure from potential Cuban refugees also continued to attract U.S. attention sporadically during the 1990s. The critical factor since the end of the Cold War in determining U.S. policy, however, has been the firm belief that Cuba no longer poses a security threat in the region and that the normalization of relations between Cuba and its Caribbean neighbors is the result of their confidence that Cuban ideological imperialism is no longer a force in the area.[5]

In the 1980s, Cuba was, nonetheless, a logical, perhaps inevitable, and certainly convenient target for the conservative, anti-communist Republican administrations of Reagan and Bush. The Cuban government of Castro was a source of material and moral support for insurgencies in Central America during that decade, whether it was as a surrogate for Soviet intentions or acting on its own in Nicaragua and El Salvador. The Central American insurgencies, along with U.S. concern over Cuban involvement in Grenada, seemed to confirm the validity of U.S. Cold War policies toward Cuba, which were premised on the containment of Cuban-supported communism in the Western Hemisphere as part of an overall global strategy of containment.

REAGAN AND THE CUBAN-AMERICAN COMMUNITY

The response of the Reagan administration to this concern over Cuba's activity in the region was multifaceted. Recognizing the potential and real political power of anti-Castro Cuban-Americans, the Reagan administration supported the formation in 1981 of the Cuban American National Foundation (CANF), a lobbying group designed to put pressure on a Congress dominated by Democrats and not enthusiastic about the Reagan administration's approach to Latin American relations. The Reagan administration appears to have played only a marginal role in the creation of CANF, with Reagan's first National Security Adviser, Richard Allen, indicating during the 1980 campaign to prominent Cuban-American leaders that it would be useful for the Cuban-American community (and the administration) to have a lobbying group comparable to the Israeli lobby in Congress. CANF ultimately developed links with the National Endowment for Democracy, which the Reagan administration created as a vehicle for the promotion of democratic institutions and movements abroad. CANF also played a role in a variety of other issues. For instance, it sought to influence U.S. immigration policy through the Operation Exodus Program, which for the first time privatized a dimension of U.S. refugee policy. CANF also became a factor in U.S. policy toward the Nicaraguan war by providing support for the Contras and for the Reagan administration's appeals for congressional funding for the anti-Sandinista organization. Further, CANF successfully lobbied Congress to have the Clark Amendment repealed in order to enable the administration to provide funding for the National Union for the Total Independence of Angola (União Nacional para a Independência Total de Angola — UNITA) insurgency in Angola against Cuban-supported forces. In addition, from the working relationship between CANF and the Reagan administration, Radio Martí emerged in 1985, and TV Martí emerged five years later during the Bush administration as foreign policy propaganda instruments directed at Cubans and heavily influenced, if not directly controlled, by anti-Castro Cuban-Americans in Miami.[6]

In 1982, the Reagan administration announced a broader approach to Caribbean policy, the Caribbean Basin Initiative (CBI), as an export-driven economic development plan for the region, a very limited version of the Alliance for Progress[7] that was more like a throwback to the private-sector-driven approach to aid policy that was characteristic of the Dwight D. Eisenhower administration (1953-1961) in the 1950s. The Reagan administration balanced that development-oriented program with large-scale funding for the Contras' military opposition to the Sandinista government in Nicaragua and with increased funding for the Salvadoran government in its efforts to fight the FMLN. In Grenada, the administration faced a range of problems: a political crisis in 1983 with the killing of deposed Prime Minister Maurice Bishop (1979-1983); a security threat with evidence of extensive Cuban involvement in Grenada, including Cuban training of Grenadan soldiers; and Cuban construction of an airfield capable of handling Cuban and Libyan jets moving between Africa and the Caribbean, a development that appeared threatening at this time when Cuba still was heavily involved in the Angolan war. Evidence also emerged of involvement of East German, Libyan, and North Korean agents on Grenada. The Reagan administration, in October 1983, took the controversial step of sending to Grenada a landing force of several thousand U.S. marines, backed by the Organization of American States (OAS) and the nations of the Caribbean Commonwealth. U.S. forces remained in Grenada for almost two years, seeking a higher level of political stability and assurances that Cuba would not gain a strategic foothold on the island.[8]

The end of the Cold War and the collapse of the Soviet Union cut off Cuba from Soviet aid, inaugurated a period of intense economic hardship, and heralded the increased isolation of Cuba in the Western Hemisphere and U.S. policy that was even more hard-line. As the Soviet Union was dismantled and withdrew from its 30-year involvement with Cuba, Cuba's impact on hemispheric affairs was diminished significantly. As Cuba posed less of a strategic threat to the region, some might have expected it to be reintegrated gradually into the hemispheric system. After all, the island nation had diplomatic relations with many nations of the hemisphere.

Countries such as Canada, Spain, and Italy had extensive investments in Cuba, and even U.S. businesspeople had found mechanisms to conduct business with the pariah state.

THE REPUBLICAN-DEMOCRATIC TRANSITION: THE 1990s

The United States remained the key to any real normalization of relations with Cuba. Instead of moving toward normalization, however, the United States under Democratic President Clinton and a Republican-dominated Congress hardened its stance on Cuba, toughening existing legislation that dealt with the bilateral relationship and introducing new legislation designed not only to curtail U.S. linkages with Cuba, but also to contain the involvement of other nationals. The stated objectives were to weaken the Castro government, undermine the already weak Cuban economy, encourage domestic political dissent in Cuba, and counter the Castro government's poor record on human rights. As the twenty-first century begins, Cuba thus continues to occupy an anomalous position in the community of nations in the Western Hemisphere, and the future of its bilateral relationship with the United States remains as contentious as ever.

U.S. pressure on the Castro government to reform has taken economic and political forms. Although the hard-line Reagan administration approach to Latin America had marginal support in the U.S. Congress in the 1980s, there was a general belief in the need to maintain strong pressure on the Castro government in order to promote political and economic reforms on the island. In 1989, as the Cold War was just beginning to wind down, Florida Republican Senator Connie Mack began to promote a bill to prohibit the subsidiaries of U.S. firms from trading with Cuba, and he pressed for passage of the legislation for the next several years. During the George Bush administration, no executive office support was forthcoming for such legislation, since senior administration officials were rightly concerned that such action would alienate U.S. allies with substantial economic interests in and normal diplomatic relations with Cuba. The issue would not die of inertia, however, and during subsequent years, a variety of factors kept it alive until ultimately it gained congressional approval. From the Bush presidency through the Clinton administration, the composition of Congress changed in a way that brought more attention to Cuban issues and policies, and this contributed to the success of the anti-Castro stance in Washington. In 1989, Ileana Ros-Lehtinen (R-Florida), a Cuban-American, was elected to the House of Representatives, to be joined in 1993 by fellow Florida Republican and Cuban-American Lincoln Díaz-Balart and New Jersey Democrat and fellow Cuban-American Robert Menéndez.[9] Republicans also gained control of Congress, with the result that they acquired chairmanships of crucial congressional committees, such as the Senate Foreign Relations Committee, led by Jesse Helms (R-North Carolina). Republicans also increasingly gained the support of key Democrats in their approach to Cuban policy. Regardless of the president's personal inclination on Cuban-American relations, the Clinton administration thus faced a better-organized Cuban-American lobby, even though the Cold War considerations that had previously driven U.S. policy were muted significantly during Clinton's terms in office. In fact, the end of the Cold War tended to reinforce the strength of the anti-Castro lobby because with the Soviet Union removed as a major security threat and Cuba now isolated and increasingly economically destitute, the Cuban lobby could focus U.S. attention more easily on what had been little more than a sideshow in the larger geopolitical considerations of U.S. foreign policy.

New Jersey Democratic Congressman Robert Torricelli introduced the CDA in the House of Representatives in early 1992, prior to the November presidential election that brought Clinton to the White House; Florida Democrat Bob Graham introduced the bill in the Senate. The measure had some similarity to the previously defeated Mack Bill, in that it was designed to maintain and increase economic pressure on the Castro government and to make it difficult to circumvent the long-standing economic embargo on trade with Cuba through measures that would prevent ships that had already made stops in Cuba from entering U.S. ports. Thus, as with the Mack Bill, this measure was aimed at U.S. multinational-controlled foreign firms with Cuban involvement.

The second dimension of the bill was also consistent with the long-standing U.S. government intent to strengthen opposition political forces in Cuba and thus weaken Castro's hold. The strategy identified was to facilitate more contacts between Cuban-Americans and their family members remaining in Cuba. The Torricelli Bill became the backbone of the legislation that was passed by Congress in 1996 as the Cuban Liberty and Democratic Solidarity (LIBERTAD) Act or Helms-Burton Act, which President Clinton signed into law on March 12, 1996. Sensitive to the importance of Cuban-American votes and also those of Democrats who shared their views of Castro, Clinton indicated in the 1992 campaign that he supported the Torricelli Bill.[10] For this reason and others, Clinton made substantial inroads into the Cuban-American vote compared with 1998 Democratic candidate Michael Dukakis.[11]

At no time early in his first administration did Clinton hint at a softer line toward Cuba, although some senior officials in his administration, including Secretary of State Warren Christopher, favored a softer line on the embargo and bilateral relations in general. Rather, Clinton demonstrated the extent to which his foreign policies on Cuba were driven by domestic political considerations more than foreign policy principles by dropping his first choice as Assistant Secretary of State for Latin America, Mario Baeza. Instead, Clinton favored Alexander Watson, who brought as his assistant Richard Nuccio, an aide of Torricelli's who was supported by CANF. Significantly, Watson's first major policy statement on Cuban relations was made at a CANF-sponsored luncheon in the fall of 1993, when he reassured his audience that the president would stay the course on Cuban policy.[12] As other authors have indicated, "For most of Clinton's tenure, a sensible Cuba policy — one that simply reflects legitimate U.S. foreign policy goals — has been held hostage to the administration's short-run political calculus." [13]

Discussions about immigration and refugee issues, advancing the human rights agenda, the place of Cuba in international narcotics trafficking, and trade and general economic linkages with Cuba dominated the first Clinton administration's Cuba policy, with the highlight of the period being the passage in 1996 of the Helms-Burton Act.

Cuba's economic crisis deepened in the late 1980s and early 1990s, with the production of foodstuffs and imports falling significantly, as the country's capacity to purchase abroad also declined. Partly to offset this decline, the Cuban government continued to encourage the expansion of tourism to the island as well as increased foreign investment. The ban on the possession of foreign currency by Cuban nationals was lifted, and agricultural product sales were opened to market conditions.

The worsening economic situation in Cuba stimulated further pressure for emigration to the United States in 1994; however, on that occasion, both U.S. and Cuban officials sought to prevent a crisis comparable to the previous decade's Mariel exodus. The Mariel exodus had placed a major organizational, institutional, and financial burden on many U.S. city and state governments as well as the federal government. U.S. and Cuban officials dreaded any repeat of the earlier situation. Clinton likely needed no reminder of his experience as governor of Arkansas in 1980 with the adverse political repercussions of prison riots caused by Cuban refugees.[14] Nor was Castro anxious to provoke a crisis with the United States because, given the dire economic situation on the island, he hoped to convince U.S. officials to discuss the economic embargo and he needed to demonstrate to the United States and to Cubans that he retained political control.

The exodus that began in August 1994 was fairly orderly at first and took place on ships that Cubans were able to hijack. However, as soon as Castro announced, as he had in 1980, that Cubans were free to leave the country, the exodus deteriorated into chaos. A large number of Cubans risked their lives by setting sail for U.S. shores on virtually anything that would float — rustic platforms or rafts made of wood — hence the origins of the *balseros* terminology. Although the magnitude of the *balseros* exodus was extreme in August-September 1994, its size, rather than the rafting phenomenon itself, was new. A constant exodus by such flimsy means had occurred during the previous decade, following the Mariel crisis.[15] Now, in barely one month, more than 31,000 Cubans left Cuba on makeshift rafts and reached U.S. shores, and some, who left from Santiago in the east, went directly to the U.S. naval base at Guantánamo. This chaotic exodus was a serious blow to Castro's prestige among Cubans and internationally, because the youth of many of the rafters underscored the fact of discontent even among those Cubans who had grown up under the Revolution. As a result, it was in Cuba's and the United States' best interests to reach a reasonable accommodation to the crisis. At the same time, no doubt, the increasingly hard line taken by the Clinton administration prevented the 1994 situation from reaching Mariel proportions. The administration ordered the U.S. Coast Guard to intercept any U.S.-based vessels attempting to go to Cuba or returning from Cuba with refugees. Individuals arriving from Cuba were ordered detained by Attorney General Janet Reno, and those intercepted at sea were to be taken to Guantánamo and detained indefinitely rather than being treated as refugees, as had happened in 1980. This series of actions directly reversed the 1966 Cuban Adjustment Act, which had guaranteed Cubans the right of asylum in the United States. With some U.S. officials hinting that, contrary to the position of Secretary of State Warren Christopher, a total military blockade of the island would be considered as a means of preventing a further exodus, the situation had reached a point at which resolution was essential.

The 1984 bilateral agreements limited Cuban immigration to the United States to 20,000 immigrants per year. In September 1994, one month after meetings with Jorge Mas Canosa of the CANF and Florida Governor Lawton Chiles (who faced a re-election bid in November 1994), the Clinton administration initiated discussions with Cuban officials in New York, an action that in itself angered Cuban-American leaders such as Mas Canosa. Even more to their dismay, an agreement was signed in which the Cuban government agreed to halt the raft exodus and the United States agreed to allow at least 20,000 Cubans to migrate to the United States annually. Perhaps even more significant, however, was the fact that U.S. negotiators refused to accede to Cuban requests to place other issues, in particular the embargo, on the table for bilateral discussions. Clearly, the September Accords were a way to end a potential crisis for both sides rather than an opening for more amicable relations between the two countries.[16]

THE HELMS-BURTON ACT

If the 1994 bilateral discussions had any potential for leading to a more open relationship between the United States and Cuba, by early 1995 that potential was marginal. Although in 1994, in the midst of the crisis, major congressional leaders and even otherwise conservative newspapers, such as *The Wall Street Journal,* favored modifying or ending the embargo and opening negotiations with the Castro government, the congressional elections in November 1994 altered the political dynamic. Republican Party congressional victories in the 1994 mid-term elections resulted in a hardening of congressional views on Cuban policy, and the new chair of the Senate Foreign Relations Committee, Jesse Helms of North Carolina, who replaced Rhode Island Democratic Senator Claiborne Pell, moved quickly to dispel any doubts about the direction in which he and fellow hard-line Republicans wished to move. The shift in the political landscape also undermined the Clinton administration's considerations about implementing a "calibrated" response to Cuba and possibly liberalizing U.S. policies as Cuba made progress toward democratization. Officials such as the National Security Council Adviser on Democratic Initiatives, Morton Halperin, favored lifting the travel ban on U.S. citizens going to Cuba, but such ideas had little chance of support in the altered post-1994 political climate.[17]

In February 1995, Helms introduced Senate Bill 381, the Cuban Liberty and Democratic Solidarity Act, which was essentially an effort to internationalize the U.S. embargo on trade with Cuba. Unfortunately, the initiative clearly ran against the international mood, as reflected in part by a strong vote in 1994 in the U.N. General Assembly condemning the embargo,[18] and it also wasted an opportunity for bilateral discussions that had been created by the immigration accords that year.

The Helms-Burton legislation was designed to tighten, not relax, the long-standing economic embargo against Cuba in an effort to bring about reforms in Cuba as well as the downfall of Castro. Congressional support for the legislation came from those who were concerned that the Clinton administration might move toward a liberalization of relations with Cuba without insisting on substantial reforms in the Castro government. These individuals viewed the U.S. president's posture during the 1994 immigration crisis as well as the administration's decision to open diplomatic relations with Vietnam as indicative of Clinton's potentially softer line on Cuba. The administration also publicly opposed the Helms-Burton legislation from the outset on grounds that the embargo and the 1991 Torricelli Bill were adequate measures to press Cuba to reform its political system.[19] Clinton administration officials were also concerned that the legislation would limit the capacity of the executive to respond to changing circumstances in Cuba and would seriously undermine relations with U.S. allies that had active economic relations with Cuba. While Congress debated the legislation in the course of 1995, the Clinton administration implemented more accommodating measures under the terms of the CDA, including the relaxation of travel restrictions for U.S. citizens wishing to visit Cuba and the establishment of U.S. news bureaus on the island.[20]

The Helms-Burton Bill, after passing the House of Representatives without difficulty, experienced more opposition in the U.S. Senate, which removed the controversial Title III and Title IV, allowing U.S. citizens to sue in U.S. courts any individuals or corporations that trafficked in property deemed to have been confiscated by the Castro government following the 1959 Revolution. Those titles also had permitted U.S. officials to refuse U.S. entry visas to executives of companies that engaged in such trafficking.[21]

Then, on February 24, 1996, an event occurred that transformed the political situation and provided the momentum for the passage and then signature of the Helms-Burton legislation, this time with the controversial sections restored. On that day, the Cuban airforce shot down two civilian aircraft operated by Brothers to the Rescue, one of several groups involved in anti-Castro activities.[22] Also on that day, a meeting had been scheduled by the Cuban Council (Concilio Cubano), which U.S. officials considered a broadly representative group of Cuban non-governmental organizations (NGOs) seeking reforms of the political system; the leaders were arrested and the rally canceled. International and domestic U.S. political backlash to this action by Cuban authorities was devastating for the Clinton administration, undermining any intent it might have had to move U.S. policy in a new and more liberal direction. Anti-Castro groups in the United States seemed justified in their claims that the Clinton administration's more conciliatory approach to achievement of political and economic democracy in Cuba was not working. The U.N. Security Council requested that the International Civil Aviation Authority investigate the Brothers to the Rescue incident, and it found that the two Cessna aircraft had been shot down in international airspace.[23]

In the immediate aftermath of the Cessna crisis, the Senate and House of Representatives voted decisively (74-22 and 336-86, respectively) in early March to pass the Helms-Burton legislation, and Clinton signed the bill into law shortly thereafter. Indicative of the public hard line the administration now took with a presidential election on the fall horizon, Jennifer Hillman, general counsel in the office of the U.S. Trade Representative, testified to the Senate Foreign Relations Committee that Cuba represented a "continuing threat." Moreover, she referred to Cuba as a "pariah state" and reasserted the right and responsibility of the United States to protect "the political and economic systems that our allies and we have built over the past decades."[24]

The Helms-Burton legislation increased support for TV Martí and reinforced restrictions on U.S. travel to Cuba and remittances to Cuban relatives from the United States. Such restrictions could be lifted only if the president could demonstrate that economic reforms had been implemented in Cuba. In general terms, Title I of the act codified all previous measures that were part of the Cuba embargo. Title II required the president to develop plans for economic assistance to Cuba as soon as a transitional government was in place. It also specified the nature of the economic aid that could be extended after a democratically elected government had been installed. Any new Cuban government had to exclude Fidel Castro or his brother Raúl; free all political prisoners; permit international investigation of Cuban prisons; dissolve the Ministry of the Interior, including the Committees for the Defense of the Revolution; legalize trade unions, and cease efforts to jam the reception of Radio and TV Martí.[25]

Title III of the Helms-Burton Act permitted former owners of property in Cuba expropriated by the Cuban government after 1959 to file suit in U.S. courts against current investors in such property. The definition of property in the legislation encompassed real and personal property as well as intellectual property, including future interests and leasehold interests in those properties. Title IV provided for the exclusion from the United States of certain third-country nationals if they trafficked in expropriated property in Cuba after March 1996. The State Department took several early actions in 1996 under this provision against executives of Canadian, Mexican, and Italian firms, although over the past several years this has not become a major issue.[26]

Section 306 (b) of the Helms-Burton legislation gave the president of the United States the power to suspend the application of Title III for successive periods of six months. In part, because of international pressure from Europe, Canada, Mexico, and other Latin American countries, President Clinton, after 1996, repeatedly suspended application of this section of the law.

The Helms-Burton law has been controversial not only in Cuba and the international community but also in the United States. Evidently, both the White House and the State Department would have preferred to follow a different course in attempting to effect political and economic change in Cuba, although they showed little willingness to go as far as Canada and the European countries in maintaining open relations with the Castro government. The situation seems unlikely to change for the better in the near future, given the domestic political balance in the United States.

Since the passage of the Helms-Burton Act, marginal progress has been made in improving U.S.-Cuban relations and in modifying the Cuban government. The death in 1997 of a major Cuban-American leader, CANF's Jorge Mas Canosa, did not change the perspective of the Cuban-American community. The major outpouring of sentiment in that community in the course of 2000 over the custody of Elián González only served to highlight the intensity of those feelings. During 1997, the Clinton administration gave approval to 10 U.S. news organizations to open bureaus in Cuba, but the Cuban government authorized only Cable News Network (CNN) to do so.

The much publicized visit to Cuba in January 1998 by Pope John Paul II underlined the extent to which the United States is isolated from the international community in its approach to relations with Cuba. Although the visit throughout the island was appropriately a religious and spiritual one, the political significance of a visit by the leader of the Roman Catholic world to the only remaining communist country in the Western Hemisphere was lost on no one. The pope demonstrated on various occasions during that visit that he disapproved of the economic embargo against Cuba and the hardships it was imposing on Cuban citizens, although he also was committed to the improvement of basic human rights in Cuba.

In the aftermath of the pope's visit, the Clinton administration announced a series of moves designed to soften U.S. tactics. The government eased the transfer of food and medicine on humanitarian grounds, restored daily charter flights to the island, and permitted Cuban-Americans to send up to $300 per month to their families in Cuba. In 1999, the Clinton government further modified these policies, permitting NGOs to send funds to independent organizations in Cuba and allowing individuals to send up to $300 every three months to Cuban families. At the same time, in an effort to encourage privatization and market development, the administration authorized the sale of foodstuffs to NGOs and private restaurants on the island and the sale of agricultural products to private and coop farmers producing for the open market. Direct mail was reestablished between the countries, and Secretary of State Madeleine Albright indicated a willingness to liberalize cultural, athletic, humanitarian, and educational linkages between the two countries.

In 2002, serious problems still remain in the bilateral relationship. One problem is the continued lack of serious political opposition and open political debate allowed in Cuba. A second problem is the related international concern over Cuba's human rights record, an issue that the Clinton administration made and the George W. Bush administration continues to make a prerequisite for liberalization of U.S. policies toward Cuba. In April 2000, the United States was among the supporters of a resolution sponsored by Poland and the Czech Republic and passed by the United Nations, drawing attention to those independent journalists in Cuba who continued to speak out for democratic reforms in Cuba.[27] A third problem in U.S.-Cuba relations is the perception that Cuba is a link in the international narcotics traffic that moves through the Caribbean. Although Cuba no longer poses a security threat to the United States in terms of military capacity or intent,[28] any Cuban linkage to narcotics traffic has to be viewed with concern, as narcotics continue to be identified as a threat to U.S. national security. Nonetheless, with narcotics as with other aspects of the U.S.-Cuba relationship, a difference of perception divides the executive and Congress. William Ledwith, chief of international operations for the U.S. Drug Enforcement Agency, indicated early in 2000 that the cocaine flow through Cuba to the United States was insignificant, especially in contrast with the roles of Jamaica, Haiti, the Bahamas, and the Dominican Republic and that cooperation between Cuban and U.S. authorities was good and improving. Ledwith also reported to Congress that Cuba had concluded antinarcotics agreements with the United Kingdom, Italy, France, the Bahamas, and the United Nations Office for Drug Control and Crime Prevention.[29]

The Republican administration of George W. Bush, with close family ties to the governor of Florida, has taken an even more aggressive stance toward Cuba. On May 20, 2001, as part of Cuban Independence Day celebrations, Bush expressed unequivocal support for two congressional initiatives designed to increase pressure on the Castro government: the Cuban Solidarity Act and the Cuban Internal Opposition Assistance Act. Bush commented, "The policy of our government is not merely to isolate Castro, but to actively support those working to bring about democratic change in Cuba. And that is why we will support legislation like the Cuban Solidarity Act and the Cuban Internal Opposition Assistance Act." President Bush went on to observe, "History tells us that forcing change upon repressive regimes requires patience. But history also proves, from Poland to South Africa, that patience and courage and resolve can eventually cause oppressive governments to fear and then to fall."[30]

Having gained control of the White House after two terms of Clinton's presidency, conservative Republicans, with bipartisan support, continued to press for more aggressive legislation to deal with Cuba, in particular to bring pressure on Castro's government to improve its dismal human rights record. In the spring of 2001, a bipartisan group of 11 senators, led by Republican Jesse Helms and Democrat Joseph Lieberman of Connecticut (Vice President Al Gore's running mate in the 2000 presidential campaign), introduced the above-mentioned Cuban Solidarity Act, providing $100 million in U.S. aid to dissidents and other NGOs in Cuba over a four-year period. The Senate proposal was a companion bill to the Cuban Internal Opposition Act, introduced in the House of Representatives in March 2001 by a bipartisan group of 96 legislators. The stated objective of the legislation was to permit U.S. support for Cuba's internal political opposition in a manner similar to the U.S. approach to the Polish opposition in the 1980s. The legislation was not intended to authorize military support but, rather, allowed for the government to send cash, food, medicine, telephones, and fax machines, among other items, to Cuban democratic organizations opposed to the Castro regime. Helms indicated that the legislation would allow the U.S. government to license private donations from people in the United States to independent Cuban groups and self-employed Cubans. The bill also would allow goods made by independent, self-employed Cubans to be imported into the United States despite the embargo on trade with Cuba.

The legislation further appealed to the Castro government to respect human rights, free political prisoners, legalize political parties, allow independent trade unions, and submit to internationally monitored free elections. In addition, the bills encouraged the U.S.-funded Radio and Television Martí services and the Voice of America to take steps to overcome the jamming of their broadcast signals by the Castro government.[31]

More than 40 years after Castro's forces marched triumphantly into Havana, having driven out the corrupt regime of President Fulgencio Batista y Zaldívar, bilateral relations between the one remaining communist government in the Western Hemisphere and the United States remain only slightly less strained than they were when Castro nationalized foreign property and allied his government with the Soviet Union. Yet, the circumstances have dramatically changed since the peak of the Cold War. Few analysts would argue that the embargo policy and the policy of isolating Cuba from hemispheric affairs have advanced the main objectives of U.S. policy, which continue to be the destabilization of Castro's government and the enhancement of democracy and political pluralism in the island.

Notes

1. Elián González was returned to Cuba at the end of June 2000.

2. Cuban Information Archives, available at <http://www.Cuban-exile.com/>.

3. It was of later significance that Bill Clinton, then governor of Arkansas, was affected negatively in his bid for re-election by a riot of Cuban-Mariel prisoners at Fort Chaffee prison. See Carmelo Mesa-Lago, 1995, *Cuba's Raft Exodus of 1994: Causes, Settlement, Effects, and Future*, North-South Agenda Paper No. 12, April (Coral Gables, Fla.: The Dante B. Fascell North-South Center at the University of Miami), 9.

4. Cuban Information Archives, available at <http://Cuban-exile.com/>.

5. Bernard Aronson and William Rogers, 1999, *Special Report: US-Cuban Relations in the 21st Century* (New York: Council on Foreign Relations). Aronson and Rogers note that this was the conclusion of a 1998 report by the U.S. Defense Intelligence Agency.

6. Walter Vanderbrush and Patrick J. Haney, 1999, "Policy Toward Cuba in the Clinton Administration," *Political Science Quarterly* 114: 387-408; Walter Vanderbrush and Patrick J. Haney, 1999, "The Role of Ethnic Interest Groups in U.S. Foreign Policy: The Case of the Cuban American National Foundation," *International Studies Quarterly* 43 (June): 341-361. President Reagan signed the legislation establishing Radio Martí in 1985.

7. The Alliance for Progress was a program of inter-American economic assistance designed by President John F. Kennedy and created within the Organization of American States (OAS) framework in 1961.

8. Aronson and Rogers 1999; Stephen J. Randall and Graeme S. Mount, 1998, *An International History of the Caribbean Basin* (London: Routledge), 154-161.

9. Vanderbrush and Haney 1999a, 392.

10. Philip Brenner and Peter Kornbluh, 1995 "Clinton's Cuba Calculus," *NACLA Report on the Americas*, 29 (2) September-October.

11. Vanderbrush and Haney 1999a, 394.

12. Vanderbrush and Haney 1999a, 396-397.

13. Brenner and Kornbluh 1995, 34.

14. Vanderbrush and Haney 1999a, 398.

15. For an excellent overview of the 1994 situation, see Mesa-Lago 1995.

16. Brenner and Kornbluh 1995, 35-36; Max Castro, 1995, *Cuba: The Continuing Crisis*, North-South Agenda Paper No. 13, April (Coral Gables, Fla.: The Dante B. Fascell North-South Center at the University of Miami), 5.

17. Brenner and Kornbluh 1995, 37.

18. Max Castro 1995, 9-10.

19. President Clinton, 1995, "Interview with CNN," *Weekly Compilation of Presidential Documents* (April 14), 624-625.

20. President Clinton, 1995, "Address at Freedom House," *Weekly Compilation of Presidential Documents* (October 6), 1780-1781.

21. U.S. House of Representatives, 1996, *Conference Report on the Cuban Liberty and Democratic Solidarity (LIBERTAD) Act of 1996,* 104th Cong., 2nd sess., March 1.

22. Originally founded in 1991, Brothers to the Rescue is an aerial surveillance mission that has assisted in the rescue of some 4,200 rafters (as of May 2002) from the waters of the Gulf of Mexico and the Florida Straits. The group's small fleet of Cessna aircraft, piloted by leader José Basulto and about 20 other individuals, has coordinated many of its surveillance efforts with U.S. Coast Guard authorities. [On February 24, 1996, a Cuban Air Force MiG-29 fired air-to-air missiles at two unarmed aircraft belonging to Brothers to the Rescue, which killed Armando Alejandre, Carlos Alberto Costa, Mario Manuel de la Peña, and Pablo Morales. See <http://www.fiu.edu/~fcf/oasfeb24rep.html> — Ed.]

23. For overviews of the Helms-Burton legislation and its impact on international reaction and on U.S. and Canadian policy, see Heather Nicol, ed., 1999, *Canada, the US and Cuba: Helms-Burton and Its Aftermath* (Kingston, Ontario: Centre for International Relations, Queen's University); and Stephen J. Randall, 1998, "A Not So Magnificent Obsession: The United States, Cuba, and Canada from Revolution to the Helms-Burton Law," *Canadian-American Public Policy* 36 (November), 1-30.

24. U.S. Senate Committee on Foreign Relations, 1996, *The Libertad Act: Implementation and International Law: Hearing Before the Subcommittee on Western Hemisphere and Peace Corps Affairs,* 104th Cong., 2nd sess., July 30, 12-13.

25. U.S. House of Representatives 1996.

26. Randall 1998, 18-19.

27. U.S. Department of State 2000, available at International Information Programs, <http://www.usinfo.state.gov/products/pdq/pdq.htm>.

28. U.S. Defense Intelligence Agency (in collaboration with the Central Intelligence Agency, Department of State Bureau of Intelligence and Research, National Security Agency, and United States Southern Command Joint Intelligence Center), 1997, *DIA Report on Cuban Threat to U.S. National Security,* available at <http://www.usinfo.state.gov/regional/ar/us-cuba/dia.htm>.

29. William Ledwith, 2000, Chief of International Operations for the Drug Enforcement Agency, Testimony before the U.S. House Committee on Government Reform, January 4, "DEA Officials Testify on Drug Trafficking in Caribbean." Available at <http://www.usinfo.state.gov/products/pdq/pdq.htm>.

30. U.S. Department of State, International Information Programs, 2001, Washington File: *Bush Signals Support for Sending Aid to Dissidents in Cuba*, May 18, 2001; available at <http://www.usinfo.state.gov/products/pdq/pdq.htm>.

31. U.S. Department of State, International Information Programs, 2001, Washington File: *U.S. Senators Propose $100 Million in Aid to Dissidents in Cuba*, May 18. Available at <http://www.usinfo.state.gov/regional/ar/us-cuba/cubaaid16.htm>. In addition to senators Helms and Lieberman, the cosponsors of the Senate bill were Rick Santorum (Republican, Pennsylvania), Bob Graham (Democrat, Florida), Robert Torricelli (Democrat, New Jersey), John Ensign (Republican, Nevada), George Allen (Republican, Virginia),

Larry Craig (Republican, Idaho), Bill Nelson (Democrat, Florida), Richard Shelby (Republican, Alabama), and Bob Smith (Republican, New Hampshire).

References

Aronson, Bernard, and William Rogers. 1999. *Special Report: U.S.-Cuban Relations in the 21st Century.* New York: Council on Foreign Relations.

Baloyra, Enrique. 1995. "Latin America, Cuba, and the United States: From the Eighties to the Nineties." In *United States Policy in Latin America: A Decade of Crisis and Change,* ed. John D. Martz. Lincoln, Neb.: University of Nebraska Press.

Boone, Douglas A. 1999. *US-Cuba Policy for the Next Millennium.* Carlisle Barracks, Pa.: U.S. Army War College.

Boraz, Steven C. 1998. *Prospects for Democratic Transition in a Post-Castro Cuba: Implications for U.S. Policy.* Monterrey, Calif.: Naval Post-graduate School.

Brenner, Philip, and Peter Kornbluh. 1995. "Clinton's Cuba Calculus." *NACLA Report on the Americas* 29 (2) (September-October): 33-40.

Brenner, Philip. 1999. "Washington Loosens the Knot (Just a Little)." *NACLA Report on the Americas* 32 (5) (March/April): 41-45.

Castro, Max. 1995. *Cuba: The Continuing Crisis.* North-South Agenda Paper No. 13, April. Coral Gables, Fla.: The Dante B. Fascell North-South Center at the University of Miami.

Clinton, William. 1995. "Address at Freedom House." *Weekly Compilation of Presidential Documents,* October 6.

Clinton, William. 1995. "Interview with CNN." *Weekly Compilation of Presidential Documents,* April 14.

Cuban Information Archives. Available at <http://www.Cuban-exile.com/>.

Economist, The. 1999. "The Disputatious Diplomacy of Drugs." 352 (8136). September 11.

González, Edward, and Richard A. Nuccio, eds. 1999. *The RAND Forum on Cuba.* Santa Monica, Calif.: RAND.

Ledwith, William. 2000. Chief of International Operations for the Drug Enforcement Agency. "DEA Officials Testify on Drug Trafficking in Caribbean." Testimony before the U.S. House Committee on Government Reform. January 4. <http://www.usinfo.state.gov/products/pdq/pdq.htm>.

LeoGrande, William M. 1997. "Enemies Evermore: U.S. Policy Towards Cuba After Helms-Burton." *Journal of Latin American Studies* 29 (1) February: 211-221.

Marquis, Christopher. 1998. "Exiles React to Clinton's Cuba Policy Shift." *The Miami Herald,* March 26.

Mesa-Lago, Carmelo. 1995. *Cuba's Raft Exodus of 1994: Causes, Settlement, Effects, and Future.* North-South Agenda Paper No. 12, April. Coral Gables, Fla.: The Dante B. Fascell North-South Center at the University of Miami.

Nelson, Jack. 1998. "Clinton Backs Bill to Ease Cuba Embargo." *Los Angeles Times,* April 14.

Nicol, Heather, ed. 1999. *Canada, the US, and Cuba: Helms-Burton and its Aftermath.* Kingston, Ontario: Centre for International Relations, Queen's University.

Pomper, Miles. 1999a. "Cuban-American Agenda Marked by New Diversity." *CQ Weekly* 57 (9) (February 27): 467-470.

Pomper, Miles. 1999b. "Farm-State Democrats' Visit to Cuba Highlights Debate over Whether to Ease Embargo." *CQ Weekly* 57 (34) (September 4): 267-268.

Portes, Alejandro. 1998. "Morning in Miami: A New Era for Cuban-American Politics." *The American Prospect* (May-June).

Purcell, Susan Kaufman. 1998. "Cuba." In *Economic Sanctions and American Diplomacy,* ed. Richard Haass. New York: Council on Foreign Relations: 35-56.

Randall, Stephen J. 1998. "A Not So Magnificent Obsession: The United States, Cuba, and Canada from Revolution to the Helms-Burton Law." *Canadian-American Public Policy* 36 (November): 1-30.

Randall, Stephen J., and Graeme S. Mount. 1998. *An International History of the Caribbean Basin.* London: Routledge.

Smith, Jonathan C. 1998. "Foreign Policy for Sale? Interest Group Influence on President Clinton's Cuba Policy, August, 1994." *Presidential Studies Quarterly* 28 (1) Winter: 207-220.

Sullivan, Mark P. 2001. *Cuba: Background and Current Issues for Congress.* Washington, D.C.: Congressional Research Services. Available at <http://www.usinfo.state.gov/products/pdq/pdq.htm>.

U.S. Defense Intelligence Agency (in collaboration with the Central Intelligence Agency, Department of State Bureau of Intelligence and Research, National Security Agency, and United States Southern Command Joint Intelligence Center). 1997. *DIA Report on Cuban Threat to U.S. National Security.* Available at <http://www.usinfo.state.gov/products/pdq/pdq.htm>.

U.S. Department of State, Bureau of Democracy, Human Rights, and Labor. 2000. *1999 Country Reports on Human Rights Practices: Cuba.* February 25. See <http://www.state.gov/index.html>.

U.S. Department of State, Bureau of Democracy, Human Rights, and Labor. 2001. *2000 Country Reports on Human Rights Practices: Cuba.* February. Available at <http://www.usinfo.state.gov/products/pdq/pdq.htm>.

U.S. Department of State, International Information Programs. 2000. *Washington File: State Department Response to U.N. Human Rights Resolution on Cuba.* April 18. Available at <http://www.usinfo.state.gov/products/pdq/pdq.htm>.

U.S. Department of State, International Information Programs. 2001. *Washington File: Bush Signals Support for Sending Aid to Dissidents in Cuba.* May 18. Available at <http://www.usinfo.state.gov/products/pdq/pdq.htm>.

U.S. Department of State. International Information Programs. May 18, 2001. *U.S. Senators Propose $100 Million in Aid to Dissidents in Cuba.* Available at <http://www.usinfo.state.gov/regional/ar/us-cuba/dia.htm>.

U.S. House of Representatives. 1996. *Conference Report on the Cuban Liberty and Democratic Solidarity (LIBERTAD) Act of 1996.* 104th Cong., 2nd sess., March.

U.S. Senate Committee on Foreign Relations and House International Affairs Committee. 1998. *Report on Cuba at the Crossroads: The Visit of Pope John Paul II and the Opportunities for U.S. Policy.* March 5. Available at <http://www.usinfo.state.gov/regional/ar/us-cuba/congress.htm>.

U.S. Senate Committee on Foreign Relations. 1996. *The LIBERTAD Act: Implementation and International Law: Hearing before the Subcommittee on Western Hemisphere and Peace Corps Affairs.* 104 Cong., 2nd sess., July 30.

U.S. Trade and Economic Council, Inc. 1999. *Foreign Investment and Cuba*. Available at <http://www.cubatrade.org/foreign.html>.

Vanderbrush, Walter, and Patrick J. Haney. *1999a.* "Policy Toward Cuba in the Clinton Administration." *Political Science Quarterly* 114: 387-408.

Vanderbrush, Walter, and Patrick J. Haney. 1999b. "The Role of Ethnic Interest Groups in U.S. Foreign Policy: The Case of the Cuban American National Foundation." *International Studies Quarterly* 43 (June): 341-361.

CHAPTER FIVE

Cuba in U.S. Foreign Policy: The Emergence of a "Post-Helms-Burton" Era?

DANIEL W. FISK

On February 24, 1996, Cuban MiG aircraft shot down two civilian airplanes,[1] killing three U.S. citizens and one permanent U.S. resident. After action by the U.S. Congress, President Bill Clinton (1993-2001) signed into law the Cuban Liberty and Democratic Solidarity (LIBERTAD) Act (Helms-Burton) on March 12, 1996. Europe, Canada, and Latin America braced for a confrontation with Washington in their bilateral relations with the United States and within the context of the North American Free Trade Agreement (NAFTA) and the World Trade Organization (WTO) over U.S. policy toward Cuba. These events appeared to presage an invigorated U.S. policy of isolating Fidel Castro with the objective of hastening democratic change on the Caribbean island.

In the four years following enactment of Helms-Burton, however, policy toward Cuba underwent a reevaluation in Congress. Several factors contributed to this development, including 1) the emergence of an aggressive lobbying effort by U.S. business allied with the farm and agriculture sector and traditional anti-embargo groups opposed to the use of sanctions in general and to the U.S. embargo on Cuba specifically; 2) Pope John Paul II's visit to Cuba in January 1998 and the impact of this event on the pro-Helms-Burton congressional coalition; 3) the ascendancy of stability in Cuba as the guiding objective of U.S. policy during Clinton's presidency; and 4) the warming of U.S. relations with other repressive communist regimes, as in the U.S. decision to extend permanent normal trade relations with the People's Republic of China (PRC), the conclusion of a trade agreement with Vietnam, and the thaw in relations and attitudes toward North Korea.

Under the influence of new actors and new dynamics and after a decade of pushing for stronger sanctions against Cuba, the U.S. Congress softened its stance on U.S. interaction with the island. U.S. policy appears to be preparing for a post-Helms-Burton era, opposing embargo supporters and calling forth elements of the embargo for revision, if not repeal.

Portions of this chapter originally appeared in the Winter 2001 edition of *The Washington Quarterly*. The views expressed in this chapter are those of the author and do not necessarily reflect the views or conclusions of The Heritage Foundation, its officers, or its board of trustees.

The dynamics of the November 2000 presidential election in Florida and the victory of George W. Bush, however, altered the Washington political equation. As a candidate and without specifically endorsing Helms-Burton, Bush pledged to maintain the embargo until current conditions in Cuba changed. Once in the White House, Bush reiterated his campaign commitment and five months into the administration endorsed a more active effort to support democratic change in Cuba. Embargo opponents, however, are not giving up. Although some no longer insist on removing the embargo completely, they appear to be limiting their priorities to selected restrictions such as easier travel to Cuba and less stringent credit sales conditions to the Castro regime. [As this volume was going to press, former President Jimmy Carter met with Fidel Castro in Havana, at the Cuban president's invitation. It will be interesting to note whether the May 2002 meeting brings about any changes in Cuba's and the United States' policies. — Ed.]

THE EVOLUTION OF U.S. POLICY

Initially, U.S. policy toward the Castro regime was a reaction to Cuba's confiscation of U.S. property and turn to the Soviet Union in the early 1960s. Concerns about Cuba's international agenda of supporting revolution in Latin America and Africa and the regime's internal repression of its own citizens also motivated U.S. efforts to isolate the Cuban government.

With the collapse of the Soviet Union and its European proxies, many people assumed that the same fate would befall Castro's rule, but U.S. policy gave little time or attention to the Cuba matter. For the administration of President George H.W. Bush (1989-1993), the fall of the Soviet Union and events in Central America were higher priorities than issues with the Castro government. Despite Clinton's 1992 campaign embrace of a tougher U.S. policy toward Cuba,[2] the subsequent Clinton administration was perceived either as not having a Cuba policy or as harboring a secret plan to normalize U.S. relations with Cuba.

The apparent policy vacuum in the executive branch prompted Congress to assert its policy vision for U.S. relations with Cuba. For example, during the first Bush administration, the Democrat-controlled Congress, out of a sense of frustration with presidential inattention, approved the Cuban Democracy Act of 1992 (CDA) over the executive's initial objections to the tightening of sanctions.[3] The CDA established a two-track policy of reaching out to the Cuban people by permitting humanitarian donations, including food and medicine, while attempting to increase economic pressure on the Cuban government by prohibiting U.S. subsidiaries from trading with Cuba and prohibiting any vessel from entering a U.S. port for a period of 180 days if that vessel had handled freight to or from a Cuban port.

Subsequently, in 1996, a Republican-controlled Congress, fearing that Clinton and his advisors were interested in giving Cuba the wrong kind of attention, that is, normalizing the relationship, introduced and approved the Helms-Burton Act.[4] This act sought to build on the CDA's dual approach by granting the president the authority to provide humanitarian assistance and prepare for a transition in Cuba, while extending sanctions to apply to third parties who conducted business transactions in confiscated U.S. properties in Cuba.

The CDA and the Helms-Burton Act marked the ascendancy of the pro-embargo coalition in Congress in the 1990s. Ironically, these acts, especially Helms-Burton, also sparked efforts to revise U.S. policy. They motivated established political actors to focus on what was for them a new issue: Cuba. In addition, the duality upon which both acts were premised — support for the Cuban people and pressure on the Castro government — contained a contradiction that could be influenced by U.S. relations with other communist societies. While the logic of a two-track approach for Cuba was easy to understand and differentiate for those who closely watched events on the island, this dual vision lost currency as U.S. relations and public attitudes softened toward the PRC, Vietnam, and North Korea. These developments occurred, moreover, at a time of new dynamics within the Cuban-American community and as a result of their presence in Washington, D.C.

STABILITY: THE BASIS OF U.S. CUBA POLICY

Under the administrations of George H.W. Bush and Bill Clinton, a general "don't-rock-the-boat" attitude prevailed toward Cuba. For varying reasons, neither administration expended a great deal of energy or political capital on promoting political change there. Stability in Cuba was the preferred course, as it allowed attention to be placed elsewhere and offered the least potential for causing negative political consequences in the United States.

Specifically during the Clinton administration, while the congressional supporters of Helms-Burton analyzed the seeming drift in policy as a failure to have a policy, the administration was focused on preventing Cuban migrants from flooding the United States. As one high-ranking Clinton administration official described U.S. policy, "Today... our primary concern is the one that did not exist 20 years ago. That is the issue of stability [in Cuba].... We [the United States] cannot permit the social dislocation in our country that would be associated with attempting to absorb a large portion of the Cuban population."[5] He continued, "This is our nightmare scenario [for Cuba]: Things become unglued, we end up with a flood of migrants, and we are pressured to stop that."[6]

The ability to avoid such a "nightmare scenario," however, is not solely within the power of the U.S. government; it depends on having a partner in Cuba. Only a stable and cooperative Cuban government and populace can minimize Washington's fears of massive migration from the island.

The Clinton administration's rationale for Cuba policy should not have been surprising, given two events. The first was Clinton's only political defeat, which came, in part, as a result of the 1980 Mariel migration (see Chapter Four in this volume). His rejection by Arkansas voters in his 1980 bid to be re-elected governor can be attributed to the reaction of voters to the relocation of *marielitos*[7] to Fort Chaffee in Arkansas. In addition, one of Clinton's first foreign policy concerns as president involved Haiti[8] and the question of how to deal with large numbers of migrants fleeing that Caribbean nation.

For U.S. policy toward Cuba during the Clinton administration, "stability" meant developing a modus operandi for curtailing any massive immigration outflows and finding a modus vivendi with the Castro government. Embargo supporters in Congress, however, did not seek stability; they sought to promote political change on the island. Thus, while congressional initiatives focused on the instruments of so-called subversion, the executive branch sought to implement and pursue a policy focused on stability first and foremost, without having to acknowledge this policy publicly.

Clinton's initiatives during his administration, including the changes in travel restrictions in June 1993, the 1994-1995 U.S.-Cuba migration talks, the approval of direct flights, the loosening of travel licensing procedures, and the go-ahead for the Cuba-Baltimore Orioles baseball games, represented efforts to create a modus vivendi with the Castro regime. Some of the initiatives were meant to send signals of reassurance to Castro, while others sought to build mechanisms to address the economic distress endemic on the island. The signing of Helms-Burton threw a wrench into this strategy; it made the Clinton administration's work harder, as it attempted to balance the negative international reaction with domestic political factors. The result was the administration's minimalist implementation strategy, which continued to allow for achievement of its overall objective: to create an incentive for Cubans to remain on the island and for the Castro regime to cooperate in keeping them there.

THE MOBILIZATION OF AN EXPANDED ANTI-EMBARGO COALITION

After years of silence on the United States' use of sanctions, including the embargo on Cuba, the enactment of Helms-Burton and the Iran-Libya Sanctions Act of 1996 (ILSA) motivated new attention to these issues on the part of established political interests. One such Washington actor was the U.S. business community. While organized and vocal on a range of economic and trade questions, the business community had given only sporadic attention, if any, to business sanctions or Cuba policies. A second set of newly motivated actors included the Latin American and European nations, most notably the Vatican.

The emergence of an active corporate lobbying effort on sanctions policy generally and on Cuba specifically became a critical element in the new policy debate in the United States on U.S. Cuba policy. As one analyst stated, "Economic sanctions have long been nettlesome to the international business community, but the issue came to the fore in the 104th Congress with the enactment of two controversial laws—the Helms-Burton Act directed against Cuba and the D'Amato-Kennedy Act aimed at Iran and Libya." [9] The D'Amato-Kennedy Act mimicked Helms-Burton in applying sanctions against third countries and entities doing business in Iran or Libya.

As no one business or commercial sector wanted to take the lead in lobbying against Congress's preference for sanctions or in taking on organizations that supported sanctions against specific countries, in 1997, elements of the U.S. corporate community established USA*Engage, a coalition of individual businesses and national and state business associations. [10] The creation of USA*Engage soon was followed by the emergence of the U.S. Chamber of Commerce in lobbying against sanctions.

This coalition quickly came to three realizations: First, they needed a grassroots strategy with local businesspeople lobbying their individual members of Congress because the political struggle over the United States' use of sanctions could not be limited to high-priced Washington lobbyists. Second, Cuba was the weak link in the sanctions structure; while the ultimate target was U.S. sanctions against Iran, Libya, and Iraq because these nations have oil revenues, attacking them meant also taking on the domestic lobby interested in strong U.S. support for Israel. This approach was to be avoided, at least initially. Third, Cuba gave the U.S. corporate sector a greater echo effect in the U.S. media; initiatives on Cuba brought wider media coverage than did the general topic of sanctions reform or any proposal to end sanctions on a Middle Eastern state.

Initially, the relationship between the traditional anti-Cuban embargo lobby and USA*Engage was uncertain. Despite their different starting points on the broader ideological spectrum (many of the traditional anti-embargo groups opposed policies supported by the business community, especially during the Reagan and first Bush administrations), both groups soon recognized that they shared a strategic goal regarding Cuba. Together, they set out to recruit the American farm and agricultural lobby, recognizing its potential to make Cuba a local issue in places where it was a nonexistent concern. The idea was to duplicate the farm community's successful effort to reverse the grain embargo President Jimmy Carter (1977-1981) imposed against the Soviet Union for its December 1979 invasion of Afghanistan. In the case of Cuba, farm bureaus in Texas, Arkansas, Illinois, Missouri, and Nebraska, among others, were recruited actively by portraying Cuba as a $3-billion market denied to them but open to Canadian, French, Brazilian, and Argentine farmers. The mobilization of these domestic constituencies has paid off, as farm-state members of Congress are among the primary movers in the effort to reverse U.S. policy toward Cuba.[11]

The emergence of these domestic U.S. pressures also has been related to the actions of international actors, especially Canada, the European Union and its member states, and the Vatican. Many in the U.S. business community first heard of Helms-Burton or ILSA from European or Canadian clients who expressed frustration with the content and course of U.S. policies. The potential economic and diplomatic fallout from a contentious transatlantic dispute over Cuba created anxiety in the U.S. business community. The reaction from European capitals, in particular, fed U.S. business fears of being caught in the crossfire or of having the rules of the international economy dramatically changed.

While European and Canadian objections to U.S. policy did register on Capitol Hill, it was the pope's January 1998 visit to Cuba that influenced the general public and members of Congress more than the concerns of long-time European and North American allies. The pope's message to the Cuban people to "be not afraid" and "open [themselves] to the world" also involved an appeal to "the world [to] open itself to Cuba." This last message resonated in the United States, particularly in the Cuban-American community.

CHANGES IN THE CUBAN-AMERICAN COMMUNITY

For years, Cuban-Americans celebrated exile, with the litmus test of opposition to Castro being whether one left the island, not whether one remained in Cuba and challenged the regime by whatever means available. Return from exile was to be considered only on the heels of an invasion or Castro's death. These attitudes were beginning to change before the pope's visit, especially among a younger generation of Cuban exile activists. When Pope John Paul II called on Cubans not to fear change, he hit a sensitive nerve in the Cuban exile community as well as among Cubans on the island.

While a majority of Cuban-Americans remain strongly anti-Castro and pro-embargo, a growing segment of the Cuban-American population sees a necessity for reconnecting with Cubans on the island, and some have voiced opposition to the U.S. embargo. Many younger Cuban-Americans are visiting Cuba to find their family roots or renew family ties disrupted by the Revolution.

The Cuban exile community's engagement with the island contains another contradiction: this population represents both a means of sustaining the regime and a powerful mechanism for undermining the authority of Castro's rule. The sustenance comes with the remittances that are sent regularly to relatives on the island. Some experts estimate the total amount of remittances to be as high as $800 million annually. These remittances give the recipients some autonomy from state-rationed goods, allowing Cubans with relatives abroad to have access to goods unavailable to those living only on the peso economy. Since remittances are one of the largest sources of hard currency, they also provide the regime with an incentive to establish mechanisms for acquiring dollars. For example, as part of its effort to acquire hard currency, the Cuban government has opened "dollar stores," once reserved for non-Cubans, to anyone with dollars.

The Cuban exile community also represents a danger to the regime, not because of fear that some exile group will threaten the regime militarily, although that possibility is a constant refrain of Cuban propaganda, but because Cubans in exile have the shared history, culture, and relationships to circumvent the regime. The exile community provides the evidence that other alternatives exist and that free Cubans can prosper economically and politically.

At the same time that attitudes in the Cuban-American community began shifting, the traditional pro-embargo Cuban-American organization, the Cuban American National Foundation (CANF), was searching for new leadership. The November 1997 death of its charismatic founder and guiding force, Jorge Mas Canosa, was a setback to CANF and to its presence in Washington.[12] Another blow to the foundation occurred in the fall of 1998 with indictments in federal court charging CANF officials and others close to CANF with involvement in a plot to assassinate Castro.[13] While they were acquitted of the charges, the allegations and trial, combined with the leadership vacuum, impacted the foundation's reputation and distracted the strongest pro-embargo entity from aggressively addressing the changing political environment in Washington.

NEW FACTORS IN UNITED STATES-CUBA RELATIONS: BASEBALL AND ELIÁN GONZÁLEZ

Two other unrelated developments also affected the evolution of U.S. Cuba policy after the enactment of the Helms-Burton Act: the Cuba-Baltimore Orioles exercise in "baseball diplomacy" and the saga of six-year-old Elián González.

While the attention surrounding Elián González is credited with changing the U.S. citizens' attitudes toward their country's embargo,[14] public opinion had become pro-engagement before young González was rescued in the Florida Straits in November 1999. This change in public opinion in the United States is attributable more to its national pastime than to Elián himself.

As part of a series of people-to-people exchanges announced by Clinton in January 1999 (and permitted under the CDA of 1992), the administration approved an exchange of baseball games between the Baltimore Orioles and a Cuban national team. In late March and early May 1999, in Havana and Baltimore, respectively, crucial changes in United States-Cuba relations occurred on a baseball diamond.

This exchange was perhaps almost as significant as the pope's visit in influencing broader U.S. public opinion. The Orioles-Cuba baseball games moved Cuba from the news and op-ed pages to the sports pages of U.S. newspapers. "*Beisbol* diplomacy" reached a huge U.S. audience, many of whom may have customarily paid little attention to international news. Over the years, U.S. public opinion has swung back and forth on the issue of normalizing relations with Cuba, with a majority in recent years favoring isolation. However, during the time period that included the pope's visit to Cuba and the two baseball games, public attitudes shifted toward support for engagement with Cuba.

In a 1998 Roper Poll, 53 percent of those surveyed expressed support for continuing the embargo, versus 42 percent who voiced opposition. According to the same survey, 56 percent favored reestablishing diplomatic relations, while 39 percent opposed such a move. By May 1999, Gallup found 51 percent in favor of lifting the embargo and 42 percent opposing the embargo's end, while those in favor of establishing diplomatic relations climbed to 71 percent, with 25 percent disapproving this action.

In both surveys, respondents continued to express strong negative feelings toward Cuba,[15] but a shift in public attitudes about the proper course for U.S. policy had occurred. This change from pro-embargo to pro-engagement is understandable, given the events of the preceding 18 months, notably the pope's visit to Cuba, the Orioles-Cuba baseball games, and the growing attention to Cuba in the farm belt.[16]

Following in the wake of these developments, the Elián González case gave the media an opportunity and an excuse to focus sustained attention on Cuba, U.S. policy, and Miami's Cuban-American community. For Washington, the González case appeared to confirm the demise of the Cuban-American lobby because of CANF's inability to lobby Congress to approve legislation granting Elián González either U.S. citizenship or permanent resident status. However, within the Cuban-American community, especially in South Florida, the Clinton administration's handling of the González case contributed to a reinvigoration of political identification with the Republican Party, something that was reflected in the November 2000 presidential elections.[17]

CONGRESS REEVALUATES U.S. POLICY TOWARD CUBA

These new actors and dynamics influenced congressional attitudes toward Cuba during the 1997-2000 period. An early indication of the changed political landscape came in the wake of Mas Canosa's death in 1997 and the pope's 1998 visit to Cuba. CANF, looking for a way to reinvigorate its profile and respond positively to the pope's Cuba initiative, proposed providing direct U.S.-funded humanitarian aid to the island. The CANF plan was endorsed by Senator Jesse Helms (Republican, North Carolina), chairman of the Senate Foreign Relations Committee, who in May 1998 introduced legislation that reflected the idea. Known as the Cuban Solidarity (SOLIDARIDAD) Act, the Helms legislation sought to provide $100 million in humanitarian assistance over four years directly to the Cuban people.

This legislation was significant for two reasons. First, it represented a shift in the U.S. congressional debate from whether to provide aid to how to do so. In previous debates, the focus was on extending sanctions and, at the most, permitting private donations. The SOLIDARIDAD proposal sought to direct U.S. government-funded humanitarian aid to the Cuban people. Second, and perhaps of greater political significance, SOLIDARIDAD created friction within the congressional Helms-Burton coalition. The reaction of the House leadership to the initiative was quick and firm: Nothing of the sort would be approved in that chamber.[18]

This reconfiguration of the congressional debate signaled the emergence of a post-Helms-Burton era in the U.S. Congress. In reality, Helms continued to oppose the loosening of the embargo; his objective in SOLIDARIDAD was consistent with provisions in Helms-Burton to authorize U.S.-funded assistance to human rights groups and victims of political repression on the island. In congressional debates, however, images often are more important than the nuances of a particular position — and the perception was that the pope's visit had opened a new opportunity for opponents of U.S. policy.

In July 1998, Senator Christopher Dodd (Democrat, Connecticut), a long-time critic of the U.S. embargo on Cuba, offered an amendment prohibiting the president from restricting exports of food and agricultural products to the island. Embargo supporters, realizing they could not defeat the Dodd Amendment, used the best weapon available, Senate parliamentary procedures, to require modification of the amendment to retain restrictions on exports to countries on the U.S. State Department's list of "terrorist countries." This meant countries that engage in terrorist acts, support terrorist groups, or provide sanctuary to terrorists. At that time, Cuba was listed as a terrorist country by the U.S. State Department, and it remains on the list. Although the Dodd Amendment did not survive as a provision in the final bill presented to the president for his approval, the fact that it was adopted by the Senate reflected the changed political consensus on U.S. policy toward Cuba in that legislative body.

In part, because of the tension in the Helms-Burton congressional coalition over the SOLIDARIDAD proposal, embargo proponents turned their attention to issues that appeared to be directed at constituency interests in South Florida more than at broader national policy. The first of these was an effort to provide compensation to the families of the four Brothers to the Rescue pilots killed in February 1996. The second issue involved the dispute between Bacardi-Martini and Pernod Ricard over ownership of the "Havana Club" rum trademark. While each of these initiatives had potentially broad policy and international law implications, they fell below the radar for most lawmakers, leaving the initiative on the larger question of U.S. policy to embargo opponents.

In the Senate, farm-state senators and long-time embargo opponents continued to press for the lifting of restrictions on food and agriculture exports and travel to and from Cuba. Senator Dodd offered another amendment on Cuba, seeking to end restrictions on U.S. citizen travel to the island nation. Actually, the amendment to the fiscal year 2000 foreign aid appropriations act was tabled, a nondebatable procedural motion used to kill floor amendments. However, the 55 to 43 vote on the motion to table was closer than embargo supporters had expected; those 43 senators, by their vote against the procedural motion, had voiced, in effect, support for lifting the travel restrictions.

Less than six weeks later, the Senate approved an initiative by Senator John Ashcroft (Republican, Missouri) that would have ended unilateral sanctions on agricultural and medical exports to any country, regardless of whether the country had been determined to be a supporter of international terrorism. Embargo supporters attempted a motion to table, losing 28 in favor to 70 against. Because the companion House legislation contained no such provision, the Republican congressional leadership was able to keep the Ashcroft language out of the final measure sent to the president.

With a clear Senate majority favoring the lifting of restrictions on the export of food, agricultural commodities, and medical products, the battle shifted to the House of Representatives during the 2000 legislative session. In May, language sponsored by Congressman George Nethercutt (Republican, Washington) to lift restrictions on food sales was affirmed when the House Appropriations Committee voted 24 to 35 to defeat an effort by Majority Whip Tom DeLay (Republican, Texas) to delete it. In contentious negotiations between Nethercutt and House Republicans who supported the embargo, an agreement eventually was reached to permit food and agricultural exports to Cuba without U.S. credit or financing, in exchange for restrictions on the president's ability to expand travel without congressional approval.

The Nethercutt compromise, reached in late June 2000, was supposed to have resolved the issue. However, the House leadership was caught by surprise when two other Republicans offered amendments on the House floor during consideration of the funding bill for the U.S. Treasury Department. Embargo opponents targeted that piece of legislation because the Treasury Department's Office of Foreign Assets Control is charged with enforcing the embargo.

The first amendment, offered by Congressman Mark Sanford (Republican, South Carolina), prohibited the spending of Treasury funds for enforcement of the restrictions on travel to Cuba. His motion passed the House by a 232 to 186 vote, with 60 Republicans voting to end travel restrictions. The second amendment, offered by Congressman Jerry Moran (Republican, Kansas), prohibited the Treasury Department from spending any funds to enforce sanctions on the sale of food or medicines to the island. The vote on ending enforcement of food and medicine restrictions was even more lopsided: 301 to 116, with 119 Republicans voting "aye" for an end to sanctions on food and medicines.[19]

Congressman Sanford summed up the attitude of many House members when he said, "We've tried 40 years of isolation. It has not worked. The will of the House is that we take this incremental step."[20] In effect, two pillars of the embargo were repudiated by the House, evidencing a dramatic change in the House as a whole on the issue of the Cuba embargo.

Meanwhile, in the Senate, the setbacks in 1998 and 1999 had not deterred embargo opponents. In fact, the sea change in the Senate was dramatic enough that Helms permitted the Senate Foreign Relations Committee to report legislation to the Senate containing sanctions reform language[21] and the modified Ashcroft amendment on agricultural and medical exports. Although he opposed both measures, Helms knew that allowing the provision through without a committee fight was less harmful to current U.S. policy than losing a committee vote on those specific provisions.[22]

To confirm that the shift in Senate attitudes had consolidated, in late July 2000, during consideration of the agriculture spending bill, an amendment to lift restrictions on the sale of food and medicines to Cuba was approved by a 79-to-13 floor vote.[23]

This new turn in the congressional debate was not driven by anything that had happened in Cuba. Cuba policy was evaluated largely in the context of the U.S. debate over trade with China and Vietnam, in which the dominant argument is that trade and "engagement" promote political and economic change in line with U.S. values. As Nethercutt argued in *The New York Times*, "Those who promoted normal trading relations with China said that trade promotes democratization. Change in Communist regimes is slow, but eventually, democratic norms take hold. Dialogue and engagement with the United States are central to this transition, as is exposure to our processes. If this is true for China, then why not for Cuba?"[24]

In the case of Cuba, no evidence suggests that fundamental political change has occurred on the island or that Castro has loosened his grip on power. In the realm of economics, the evolution in Cuban policies has been necessitated by the disappearance of Cuba's Soviet benefactor. Use of the dollar has been legalized; several categories of work have been authorized for self-employment; cooperative farms have been granted more autonomy, including some latitude to sell their products directly; and the regime has aggressively attempted to attract foreign investment through joint ventures with Cuban state entities. All these changes represent tactical responses to the Cuban regime's need for hard currency. The basic nature of Cuba's repressive, controlling system remains unchanged.

The shift in Congress, then, appears to be based on its changing perceptions of domestic constituencies and their relative power and priorities as much as, if not more than, on specific conclusions about the prospects for reform under Castro.

THE 2000 ELECTIONS AND THE BUSH ADMINISTRATION

As the year 2000 ended, the U.S. debate over Cuba policy appeared to be firmly embarked on a new phase, with the debate being driven by opponents of the embargo and the demise of the embargo appearing no longer unalterably tied to the demise of Mr. Castro's regime.

The November 2000 elections did not alter the new consensus in Congress: The majority in both chambers were still opposed to many of the major components of the U.S. embargo on Cuba.

The election of George W. Bush and "Elián's revenge," however, did change the political calculus. The 2000 election outcome in Florida serves as a reminder to Republicans and Democrats to keep the demographics of that state in mind when contemplating policy toward Cuba and its potential impact on the 2004 presidential election. The 2000 election also gave a new twist to the executive-legislative rivalry that had existed between a Republican Congress and a Democratic (Clinton) White House.

For congressional Republicans, having a Republican administration requires that their actions not embarrass or confront the president head-on over issues for which the domestic political downside is greater than any political advantage to be gained. Recent history strongly suggests that Cuba can be an issue for which the negatives are greater than the positives. Cuban-Americans, concentrated in two key electoral states, Florida and New Jersey, vote with that issue primarily in mind. Anti-embargo groups, including farmers, have too many factors to weigh in their voting calculations, and Cuba is not a big enough market to turn that group into a one-issue constituency. As for the business lobby, they, too, have a multiple agenda, and members of Congress grow weary of the "What have you done for me today?" argument of many corporate lobbyists.

Further, for the 2001-2002 congressional session, each party has reasons to downplay the Cuba issue, especially if the resulting fallout penalizes their respective political interests. For Republicans, the re-election of Jeb Bush, the president's brother, as governor of Florida should give pause to too vigorous an onslaught on Cuba policy. Further, with this period representing Helms' valedictory time on the political scene,[25] his colleagues are unlikely to reverse in any significant way the legislation that bears his name.

For their part, the Democrats face several calculations: their belief that Governor Jeb Bush of Florida may be vulnerable and the hope that they can pick up another southern governor's office in 2002; the 2004 re-election campaign of Senator Bob Graham, Florida's senior Democrat and a seat critical to the Democrats' hold on the Senate; and the desire of some in the Democratic Party to mend fences with Cuban-Americans and revive the success of Clinton in attracting significant numbers of that constituency back to the Democrats' fold in 2004. Already, Senator Joseph Lieberman (Democrat, Connecticut), the 2000 Democratic vice presidential candidate, and other senior Democrats are wooing the Cuban American National Foundation's leadership.[26]

These dynamics will not stop the Cuba debate in Congress. Both sides have introduced legislation outlining their agendas for U.S. policy on Cuba. President

Bush, however, has made it clear that his pro-embargo campaign comments were not based on political expediency but reflect his commitment to the basic aspects of U.S. policy. As he reiterated at the 2001 White House celebration of Cuban Independence Day,

> The sanctions our government enforces against the Castro regime are not just a policy tool; they're a moral statement. My administration will oppose any attempt to weaken sanctions against Cuba's government until the regime — and I will fight such attempts — until this regime frees its political prisoners, holds democratic, free elections, and allows for free speech.[27]

The president further outlined his administration's policy as favoring efforts "to actively support those working to bring about democratic change in Cuba," endorsing the substance of proposals by Helms and Congressman Lincoln Díaz-Balart (Republican, Florida) to provide direct assistance to Cuban civic movements and independent non-governmental organizations.[28]

Moreover, the Bush administration has indicated that it is giving serious consideration to allowing the right-of-action provision (Title III) of Helms-Burton to go into effect.[29] This provision would allow those individuals whose properties were confiscated in Cuba to pursue compensation through judicial avenues from third parties who use, occupy, invest in, manage, or otherwise benefit from such properties. The law provides the president with the authority to waive the implementation of this provision every six months if he determines that it is "necessary to the national interests of the United States and will expedite a transition to democracy in Cuba." From its enactment in March 1996 through the end of his presidency in January 2001, Clinton waived the Title III provision, leading many to the conclusion that the waiver was guaranteed regardless of the behavior of the Castro regime or those who did business with it. The early signals from the Bush administration are that waivers of the right-of-action provision will not be automatic.

CONCLUSION

On several levels, the Helms-Burton Act has helped shape a post-Helms-Burton era. The statute inadvertently helped energize an anti-embargo coalition that has been more successful in reshaping attitudes and policy than many thought possible when Clinton signed the act into law. The Helms-Burton Act also opened the door wider to some level of engagement by building on the dual approach of the CDA and exploring ways to provide help directly to the people of Cuba, while minimizing any consequent succor provided thereby to the Cuban government.

While the debate on policy toward Cuba previously focused primarily on enforcing punitive measures versus lifting of the embargo, the debate subsequent to Helms-Burton has shifted to a more targeted set of approaches. Various legislative proposals have been introduced to refine the embargo and allow more engagement, ranging from humanitarian aid to exceptions that would virtually nullify the embargo. However, underlying these proposals, there is a fundamental difference of approach. The struggle is between the following two distinct strategies: engaging the Castro regime through such means as agricultural sales, credits, commerce with Cuban state entities, and lifting of travel restrictions versus the approach of engaging the Cuban people through programs that seek to go around the regime and reach the Cuban people directly. The resolution of this debate will shape the future of U.S. policy toward Cuba.

Notes

1. The two planes, which were shot down in international waters, belonged to the anti-Castro, Miami-based organization, "Brothers to the Rescue." Founded in 1991, Brothers to the Rescue claims to have helped some 4,200 rafters reach safety in the waters of the Gulf of Mexico and the Florida Straits as of May 2002. See <http://www.cubainfolinks.net/links/hermanos.htm>.

2. Tom Fiedler, 1992, "Clinton Backs Torricelli Bill: 'I Like It,' He Tells Cuban Exiles," *The Miami Herald*, April 24.

3. Public Law 102-484, 106 Stat. 2315, October 23, 1992. The CDA was approved as Title XVII of the National Defense Authorization Act for Fiscal Year 1993.

4. Public Law 104-114, 110 Stat. 785, March 12, 1996.

5. Michael Kozak, 1998, "The Prospects for a Peaceful Transition in Cuba: Six Months After the Papal Visit" (remarks before "Cuba in Evolution," sponsored by the *The Dallas Morning News*, Dallas, Texas, September 29). At the time of his remarks, Kozak was the chief of the U.S. Interests Section in Havana, Cuba.

6. Laurence Iliff, 1998, "U.S. Concerned that Changes in Cuba Will Bring Influx," *The Dallas Morning News*, September 30.

7. In Cuban vernacular, the term *marielitos* is used to refer to immigrants who left the island during the 1980 exodus out of the port of Mariel.

8. Initially, U.S. policy toward Haiti was unsympathetic to Haitian refugees. Those intercepted at sea or those who successfully landed in the United States were returned to Haiti. However, dissatisfaction with this policy created a national and international outcry, along with charges that the United States was discriminating against Haitians, while unconditionally accepting Cubans and Nicaraguan refugees. In 1994, U.S. policy toward Haitian immigration was reversed. President Bill Clinton announced that the Immigration and Naturalization Service (INS) would conduct asylum hearings for Haitian refugees intercepted at sea and allow them to submit their applications for U.S. asylum. Clinton also announced the appointment of a Haitian special envoy. Despite these changes, Haitians were not allowed to immigrate en masse to the United States. For example, well over 1,000 boat people were returned to Haiti in May, 1994, even after the change in policy was announced. The Clinton administration was worried about mass immigration of Haitians, should the United States appear sympathetic to Haitian refugee claims. This, in fact, was one of the major reasons why the United States subsequently participated in the project to restore to power to Haiti's democratically elected former President Jean-Bertrand Aristide. — Heather N. Nicol, ed.

9. Dick Kirschten, 1997, "Chicken Soup Diplomacy," *The National Journal*, January 4.

10. For background on USA*Engage, see Kirschten 1997. For critical reports on USA*Engage, see Ken Silverstein, 1998, "So You Want To Trade With a Dictator," *Mother Jones*, May/June; and Jacob Heilbrunn, 1998, "The Sanctions Sellout: The Corporate Takeover of Foreign Policy," *The New Republic*, May 25, 21-25. Additional information on USA*Engage can be found on its website at <http://www.usaengage.org>.

11. Juan O. Tamayo, 2000, "Farmers Fuel Drive to Repeal Sanctions; Big Business Eyes Sales to Havana," *The Miami Herald*, June 25.

12. Rick Bragg, 1999, "For Cuban-Americans, a Void Lingers 2 Years after a Leader's Death," *The New York Times*, September 12.

13. Mark Fineman and Mike Clary, 1998, "In Shift, U.S. Indicts Crew of Leaky Boat for Castro Plot," *The Los Angeles Times*, September 8. See also, Larry Rohter and Ann Louise Bardach, 1998, "Cuban Exile Leader among 7 Accused of Plot on Castro," *The New York Times*, August 26; Deborah Ramírez, 1998, "U.S. Charges Exiles in Castro Death Plot; Grand Jury Names 3 New Defendants; More Are Expected," *The Sun-Sentinel*, August 26; and Tim Golden, 1999, "5 Cuban Exiles Charged with Plotting to Kill Castro Are Acquitted," *The New York Times*, December 9.

14. For example, see William Raspberry, 2000, "The Boy and the Embargo," *The Washington Post*, July 28.

15. David W. Moore, 1999, "Americans Support Renewed Diplomatic Relations with Cuba," *Gallup News Service*, May 24.

16. For a more detailed discussion of U.S. public opinion toward Cuba, see Daniel W. Fisk, 1999, "Cuba and American Public Opinion," *Cuba in Transition, Vol. 9: Papers and Proceedings of the Eighth Annual Meeting of the Association for the Study of the Cuban Economy*, August.

17. See William Schneider, 2001, "Elián González Defeated Al Gore," *The National Journal*, April 28.

18. Tom Carter, 1999, "Anti-Castro Camp Opposes Measure on Food, Medicine," *The Washington Times*, June 24.

19. Karen DeYoung, 2000, "Momentum Grows on Hill to Ease Sanctions on Cuba," *The Washington Post*, July 22.

20. As quoted in *Newsweek*, 2000, "Perspectives" section, July 31, 11.

21. Since its founding, one of the objectives of USA*Engage has been the enactment of legislation to require that before economic sanctions are implemented, the president and Congress assess the impact of sanctions on domestic industries and the likelihood that such sanctions will achieve their intended objectives. The legislation also would require an automatic sunset provision for sanctions. This legislation, known as the "Unilateral Sanctions Reform Act" or the "Sanctions Process Reform Act," originally was introduced in Congress in late 1997.

22. The provisions were part of S. 2382, the Technical Assistance, Trade Promotion, and Anti-Corruption Act of 2000, reported out of the Senate Foreign Relations Committee on April 7 by a voice vote. See U.S. Senate, 2000, Senate Report 106-257, 106th Congress, 2nd session, April 7.

23. DeYoung 2000.

24. George R. Nethercutt, Jr., 2000, "What's Good for China Is Good for Cuba," *The New York Times*, May 26. Also see William Neikirk, 2000, "House Warms to Relaxing Cuba Embargo; China Trade Vote Weakens Opposition," *Chicago Tribune*, May 26; and Rafael Llorente, 2000, "China Trade Bill Helps Foes of Cuba Embargo; Farming Groups Back Legislation," *The Sun-Sentinel*, May 26.

25. For example, see Walter Russell Mead, 2001, "Why the World Is Better for Jesse Helms," *The New York Times*, April 22.

26. For an analysis of Senator Lieberman's efforts among the Cuban-American community during the 2000 election campaign, see Ralph J. Galliano, ed., 2000, "Lieberman's Inroads into the Cuban-American Vote," 2000, *US-Cuba Policy Report*, November 30.

27. The White House, 2001, Office of the Press Secretary, "Remarks by the President in Recognition of Cuba Independence Day," May 18. Available at <http://www.whitehouse.gov/news/releases/2001/05/20010518-7.html>.

28. The White House, 2001, "Remarks by the President," May 18.

29. Tom Carter, 2001, "Bush Weighs Helms-Burton Law," *The Washington Times*, June 11.

References

Bragg, Rick. 1999. "For Cuban-Americans, a Void Lingers 2 Years after a Leader's Death." *The New York Times,* September 12.

Carter, Tom. 1999. "Anti-Castro Camp Opposes Measure on Food, Medicine." *The Washington Times,* June 24.

Carter, Tom. 2001. "Bush Weighs Helms-Burton Law." *The Washington Times,* June 11.

DeYoung, Karen. 2000. "Momentum Grows on Hill to Ease Sanctions on Cuba." *The Washington Post,* July 22.

Fineman, Mark, and Mike Clary. 1998. "In Shift, U.S. Indicts Crew of Leaky Boat for Castro Plot." *The Los Angeles Times,* September 8.

Fisk, Daniel W. 1999. "Cuba and American Public Opinion." *Cuba in Transition, Vol. 9: Papers and Proceedings of the Eighth Annual Meeting of the Association for the Study of the Cuban Economy.* August.

Galliano, Ralph J., 2000. "Lieberman's Inroads into the Cuban-American Vote." In *U.S.-Cuba Policy Report,* ed. Ralph J. Galliano. November 30.

Golden, Tim. 1999. "5 Cuban Exiles Charged with Plotting to Kill Castro Are Acquitted." *The New York Times,* December 9.

Heilbrunn, Jacob. 1998. "The Sanctions Sellout: The Corporate Takeover of Foreign Policy." *The New Republic,* May 25.

Iliff, Laurence. 1998. "U.S. Concerned That Changes in Cuba Will Bring Influx." *The Dallas Morning News,* September 30.

Kirschten, Dick. 1997. "Chicken Soup Diplomacy." *The National Journal,* January 4.

Kozak, Michael. 1998. The Prospects for a Peaceful Transition in Cuba: Six Months After the Papal Visit. Remarks before "Cuba in Evolution," sponsored by *The Dallas Morning News,* Dallas, Texas, September 29.

Llorente, Rafael. 2000. China Trade Bill Helps Foes of Cuba Embargo; Farming Groups Back Legislation." *The Sun Sentinel,* May 26.

Mead, Walter Russell. 2001. "Why the World Is Better for Jesse Helms." *The New York Times,* April 22.

Moore, David W. 1999. "Americans Support Renewed Diplomatic Relations with Cuba." *Gallup News Service,* May 24.

Neikirk, William. 2000. "House Warms to Relaxing Cuba Embargo; China Trade Vote Weakens Opposition." *The Chicago Tribune*, May 26.

Nethercutt, George R., Jr. 2000. "What's Good for China Is Good for Cuba." *The New York Times*, May 26.

Newsweek. 2000. "Perspectives," July 31.

Ramírez, Deborah. 1998. "U.S. Charges Exiles in Castro Death Plot; Grand Jury Names 3 New Defendants; More Are Expected." *The Sun-Sentinel*, August 26.

Raspberry, William. 2000. "The Boy and the Embargo." *The Washington Post*, July 28.

Rohter, Larry, and Ann Louise Bardach. 1998. "Cuban Exile Leader Among 7 Accused of Plot on Castro." *The New York Times*, August 26.

Schneider, William. 2001. "Elián González Defeated Al Gore." *The National Journal*, April 28.

Silverstein, Ken. 1998. "So You Want to Trade With a Dictator." *Mother Jones*, May/June.

Tamayo, Juan O. 2000. "Farmers Fuel Drive to Repeal Sanctions; Big Business Eyes Sales to Havana." *The Miami Herald*, June 25.

U.S. Public Law 102-484, 106 Stat. 2315, October 23, 1992. The Cuban Democracy Act of 1992.

U.S. Public Law 104-114, 110 Stat. 785, March 12, 1996. Helms-Burton Act.

U.S. Senate. 1993. *National Defense Authorization Act for Fiscal Year 1993*.

U.S. Senate. 2000. Foreign Relations Committee. *Technical Assistance, Trade Promotion, and Anti-Corruption Act of 2000*. April 7.

U.S. Senate. 2000. Senate Report 106-257, 106th Congress, 2nd session. April 27.

The White House. 2001. Office of the Press Secretary. Remarks by the President in Recognition of Cuba Independence Day. May 18. Available at <http://www.whitehouse.gov/news/releases/2001/05/20010518-7.html>.

CHAPTER SIX

Cuba: The "Nerve-Racking Silence"[1] of Liminality

KARL B. KOTH

As we enter the second millennium, we are influenced by the opinions of Francis Fukuyama and others[2] in the belief that neoliberalism, the triumph of the new capitalist world order, offers the most viable possibility for economic progress. Yet, the critical contemporary observer must recognize that all the pieces do not fit neatly into this puzzle. One difficulty is that some people are not convinced that neoliberalism is the answer to their developmental necessities. The 1994 uprising in Chiapas, Mexico, for example, reminds us that the search for social and economic justice and a more humane economic model of change is still a burning issue for many marginalized peoples around the globe.[3]

The demonstrations against the deliberations of the World Trade Organization (WTO) meetings in Seattle, Davos, and Quebec City have been instructive in this context. They signaled that not only the less fortunate but also many in the most privileged nations of the world were equally adamant in expressing that the dictates of the new capitalist global order were not to their liking. Characterized as the "biggest fiasco in commercial negotiations of the last 20 years,"[4] the Seattle negotiations provided recent proof that simply taking for granted the victory of globalization and neoliberalism begs the question of future developmental possibilities around the world.

Even more illustrative of the fundamental debate over the new world order is the new developmental path on which the world's most insistently anticapitalist and anti-imperialist state, Cuba, has embarked, in order to address the compelling economic problems it has faced since the Soviet Union's withdrawal of support in 1991. What is Cuba's new developmental path in the short run? And what is it most likely to become in the future? These are two of the issues this chapter will probe. The third issue is the effect, if any, of Cuba's new trajectory on future Canada-Cuba relations.

Clearly, answers to the second question — Cuba's developmental path for the future — will remain speculative at best. However, certain significant signs may help predict to some extent what the future holds for this very important Caribbean nation.[5] If Cuba is able to navigate the turbulent waters of national development successfully and produce a humane developmental strategy and, with it, a relatively prosperous society, might its model still become an acceptable second option? In a world largely convinced that only a free-market model of unrestrained capitalism is feasible, this would be no mean feat for Cuba, a nation straddling the liminal position between efforts to remain true to its revolutionary principles and strategies to provide a better standard of living for its people.

CUBA'S ECONOMIC AND DEVELOPMENTAL CHALLENGES

Despite economic travails, Cuba displays tremendous promise. The island possesses many crucial preconditions for real and sustained development, not least of which is a highly educated and trained population. Cuba is just beginning to emerge from a most terrifying economic tailspin that began in 1991. Although the situation has been documented elsewhere, few people in the developed world can imagine what it is like for a country to have lost virtually all of its foreign trade and support overnight.[6] By 1994, gasoline was almost nonexistent, as were many items of food and medicine and other basic amenities of life. The bleak situation worsened upon the reappearance of a structural impediment, the proverbial one-crop economy that still plagues the Caribbean, and to a certain extent Cuba, despite or because of decades of partnership with the Soviet Bloc.[7]

Cuba's one-crop economy results from an earlier globalization forged by the advance of Western imperialism. Such economic structuring renders the Caribbean nations, geographically each other's natural trading partners, virtually incapable of trading because of a commodity structure imposed by centuries of control by European nations that did not take into account the well-being of the people they were ruling. Unfortunately, because of their inherent weakness imposed by their small size, none of the Caribbean nations was able to overcome this deficiency. Arguably, today, the Caribbean region continues to be exploited, as its primary value to the United States, Canada, and Europe is as a tourist "paradise," where their working populations can go for relaxation, according to political science professor Peter Schwab.[8] A central irony here is that this very same exploitation was one of the reasons for the Cuban Revolution. Initially, the government of Fidel Castro attempted to break centuries of foreign domination without outside assistance or foreign aid.

The results of foreign domination cannot be overemphasized, nor should one fail to draw comparisons between Cuba's present dilemma and its historical efforts to overcome domination. Interesting in this regard is the assessment of historian Geoff Simons regarding Cuba's early and forced inclusion in the world trading system in the fifteenth century. It was the misfortune of the native Taíno inhabitants of Cuba, Simons argues, ". . . to clash with foreign adventurers equipped with a superior military technology, an implacable racist ideology, and a merciless religious absolutism." [9] The reference, of course, is to the arrival of Christopher Columbus in 1492 and the development of the Spanish empire. The very first result of the Spanish conquest of Cuba was the enslavement and subsequent virtual extinction of Cuba's native population. By the mid-sixteenth century, more than 100,000 Taínos were reduced to fewer than 3,000, an enormous carnage caused by disease and Spanish brutality.[10]

What followed in the island's history was no less brutal a regime based on the production of sugar. For the next 406 years, Cuba endured Spanish rule characterized by the monopoly of the sugar industry and the attendant slave system. Over this period, the Cuban economy gradually emerged as a one-crop-dependent economy at the mercy of a single market, Spain. For example, although the island was a net exporter of jerked beef in 1761, fewer than 30 years later it had to satisfy its requirements for this product through imports. The reverse statistic could be observed in the case of sugar, which before the end of the eighteenth century had become almost the only export item in the island's economy worth mentioning.[11]

Part of the increase in Cuban sugar exports was due to the independence of the United States from Great Britain. That event had other consequences as well. Increasingly, the United States assumed the role of Cuba's main trading partner, as the island's commercial relationship with Spain declined. This, in turn, resulted in a dramatic increase in Cuba's population because more slaves had to be imported from Africa to work on the sugar plantations. In addition, and more important, U.S. influence created an increasing divide between the interests of the commercial and administrative elites, composed for the most part of *peninsulares* (people born in Spain) and the interests of *criollo* (island-born) planters, who wanted freer trade. The latter were joined by other classes of Cubans, consumers all, whose interests focused on obtaining goods at the lowest possible price.

This rift increased in the nineteenth century and was exacerbated by another sociopolitical problem. Between the numerous slave revolts that continued into the nineteenth century and the 1807 British ban on the African slave trade, it was becoming apparent that slavery itself was doomed. For that reason, among other factors, many Cuban slave owners agitated during the first part of the nineteenth century for annexation by the United States. With the U.S. Civil War and the abolition of slavery, however, that possibility became nonexistent. Nevertheless, the outcome of the Civil War significantly affected colonial Cuba.

Bereft of the preferred option of joining the United States, some Cuban planters allied with their more nationalistic colleagues to plan an eventual uprising against Spanish rule. The *casus belli* was the imposition on February 12, 1867, of a new 6 to 12 percent increase in income tax to sustain the colonial government.[12] General *criollo* dissatisfaction finally led to the Ten Years' War for independence, with the issue of slavery at the forefront. However, the Spanish army and the prospect of total emancipation were enough to keep Cubans divided on the issue of independence. As a result, the Pact of Zanjón, initiating an uneasy peace, was signed in February 1878.

The years between the Zanjón peace treaty and the outbreak of the second war for independence saw U.S. interest in the island increase. Railways were built, and U.S. capital was invested in the island, mainly in the sugar industry. At this time, Cuba was drawn fully into the orbit of the expanding U.S. commercial empire, to the extent that it came to depend almost entirely on the United States for investment and a market for sugar. The United States had effectively replaced Spain in that domain, although not officially. This commercial nexus, a product of the years after the U.S. Civil War, actually had many proponents on the political side many years before that event.

Throughout the nineteenth century, various voices in the United States clamored for the annexation or control of Cuba, many from a frankly racist perspective.[13] A few Cubans also ardently wished for such an outcome With the outbreak of Cuba's second independence war in 1895, the United States was able to convert that wish into action: What began as a war for Cuban independence soon was converted by the United States into a pretext for invasion. After three years of bitter warfare, all signs pointed to the inevitable triumph of Cuban arms. In other words, the Cubans had fought Spain to a standstill. Little was left for Cubans to oust the Spaniards completely, throw off the colonial yoke, and organize their own destiny. After almost three years of fighting, the Cuban revolutionaries controlled most of the countryside. Yet, the final victory would not be theirs because the independence they had fought so hard for was taken from them by the United States.

On February 15, 1898, the U.S. battleship *Maine* sank in Havana harbor after an explosion. The cause of the sinking has never been ascertained. However, it was the pretext the United States sought, and war was declared on Spain as a result of the incident. Overnight, what had been the Cuban Independence War was transformed into the Spanish-American War. The United States began a military occupation that later gave way to civilian government but always under U.S. tutelage. One has to employ the term "tutelage" because, in fact, with the imposed Platt Amendment[14] as part of the Cuban Constitution, the United States was allowed to intervene *ad arbitrium* in Cuban affairs.

Most Cubans resented the United States' cheating them of their victory over Spain and declaring them unfit to govern themselves.[15] Between 1898 and 1959, Cuba found itself in a dependent relationship with a second foreign power after having fought a war to free itself from Spanish rule. In the events that prefigured the Cuban Revolution's victory of January 1, 1959, over the forces of dictator and President Fulgencio Batista y Zaldívar, anti-U.S. feeling came strongly to the fore among part of Cuba's population. With the triumph of Castro's rebel army on January 1, Cuban nationalism was able to assert itself and be officially recognized for the first time in its history. However, there was more to that revolutionary struggle than mere recognition. True independence was still some decades away, as Cuba chose to seek a developmental path intertwined with the Soviet Bloc's economic system, known as the Council for Mutual Economic Aid (COMECON). Thus, another dependent relationship was formed, as the Cuban economy came to be dominated by its adherence to the dictates of the Soviet empire. The only difference was that this third dependence was voluntary, although forced, one might say, by circumstances.

To summarize, until 1898, the island had been a colony of Spain for almost four centuries. Thereafter, until 1959, it was under the tutelage, if not outright control, of the United States. This political and economic domination was exchanged in 1961 for an economic dependency upon and political connection with the Soviet Union. Although Cuba was free to develop its economic conceptions to a certain extent, it was a member of the Council for Mutual Economic Assistance (CMEA) and fully integrated into the trading world of the Soviet Union and its satellites. However, this dependency was entirely in Cuba's favor, as it received the equivalent of US$6 billion in annual subsidies from the Soviet Union.[16] By 1989, the Caribbean island's exports had grown to US$5.4 billion. Consequently, when the Soviet trading bloc disintegrated and the aid was discontinued in 1991, the Cuban economy collapsed. By 1992, its exports had fallen to just over half of what it usually exported to the Soviet Bloc; three years later, exports reached the pathetically low level of US$1.6 billion.[17]

The indelible fact of Cuban history is, therefore, that except for the brief period of 1959-1961, Cuba's leadership never had to, nor was allowed to, think for itself in economic, if not political and social terms. The key word here is *allowed*, because very important exceptions were the Ten Years' War against Spain, 1868-1878, and the War of Independence, 1895-1898, which was co-opted by the United States and turned into an occupation of Cuba from 1899 to 1902.[18] So there never was a fully independent Cuba, left entirely to its own devices, by imperial powers or by others, until the collapse of the Soviet Union in 1991. With the collapse of that trading bloc and the termination of important subsidies and trade agreements that kept the island nation afloat economically, Cuba was literally on its own in every sense of the word. Worse yet, with the passage of the Torricelli Act of 1992 and the Helms-Burton Act (officially, the Cuban Liberty and Democratic Solidarity (LIBERTAD) Act of 1996), the U.S. economic blockade of Cuba, first implemented during the Eisenhower administration (1953-1961), became a virtually complete blockade of the island.

THE HISTORICAL DIVIDE

After the collapse of the Soviet empire, Cuba was faced with no other possibility than to begin to think independently in a global context. In 1991, the world presented Cuba no other models of an alternative economic and social vision, following the demise of the Soviet experiment, seeming only to fulfill Fukuyama's assumptions about the supposed triumph of liberalism, in which the only feasible economic polity is that nations earn hard cash by whatever means possible in a global, pro-capitalist, and competitive market.[19]

The problem facing Cuba, therefore, was how to accommodate this reality and at the same time maintain the social revolution. How would Cuba adjust to the demands of the market-driven world economy and also maintain social equality in the areas of health, education, and employment? Added to this sudden "emancipation" into harsh reality was the other dilemma of being cut off from a natural and historical market, the United States. Many thought that Cuba would have no other choice than to ask the United States for a bailout; the U.S. Central Intelligence Agency (CIA) certainly thought so in 1993.[20]

Even though it was estimated that the island's economy shrank by more than 50 percent after the collapse of the Soviet empire, Cuba did not succumb to easy temptations.[21] In 1994, at the nadir of its fortunes, when riots broke out in Havana and 30,000 Cubans boarded flimsy rafts in an attempt to flee the economic disaster and reach better climes, mainly in the United States, the government held fast.[22] Castro and a majority of Cubans persevered, and a nation that appeared beaten soon proved itself determined. It is well-known that other Cubans who openly disagreed with Castro's policies and philosophy were subjected to harsh repression in the form of imprisonment or torture.[23] And many Cubans who fled the Castro regime did so not for economic reasons but in search of freedom.

THE SOLUTIONS

A significant and daunting problem had to be overcome by the Cubans in 1994. After 450 years of colonial and imperialist domination, Cuba was in the same position as most of its Caribbean neighbors: It had basically a one-crop economy and some of the world's most pristine and unexploited beaches. How could Cuba overcome its problems? Common speculation was that Castro and the system under which Cubans had lived for 40 years were about to disappear.[24] Why not, since the Soviet Union, a much larger nation and better endowed with economic resources, had been unable to chart significant growth under a similar command economy? What were Cuba's options? The realities of the collapse of the Soviet Union and the end of Soviet aid forced Castro and Cuba to contemplate some far-reaching changes. What this meant for Cuba was an adjustment as profound as the one that took place after 1961, when Castro chose a Marxist-Leninist economic and political model. Sugar was not going to be the answer to development growth and rescue from the economic slump. After 1990, sugar production went into a tailspin. The 1993 crop brought in 4.2 million tons; the 1994 crop, only 3.6 million. This was due to the curtailment of oil shipments from the Soviet Union, cut to about one-quarter of normal deliveries.[25] Without oil, the sugar factories had no fuel for their boilers, which had much less sugar to process because the entire mechanized harvesting process literally ran out of gasoline. Suddenly, hauling of cane had to be improvised by harnessing bullocks to wains in the traditional way, but even this was easier said than done because some of the subsidies from the former Soviet Union had been used to buy animal fodder. Cuba literally had to begin organizing its economy from scratch.

To overcome the immediate transportation shortage, bicycles were substituted for buses. All over Havana today, one can still see numerous bicycle parking lots set up in the patios of ground-floor apartments. Then, the *camellos* were constructed: bus bodies were welded together with a tractor in front that could haul up to three times as many people as a regular bus. Rickshaws propelled by entrepreneurial young Cubans also appeared; this new development was allowed by the Cuban government, which had decided to relax some prohibitions on private business in order to kick-start the economy. In fact, the Cuban government was admitting that it lacked the resources to sustain the population in the expected way and now would have to allow Cubans to fend for themselves. The irony was inescapable: Cuba now was practicing, in its own manner, the capitalist system.

This new government policy was called the Special Period. One of the first internal measures adopted to stimulate the economy was the creation of government-sponsored farmers' markets in October 1994. Under this measure, farmers were allowed to sell their surplus crops on the market at a profit. The result was "an 11 percent increase in food production" with a resultant halving of food prices.[26] A further liberalization of the economy also took place. The currency was made convertible; indeed, Cubans were allowed to hold and use U.S. dollars. They also were allowed to set up small private business ventures: from running bars, restaurants, and cafes, to driving taxis and renting out bed-and-breakfast rooms to foreigners. It is now quite common to see signs in the formerly affluent neighborhood of Vedado advertising rooms for tourists. The owners have to pay a hefty license fee to the government for the privilege (regardless of how often they rent the rooms), but they do not seem to mind.[27]

In addition, Cuba announced that it was open for business and foreign investment. Agreements were signed almost from the moment Cuba was cut free from the Soviet economic network. One of the first entrepreneurs to take advantage of the new policy was Canada's Ian Delaney of Calgary, the first of a number of Canadian businesspeople to pioneer the Cuban business connection. In 1991, searching for nickel to feed his refinery at Fort Saskatchewan, Alberta, Delaney made a deal with Cuba that not only rescued his company and initiated a spate of lucrative joint industrial ventures for the Cuban government, but also earned him a place on the U.S. Treasury Department's blacklist, resulting in his being "barred from entering the [United States] under the Helms-Burton Act."[28] Delaney's Sherritt International Inc. is the largest investor in Cuba today, having obtained permission to deal in Cuban real estate, communications, transportation, finance, and sugar.[29] Since Delaney's success, many more Canadian firms have signed joint deals with the Cuban government.

Lest anyone should think that Canada has merely been quick to cash in on the U.S. blockade, taking advantage of its neighbor's adamant foreign policy, Delaney's success actually represents the historic culmination of decades of Canadian support for Castro and the Cuban Revolution. Canada never broke off diplomatic relations with Cuba, and in 1976 Prime Minister Pierre Elliot Trudeau (1968-1979, 1980-1984) "was the first NATO leader to visit the island."[30] In 1994, Nova Scotian Premier John Savage took a number of businesspeople to Cuba, which resulted in increased bilateral trade. The province of Saskatchewan has invested capital in one of its companies, York Medical, which enjoys a private contract to commercialize Cuban pharmaceuticals.[31]

In addition to Sheritt International and York Medical, other Canadian firms have been busy positioning themselves to take advantage of the positive business climate. Another big player, Wilton Properties Ltd, owned by Vancouver business-man Wally Berukoff, invested some $400 million dollars in a joint Canada-Cuban venture to build 11 new hotels and other facilities. Berukoff's Miramar Mining Corp. has also been exploring a copper-gold project on the mainland and another gold lode on the Isle of Youth.[32]

However, most telling has been the rise in the number of Canadian visitors to Cuba annually, Canada being, in fact, one of the island's largest providers of tourists. In fact, Cuba has become the preeminent destination for Canadian tourists, so much so that the Pizza Nova chain as well as Labatt Breweries have increased their investments to service this home market. Total Canadian investments in Cuba rose above $600 million in 1996, and Canada has become one of Cuba's largest trading partners.[33]

This *apertura* or opening of the economy to foreign investors seems to have become more than the whimsical stopgap measure it was when Castro first confronted economic collapse in 1991. The reason is that solid gains have been achieved since the nadir of the Cuban economy in 1994. After one year, the economy was sputtering along with a 2.5-percent growth rate that was slated to increase after 1995. Oil production, for example, historically the bane of the Cuban economy because the energy-deficient island depended upon the Soviet Bloc for oil, received a much needed boost with the signing of joint ventures between Cuba and foreign investors. As a result, capital as well as spare parts and modern deep-sea drilling and refining methods have bolstered this sector. Moreover, local oil production currently meets about one-quarter of Cuban needs and is expected to increase to one-half by the year 2004.[34]

During my visits to Cuba in the spring and summer of 1999, practically every day brought some report or evidence of new foreign investments and joint ventures with various countries. Walking just outside downtown Havana, I came across a small building where some special equipment was being installed. Upon inquiry, I was told that it was a new sausage factory being built by a German firm. Indeed, the Germans, though slow to get off the mark, sent a high-level delegation led by Hans Olaf Henkel, president of the Federation of German Industries, to confer with the Cuban government on the possibility of increased cooperation and trade between the two countries. DaimlerChrysler, which already supplies agricultural machinery to Cuba, is building a bus assembly plant for the very needy Cuban transportation network.[35] One could add to these examples *ad infinitum*; they are cited to show that the Cuban government has enacted what appear to be fundamental economic policy changes since the end of its economic dependency on the Soviet Bloc.

Industrial production is not the only resource Cubans intend to explore. Another part of the reason for the turnaround was the Cuban government's decision to develop, at last, the one unexploited resource it has in abundance: its beautiful beaches, that is, the tourism sector. Understandably, this sector has grown the fastest, while creating conditions that have given rise to the social problems associated with this industry. In 1995, the tourist industry brought Cuba US$1.4 billion, an increase of one-third over the previous two years.[36] The trend continues. In 1990, some 320,000 tourists visited Cuba. That number increased to 1.4 million in 1998, and an additional 300,000 came in 1999, representing an annual growth rate of some 20 percent. Canada contributes the highest number of visitors, followed by Germany, but a heavy mix of tourists also come from other Latin American countries. The attractions include not only the pristine beaches but also the nature of the tourist venture. Recognizing that today's tourists are looking for more than simply beaches and sun, Cuba has developed its tourism around themes such as health, beauty, culture, education, and business.[37]

Fundamental changes have occurred in the way the Cuban government imagines the future development of the island. Without a capital base of its own, Cuba has been forced by circumstances to do business with what Castro has called the "filthy and repugnant" capitalist world market.[38] As the government recognizes that for many Cubans, especially younger people, the right to shop is an imperative that it cannot ignore, the Special Period is probably here to stay. Moreover, the government continually searches for ways to satisfy the people's demands without generating the attendant drawbacks that more capitalism has brought and will bring in its train.

THE SPECIAL PERIOD

Government intentions and policies aside, however, what has been the impact of the Special Period on ordinary Cubans? The first issue is how ordinary Cubans negotiate the curious phenomenon of a dual economy. Some Cubans have access to U.S. dollars, while others do not. Tourists can be unaware of this fact because it is possible to spend one's entire holiday in Cuba and never know that two economies actually operate side by side, those of the U.S. dollar and the Cuban peso. Business in Cuba can be conducted either in dollars or in pesos, but access to dollars means having the ability to buy almost anything one wants. New cars, hardware, furniture, and food, including meat, are for sale and affordable if one has access to dollars. Holding U.S. dollars has also been legalized. Some Cubans work very hard indeed to obtain even a few dollars. As a taxi driver explained when I asked how he made ends meet, "When I leave my shift at three in the afternoon, I work freelance as a tile layer for people whose relatives in Miami send them money. I have to make do this way. Since I have no relatives abroad to send me dollars, how can I exist with a family of four on only 140 pesos a month?" One peso is worth about US$0.05 (5 cents). A tourist can buy a bottle of good quality Cuban rum for US$4, the equivalent of 80 pesos, which represents one month's salary for some Cubans. What feelings of deprivation or of being underprivileged might this situation create in the average Cuban's mind? Surprisingly, I could not detect any resentment.

Perhaps this apparent acceptance is due to the high level of education in Cuba. However, there is another factor: The government, despite the difficulty of the Special Period, has not abandoned its revolutionary accomplishments. Time and time again, during my two visits to Cuba in 1999, people spoke to me of their appreciation for Cuba's egalitarian distribution of health, education, and basic services. Yet, could Cuba be witnessing a profound change in mentality, or rather, the resurgence of a way of thinking that had been submerged for some decades? Were Cubans reverting to an older, capitalistic, individualistic mentality while still accepting free government services? And would that type of thinking eventually generate problems for the Cuban government and for those sectors of the population that traditionally are marginalized in capitalist countries? What exactly were the changes attendant on the *apertura*, the introduction of the Special Period?

Visitors to Cuba today, certainly in Havana, might well wonder what Cuba they are visiting — the Cuba of pre-revolutionary days or Castro's Cuba? As an example, prostitution, once the bane of "Yankee Cuba" and mentioned often by Castro during the early years of his regime as a symbol of the exploitation of Cubans by the United States, is flourishing again. Prostitutes can be found on street corners, especially near hotels. Girls who appear to be only 13 or 14 years old brazenly approach any male who looks like a tourist, in search of dollars to buy food (to supplement what is available through the official food rationing book) as well as luxury items for themselves and their families.[39]

This reappearance of prostitution, however, cannot be entirely blamed on the Special Period, just as the return to a capitalist mentality cannot be blamed on tourism and Cuba's new policies. The fact is that some of the policies and phenomena are not new. Faced with a stagnant economy and worker absenteeism, the Cuban government returned to a system of material rewards for workers in 1973, in the form of more luxury items. Not surprisingly, because Cubans had so much cash and so little to spend it on, especially as basic services were free, many people chose not to work at all. In the early 1970s, in an attempt to soak up extra cash, the government opened some high-priced restaurants and provided some luxury goods at high prices. Thus, money became attractive again. In a further attempt to translate this new value into productive work, the government reintroduced material incentives, which resulted in a very significant increase in productivity.[40]

After the collapse of the Soviet Union in 1991, when the Cuban economy nearly came to a standstill, economic life was seriously curtailed. The government found it increasingly difficult to provide the basic services that Cubans had become accustomed to receiving. Food became scarce, and the rationing book could not cover even basic minimum daily requirements.[41] The distribution of health services also suffered, so that it was difficult to find even an aspirin in the government pharmacies. Subsequently, the economy was liberalized, both to tap into Cubans' ingenuity for survival and to allow minimal private enterprise to fill gaps that the command or socialist economy could not sustain. In 1993, for example, self-employment in a number of trades was permitted. In addition, the government legalized the holding of dollars and individual entrepreneurs' sale of agricultural products.[42]

Unfortunately, with the resurgence of Cuba's unique form of "mini-capitalism," called the Special Period, has come a resurgence of racism. This seems odd because of all the sectors of Cuban society, the group that was supposed to have benefited the most from Castro's policies were Cubans of African origin. Anti-black jokes, at a minimum during the first years of the Revolution, have appeared openly once again. During my visits in 1999, I noticed that many young blacks seemed to be hanging around the streets; some were hawking black-market cigars to tourists, and many of the women were prostitutes. The racial tension in Havana manifests itself even to the casual observer. In the administrative levels of the hotel and tourist industry, for example, whites predominate, as they seem to in other emerging sectors of the new economy, such as foreign-run enterprises and national corporations that utilize dollars. Whites also appear to be the majority among university students, at least at the University of Havana. In contrast, blacks tend to be employed in jobs requiring little education, such as those in construction, sugar cane cutting, and the service sector.[43] Why this should still be so, given the revolutionary government's emphasis on egalitarianism, is a mystery. Still, this renewed racism seems to be partially a product of the recent changes in the economic approach of the Cuban government, and it is unlikely to disappear.[44]

POLITICAL INDICATORS FOR THE FUTURE

Given the very short period of time that Cuba's mini-capitalism has been in effect, it is still too early to test its efficacy. Economic decisions taken in the early 1990s have not had sufficient time to produce a visible betterment of the standard of living of the Cuban population. One thing, however, is certain. Without the support of the Soviet Union and cut off from a natural market by the U.S. blockade, Cuba, for the first time in its history, has had to function by and for itself and devise national solutions to its problems. There are no exploiters to blame for Cuba's predicament and no supporters with ready cash and subsidies; there are only the raw worlds of business and the global market. Nevertheless, despite the lack of evidence of any substantial improvement at the individual level, the Cuban economy appears to have grown considerably. Unfortunately, serious social problems such as prostitution and racism have returned, particularly in connection with the tourist industry.

Cuba's economic and social policies will be debated seriously, and a new government will be formed when Castro dies or is no longer able to function as president; however, these policies will be debated by a younger group of politicians who have no memory of the pre-Castro days. No one can predict the future; the only certainty is that a fresh approach to economic and social affairs cannot be too far away.

At the moment, however, that fresh approach is nowhere in sight. The new cadre of leaders who came to the fore in the early 1990s — Roberto Robaina, Carlos Aldana, and Ricardo Alarcón — were not given any real power.[45] Although former Foreign Minister Robaina once was touted as a possible replacement for Castro and supposedly was so close to Fidel that the president referred to him affectionately as Robertico,[46] in barely two years he was relieved of his position and shunted to the background. Reportedly, his dismissal from the position as chancellor (foreign minister) was due to his wife's employment by one of the tourist agencies that promoted the tourist sex trade.[47] Although there may be some truth to this, a more compelling reason has been advanced: Robaina represented the soft touch; he was the *aperturista* (the opener) instead of the hard-liner — and it was and is the hard line that Castro expects to be applied to Cuba's mounting social problems.[48]

In 1999, Robaina was replaced by Felipe Pérez Roque, a 34-year-old engineer with relatively little experience in either politics or international relations. Pérez Roque was director of the Federation of University Students in the 1980s. He then joined the president's Group of Coordinators and Assistance (Grupo de Coordinación y Apoyo), a group of some 20 individuals whose job was to supply President Castro with information on various important topics. In 1993, Pérez Roque was designated as Castro's private secretary; subsequently, he was always seen at Castro's side, taking notes and consulting frequently with him. Because of his closeness to the president, he has become, as noted by the official newspaper *Granma*, one of the few people familiar with Castro's "ideas and thoughts."[49] The fact is that Castro still is very much in control and very concerned about the problems his Special Period has seemingly generated. The "major crisis" touted by the CIA in 1993, which supposedly was going to overwhelm Cuba, not only has not taken place, but seems not even to be in the offing. Castro remains firmly in control, and, contrary to some reports, seems quite healthy.[50]

Still, the problems besetting Cuba raise questions about the future. What is Cuba's solution to its current economic problems likely to be? What are the policy options facing countries such as Canada, which have continued relations with Cuba and whose citizens and enterprises have taken advantage of the U.S. blockade to deepen their relations and their investment positions in Cuba?

No one can second-guess future decisions of Cuba's resilient and powerful president, and yet some indications can be noted. The first is that Castro does not appear to intend to give an inch in Cuba's relations with other countries. This essentially is the meaning of Pérez Roque's replacement of Robaina. Internally, Cuba probably will not introduce any "reforms" on the western model; that is, no change will occur in the internal governing system under which the island has lived for the past few decades.

Nevertheless, Castro has tried to conduct a certain kind of rapprochement, both with the rest of the world and internally. This has taken the form of inviting Western leaders to visit Cuba The first such leader was Pope John Paul II, who visited Cuba for five days in January 1998. The second was Canada's Prime Minister Jean Chrétien in April 1998. Both visits had their successes and failures. Certainly, as has been reported elsewhere, Canada-Cuba relations suffered a setback because Prime Minister Chrétien apparently was too quick to make demands without carefully thinking through the logic of his position. Mr. Chrétien accosted President Castro regarding Cuba's dismal human rights record and the detention without trial of certain Cuban opposition leaders. Chrétien's position earned, and still earns, substantial criticism in the Canadian press, where he has been accused of considerable dilettantism.[51]The point here, though, is whether these visits had any effect in regard to changing Cuba's positions — and I would say that they did not. It is true that some sectors of Cuban society that were largely marginalized or driven underground in the past are now officially sanctioned, but that is because Castro's politics and policies have changed and softened over the years. For example, Roman Catholic churches and those of other denominations are filled again on Sundays.[52] In June 1999, a mass rally of Cuban Protestants was held in the Plaza de la Revolución in Havana. Castro himself attended, as did other members of the National Assembly of People's Power (Asemblea Nacional del Poder Popular). Also present were representatives from the National Council of Churches, Pastors for Peace, and many Latin American countries. As many people, if not more, were present in the plaza on June 20, 1999, as had attended the May Day parade one month earlier. It is clear from the mass rally of Cuban Protestants that the once-vilified churches are no longer seen as enemies and that religious freedom is acceptable, although without any firm legislative basis, in the Cuban system.[53]

Cuba's external policy also reflects change, as relations with the rest of the world and particularly with the other nations of the Americas have expanded. The year 1999 was a time for deepening relations with neighboring countries, with visits in June by the Barbadian prime minister and the Haitian president. Both of those Caribbean leaders signed important bilateral agreements that are indicative of Cuba's continuing intention to resume and extend economic and other sorts of relations with its Caribbean neighbors.[54]

SOCIALISM WITH TOURIST DOLLARS

Given the Cubans' evident taste for consumerism and the resistance or indifference to socialism of many young people, is it possible to continue reforms without changing the basic system of government? Or, as I recall a conference participant asking at the 1999 III Taller Científico, Primero de Mayo, "How does one construct socialism with tourist dollars?"[55] The Cuban government has been unable to address this difficult question, which appears to defy solution. While tourists enjoy both the means and the right to travel, Cuban citizens surely must ask themselves the obvious question: "Why not us?"

Arguably, therefore, the Cuban government will be unable to retreat from the reforms that have been put in place. Rather, Cuba will have to continue restructuring its economy in an ingenious way so as to maintain growth without discarding its social programs.[56] The *apertura* likely will continue for some time. One could argue that the doctrinaire socialism of the past, with its ban on religious services and festivities and its requirement of conformity to atheism in order to get into a university or obtain a good job, might possibly be reinstated at some point, though this is unlikely. However, the citizens' desire for consumer goods and for more freedom to buy, travel, and read probably would not disappear even if the government were to attempt to reimpose restrictions. Thus, the economic policies of the last decade and Cuba's agreements with individual foreign companies, which bring needed capital for the expansion of the economy, will likely continue in their present forms. Capitalist investors such as Delaney will continue to come to Cuba, as will corporate giants such as DaimlerChrysler, because there is money to be made from such ventures. Some analysts even think it probable that the U.S. embargo may be lifted in the not too distant future.

One thing seems obvious: As long as Castro is alive and at the helm, no substantive changes will occur in the internal affairs of Cuba. And whether Canada's Chrétien likes it or not, Cuban dissidents will be treated no differently, nor will most Cubans demand it. Thus far, Cuba's system of government has proved itself able to withstand the kinds of shocks that brought down the larger, more prosperous former Soviet Union. Now that the island's economy is growing again, Cuba is not likely to change. Business will continue as usual.

One major roadblock looms, however. Despite the *apertura* and the relatively high awareness of the populace regarding world affairs, no freedom of speech, as we understand it, exists in Cuba.[57] Without this freedom, any major restructuring of the Cuban economy will be only in the nature of government-sponsored foreign investment. Without free speech, no revival can take place in Cuba's internal economy, the driving force that could produce sufficient improvement in the nation's standard of living. In the long run, I believe, Cuba will come to realize that efforts to restrict information and control dissent are counterproductive. Although I may be wrong, I am convinced that free enterprise necessitates a climate of free expression and criticism.

Even so, some signs point to changes that may come. Dissent of any official kind certainly has been treated harshly, as with the 1997 arrest of Cuba's four most famous dissidents. Three of the four were released in May 2000. A few weeks before this volume was to go to press, on May 5, 2002, Vladimiro Roca Antúnez was released from prison. In an article in *The Miami Herald* by Nancy San Martin, Roca is quoted, via a telephone interview, as follows: "Dialogue and reconciliation without exclusion — that has always been and will continue to be my mantra. . . . The things that are good about this country, such as health and education, should not be touched. But the things that are bad, like the economy and lack of freedom, that must change." The article continues with this observation: "Roca's release came a week ahead of a scheduled visit to Cuba by former President Jimmy Carter, raising speculation that freeing Roca was a goodwill gesture on the part of the Havana government."[58]

During one of my visits to Cuba in 1999, a taxi driver told me, "One has to be careful with criticism. The police and army are everywhere." In stark contrast with this citizen's caution, I witnessed a remarkable example of opposition that same year. While I was visiting the home of a friend in Havana, someone criticized the government and Castro relentlessly and gave reasons for refusing to attend the upcoming May First parade, which is obligatory for many workers. This person's fervent and prolonged tirade could be heard throughout the small apartment building. When asked about fears of being overheard by a member of the local Committees for the Defense of the Revolution (Comités de Defensa de la Revolución — CDR), the dissenter said the CDR already knew about the views being expressed. At the time, no one offered an explanation for this individual's behavior.[59]

How long will Castro's government be able to cope with the massive influx of tourists who bring with them democratic attitudes about freedom of speech? How long can the island's strict socialist tenets overpower the temptations that consumerism holds out to the Cuban people? Regarding demands for change by the Cuban people, I believe the present government has secured a grace period through its Special Period measures. Cubans want more consumer goods and a higher standard of living, and the government is aware of this. On the other hand, Cubans feel entitled to the social services that are part of everyday life in Cuba. Can the consumer market be developed further for Cubans without sacrificing their hard-won social achievements? The possibility exists, I believe, if the government is willing to codify some recent measures and permit more personal freedom. The end result could well be a system that is partly socialist and partly capitalist, but certainly more humane and responsive to the needs of the broad mass of citizens than obtains even in the United States. I do not believe that Cubans are willing to trade their quality of life for the uncertainties of uncontrolled capitalism. Now and in the future, any government that attempts to undo the Cuban labor movement, the equality won by blacks, and the awareness created by feminism will be ushered unceremoniously out the door. Even though blacks apparently have been subjected to some forms of prejudice through recent changes in Cuba, it is unlikely that they will be accepting of more serious forms of racism if and when there is a change to a more liberal economic and social system. Nor should it be expected that Cuban women, emancipated at least in the ideological sense, will accept a return to pre-Revolutionary forms of sexual politics. In other words, the social gains and awareness won by the Cuban Revolution will remain in place, even though the means of sustaining them may be subject to revision and experiment.

Cuba's new experience of careful excursion into capitalism may be less nuanced than the experiments of some other socialist countries charting the transition, but members of today's younger generation, who were not present at the beginning of the Revolution, definitely want change and access to greater material prosperity.

Is there any message for Canada in this picture of contemporary Cuban society, especially regarding Canada-Cuba relations? In my opinion, no changes that Cuba might undergo would have serious adverse effects on relations between the two nations. Canadian business leaders have been able to work with Castro, and they also will be able to work with his successors, socialist or not. Given Canada's historic and intensive commitment to social programs and to a social safety net, the two countries may very well have a basis for a mutually beneficial extended dialogue in the near future.

Notes

1. These words were taken from a statement by Jesús Díaz, a Cuban writer living in Berlin. He was referring to the manner in which Cubans are expressing a call for change. The statement was written in 1994. See Marco Meier, 1998, *René Burri: Cuba y Cuba* (Washington, D.C.: Smithsonian Institution Press), 22.

2. Francis Fukuyama, 1992, *The End of History and the Last Man* (New York: Free Press).

3. Jaime Avilés, 1999, "Chiapas: los mecánicos del general Uribe," *La Jornada*, December 11, 4.

4. Gerardo Fujii, 1999, "La batalla de Seattle," *La Jornada*, December 11, 24. This fiasco coincided with the convening in Belem, Brazil, on December 10, of the Second Meeting against Neoliberalism. See Fujii 1999, 66.

5. Cuba is the largest and one of the best-educated nations in the Caribbean, according to the United Nations Development Programme's "Human Development Report 2001: Addendum, Human Development Index for 12 Countries Not Included in the Main Indicator Tables." Cuba also has an outstanding record in health care, with life expectancy at 75.9 years. See <http://www.undp.org/hdr2001/Addendum4.pdf>. In addition, it may well be that Cuba will emerge to play a leadership role in the area, uniting a region that has common historical and cultural ties.

6. See Peter Schwab, 1999, *Cuba: Confronting the U.S. Embargo* (New York: St. Martin's Press), 116. This author calculates Cuba's loss of trade at 93 percent. The island's economic problems began in 1991 with the collapse of the Soviet Union, and by 1994, Cuba's situation had reached a nadir.

7. Although Cuba mainly relied on sugar in the past, it should not be expected to remain strictly in the typical Caribbean sugar-and-banana syndrome. The island's other commodity exports include nickel and cobalt, other agricultural products, and biotechnology manufacturing. Its potential to become a broad-based economy is quite high.

8. Schwab 1999, 36-37.

9. Geoff Simons, 1996, *Cuba: From Conquistador to Castro* (New York: St. Martin's Press), 65.

10. The tragic decimation of the Taíno was replicated all across Spanish America. There was even a scheme to cure this dearth of labor in Cuba with people exported from the Mexican Huasteca. See Michael T. Ducey, 2001, "Indian Communities and Ayuntamientos in the Mexican Huasteca: Sujeto Revolts, Pronunciamientos and Caste War," *The Americas* 57 (4): 525-550.

11. Louis A. Pérez, Jr., 1988, *Cuba: Between Reform and Revolution* (New York: Oxford University Press), 82.

12. Simons 1996, 139.

13. See statements by J.C. Breckenridge and José Martí's fears in Simons 1996, 184-185.

14. Designed by U.S. Secretary of War Elihu Root and presented before the Senate by Senator Orville H. Platt, the amendment was entered into the U.S. Army Appropriations Bill of March 1901, defining, among other things, Cuba's own rights to negotiate treaties with other countries and henceforth granting the United States permission to intervene in Cuban political affairs, purportedly to preserve Cuban independence. In 1934, as part of his Good Neighbor Policy, U.S. President Franklin D. Roosevelt supported the termination of all of the Platt Amendment's provisions, except for the U.S. "right" to keep a naval base in Guantánamo Bay, Cuba.

15. Hugh Thomas, 1971, *The Pursuit of Freedom* (New York: Harper & Row), 404, 410, 437, 453-54; Louis Pérez, Jr., 1988, 179-183.

16. By the mid-1980s, Cuban exports to and imports from the Soviet Union were 64 percent and 62 percent, respectively, of the total. See Pérez 1988, 355.

17. Juan M. del Águila, 1996, "Cuba Adapts to a Brave New World," in *Latin American Nations in World Politics*, eds. Heraldo Muñoz and Joseph S. Tulchin (Boulder, Colo.: Westview Press), 89.

18. In this regard, it is instructive that the 1991 Party Congress met on the one hundred twenty-third anniversary of the start of the Ten Years' War. The main argument here is that Cuba is attempting to invoke its national history as its source of "ideological legitimization." See Marifeli Pérez-Stable, 1997, "The Invisible Crisis: The Exhaustion of Politics in 1990s Cuba," in *Toward a New Cuba? Legacies of A Revolution,* eds. Miguel Ángel Centeno and Mauricio Font (Boulder, Colo.: Lynne Rienner Publishers), 27.

19. The extent of the harshness and brutality of this "liberalism" and the suffering it has caused for the poorer people of the world never have been fully documented. See David Jones, 1994, "The Trade in Flesh: Gruesome Face of the New World Market," *Latin American Connections*, January-February: 7.

20. Carla Anne Robbins, 1993, "Major Crisis in Cuba Possible 'at Any Time,' CIA Warns," *Globe and Mail*, November 23.

21. Patrick Symmes, 1996, "Taking the Measure of Castro, Ounce by Ounce," *Harper's Magazine,* January, 58.

22. Peter C. Newman, 1995, "Going Capitalist on the Canbuck," *Maclean's*, February 13: 45.

23. It seems to be standard practice to accuse Cuba generally of an abominable record in human rights, without making the distinction among a number of these rights. In that sense, the UN High Commissioner for Human Rights' Commission on Human Rights Resolution 2002/18 (April 19, 2002), "Situation of Human Rights in Cuba," does congratulate Cuba on ". . . efforts to give effect to the social rights of the population despite an adverse international environment . . .," while inviting it "to make efforts to achieve similar progress in respect of human, civil and political rights, in accordance with the provisions of the Universal Declaration of Human Rights and the principles and standards of the rule of law; . . ." This resolution was adopted on April 19, 2002, by a recorded vote of 23 to 21, with 9 abstentions. For the document, see <http://www.unhchr.ch/huridocda/huridoca.nsf/(Symbol)/ E.CN.4.RES.2002.18.En?Opendocument>. See also, "Acusa Cuba a América Latina de ser 'judas,'" *La Prensa* (Mexico City), April 19, 2002, 3. For a strident criticism of Cuba's record, see Thomas A. Leonard, 1999, *Castro and the Cuban Revolution* (Westport, Conn.:

Greenwood Press), 85, who remarks, "According to Amnesty International, The U.N. Human Rights Commission, and the U.S. Congress, Cuba's human rights' record remains among the most horrific in the world." See also, Peter Morici, 1997, "The United States, World Trade, and The Helms-Burton Act," *Current History* (February): 87-88.

24. Leonard 1999, 86.

25. del Águila 1996, 89.

26. Symmes 1996, 59.

27. Jonathan Steele, 1997, "Havana Good Time," *Guardian Weekly*, October 26: 30.

28. Nomi Morris, 1996, "Can Cuba Change?" *Maclean's*, January 15: 22-23.

29. Morris, 1996, 22-23. According to William C. Symonds, "Delaney was among the first to be barred from entering the U.S. under the Helms-Burton Act." See William C. Symonds, 1997, "Castro's Capitalist: Canada's Sheritt Cleans Up in Cuba," *Business Week*, March 17: 48.

30. Newman 1995, 45.

31. Morris 1996, 23; Liliam Riera, 1999, "Helms-Burton Act Loses Credibility with Canadian Business," *Granma International*, May 23: 3.

32. *Financial Post Daily*, July 3, 1996. Cited in Sahadeo Basdeo, 1999, "Helms Burton Controversy: An Issue in Canada-US Foreign Relations," in *Canada, the US and Cuba: Helms-Burton and Its Aftermath*, ed. Heather N. Nicol (Kingston, Ontario: Centre for International Relations, Queen's University), 15-16.

33. According to Marc Frank, 2002, "U.S. Agents to Sell Cuban Resorts," *Maclean's* (Internet), April 13: "The Cuban Tourism Ministry reported about 1.8 million visitors in 2001, mostly from Europe and Canada."

34. Joaquín Oramas, 1999, "Petroleum: Utopias and Realities," *Granma International*, May 23:5.

35. Hans-Werner Richert, 1999, "German Industry Wants to Be Number One in Cuba," *Granma International*, May 23:5.

36. Morris 1996, 17.

37. Ma Eugenia Monroy, 1999, "Difunden atractivos de la isla," *Reforma*, November 21, 301. For example, a high-quality health center is under construction in Villa Clara province. It will have a capacity of 400 tourist-days per year and is expected to open in 2001. See *Granma International*, 1993, "Health and Beauty Center," May 23: 3.

38. Fidel Castro, quoted in Newman 1995, 45.

39. The reappearance of prostitution is not recent. It does date back, however, to the increase in foreign tourism from the mid-1970s. See *Washington Post*, 1977, "Young Prostitutes Back in Havana," December 13.

40. *Toronto Star*, 1976, "Money's Back in Style," May 25.

41. Symmes 1996, 59.

42. *Latin American Weekly Report*, 1993, "After Dollarisation, Self-employment," September 23: 441.

43. Homero Campa, 1999c, "En la crisis, resabios históricos y socioculturales," *Proceso* (June 6): 44.

44. One author attributes Cuba's increasing racism to "dollar apartheid." See Centeno, 1997, "Cuba's Search for Alternatives," 12, in Miguel Ángel Centeno and Mauricio Font, eds., 1997, *Toward a New Cuba? Legacies of a Revolution* (Boulder, Colo.: Lynne Rienner Publishers). Other authors attribute the racial climate to a preference for whites in the tourist industry as well as a preference for foreign managers in joint ventures. See Alejandro de la Fuente and Laurence Celasco, 1997, "Are Blacks 'Getting Out of Control'? Racial Attitudes, Revolution, and Political Transition in Cuba," 30, in Centeno and Font, 1997.

45. John M. Kirk, 1990, "Cuba at the Crossroads," *International Perspectives* 19 (8): 91.

46. *Maclean's*, 1996, "A Hard Act to Follow," January 15: 19.

47. Homero Campa, 1999b, "El gobierno canceló las oficinas de la empresa mexicana Cubamor, acusada de promover el turismo sexual de la isla," *Proceso* (June 13): 47.

48. Homero Campa, 1999a, "'De línea dura,' el nuevo canciller cubano está muy 'familiarizado con el pensamiento de Fidel,'" *Proceso* (June 6): 46.

49. Quoted in Campa, 1999a, 47.

50. Cuba watchers and travelers seem to be in agreement about the tenacity of the regime. See Gillian Gunn Clissold, 1997, "Cuban-U.S. Relations and the Process of Transition: Possible Consequences of Covert Agendas," in *Toward a New Cuba? Legacies of a Revolution*, eds. Miguel Ángel Centeno and Mauricio Font (Boulder, Colo.: Lynne Rienner Publishers), 84.

51. See Bruce Wallace, 1999, "Canada's Accidental Tourist,"*Maclean's* 113: 17 (April 24), 29. See also Allan Fotheringham, 1998, "Chrétien a Hostage to Castro's Outrageous Exaggeration," *Financial Post* 91: 18 (May 2), 27; and Bruce Wallace, 1998, "Connecting with Castro," *Maclean's* 111: 19 (May 11), 5.

52. Schwab 1999, 118.

53. *Trabajadores*, 1999, "Exitosa culminación de la celebración evangélica cubana," June 21:1.

54. Orlando Oramas León, 1999, "Barbados y Cuba" and "Llega hoy el presidente haitiano René Preval," *Granma*, June 18:1. Fidel Castro led a high-level delegation to the Association of Caribbean States' 1995 Summit in Port-of-Spain. Andrés Serbin argues that with the withdrawal of U.S. interest from the Caribbean, the way is open for Cuba to head a process of regional consolidation. See Andrés Serbin, 1997, "The Geopolitical Context of the Caribbean Basin in the 1990s: Geoeconomic Reconfigurations and Political Transitions," in *Cuba and the Caribbean: Regional Issues and Trends in the Post-Cold War Era*, eds. Joseph S. Tulchin, Andrés Serbin, and Rafael Hernández, (Wilmington, Del.: Scholarly Resources, Inc.), 30-31.

55. I was asked to present an historical paper at the Third "First of May" Scientific Workshop (III Taller Científico, Primero de Mayo), held in Havana in the spring of 1999. One of the conference participants asked this question, to which no one offered an answer.

56. Julio Carranza Valdés, "Economic Changes in Cuba: Problems and Challenges," in *Cuba and the Caribbean: Regional Issues and Trends in the Post-Cold War Era*, eds. Joseph S. Tulchin, Andrés Serbin, and Rafael Hernández, (Wilmington, Del.: Scholarly Resources, Inc.), 206.

57. One has to strive to be objective in this regard. Certainly, no newspapers are offering critical views of the government or Cuban politics. However, what does one make of the films by the late Tomás Alea, for example? Alea's "Strawberry and Chocolate" contained very explicit condemnations of some aspects of official Cuban life, and some of its characters displayed an indomitable yearning for a free society.

58. The dissidents were Marta Beatriz Roque Cabello, Vladimiro Roca Antúnez, René Gómez Manzano, and Félix Bonne Carcassés. See Schwab 1999, 148. On July 16, 1997, after publishing their document entitled *The Homeland Is for All* (*La Patria es de Todos*) and sending a copy of the text to Havana's Central Communist Party Committee (Comité Central del Partido Comunista), these four individuals were arrested and incarcerated without trial. All but one of the four dissidents — Vladimiro Roca — were released in May 2000. See <http://www.state.gov/www/regions/wha/cuba/release_dissidents.html>. On May 5, 2002, Roca was finally released. See <http://www.miami.com/mld/miami/3204646.htm>.

59. The CDRs were set up in the first days of the Revolution primarily to oversee the distribution of food rations. Thereafter, they became a sort of watchdog of the government, reporting on every aspect of daily life from absenteeism to political deviance. Literally, the CDRs were there to ensure that the Revolution worked from the level of the individual household. Although still in existence, the CDRs have tended to lose their singular importance in recent years.

References

Avilés, Jaime.1999. "La Ley de Herodes." *La Jornada*, December 11.

Basdeo, Sahadeo. 1999. "Helms Burton Controversy: An Issue in Canada-US Foreign Relations." In *Canada, the US and Cuba: Helms-Burton and Its Aftermath*, ed. Heather N. Nicol. Kingston, Ontario: Centre for International Relations, Queen's University.

Campa, Homero. 1999a. "'De línea dura,' el nuevo canciller cubano está muy 'familiarizado con el pensamiento de Fidel.'" *Proceso*, June 6.

Campa, Homero. 1999b. "El gobierno canceló las oficinas de la empresa mexicana Cubamor, acusada de promover el turismo sexual de la isla." *Proceso*, June 13.

Campa, Homero. 1999c. "En la crisis, resabios históricos y socioculturales." *Proceso*, June 6.

Carranza Valdes, Julio. 1997. "Economic Changes in Cuba: Problems and Challenges. In *Cuba and the Caribbean: Regional Issues and Trends in the Post-Cold War Era*, eds. Joseph S.Tulchin, Andrés Serbin, and Rafael Hernández. Wilmington, Del.: Scholarly Resources, Inc.

Centeno, Miguel Ángel, and Mauricio Font, eds., 1997. *Toward a New Cuba? Legacies of a Revolution*. Boulder, Colo.: Lynne Rienner Publishers.

del Águila, Juan M. 1996. "Cuba Adapts to a Brave New World." In *Latin American Nations in World Politics*, eds. Heraldo Muñoz and Joseph S. Tulchin. Boulder, Colo.: Westview Press.

De la Fuente, Alejandro, and Laurence Celasco. 1997. "Are Blacks 'Getting Out of Control'? Racial Attitudes, Revolution, and Political Transition in Cuba." In *Toward a New Cuba? Legacies of a Revolution*, eds. Miguel Ángel Centeno and Mauricio Font Boulder, Colo.: Lynne Rienner Publishers.

Ducey, Michael T. 2001. "Indian Communities and Ayuntamientos in the Mexican Huasteca: Sujeto Revolts, Pronunciamientos, and the Caste War." *The Americas* 57 (4): 525-550.

Fotheringham, Allan. 1998. "Chrétien a Hostage to Castro's Outrageous Exaggeration." *Financial Post* 91: 18 (May 2).

Frank, Marc. 2002. "U.S. Agents to Sell Cuban Resorts." *Maclean's* (April 13, internet).

Fukuyama, Francis. 1992. *The End of History and the Last Man*. New York: Free Press.

Fujii, Gerardo. 1999. "La batalla de Seattle." *La Jornada*, December 11.

Granma International. 1999. "Health and Beauty Center," May 23.

Gunn Clissold, Gillian. 1997. "Cuban-U.S. Relations and the Process of Transition: Possible Consequences of Covert Agendas." In *Toward a New Cuba? Legacies of a Revolution*, eds. Miguel Angel Centeno and Mauricio Font. Boulder, Colo.: Lynne Rienner Publishers.

Jones, David. 1994. "The Trade in Flesh: Gruesome Face of the New World Market." *Latin American Connections* (January-February).

Kirk, John M. 1990. "Cuba at the Crossroads." *International Perspectives* 19 (8).

Latin American Weekly Report. 1993. "After Dollarisation, Self-employment," September 23.

Leonard, Thomas A. 1999. *Castro and the Cuban Revolution.* Westport, Conn.: Greenwood Press.

Maclean's. 1996. "A Hard Act to Follow," January 15.

Meier, Marco. 1998. *René Burri: Cuba y Cuba.* Washington, D.C.: Smithsonian Institution Press.

Monroy, María Eugenia. 1999. "Difunden atractivos de la isla." *Reforma,* November 21.

Morici, Peter. 1997. "The United States, World Trade, and The Helms-Burton Act." *Current History* (February).

Morris, Nomi. 1996. "Can Cuba Change?" *Maclean's,* January 15.

Muñoz, Heraldo, and Joseph S. Tulchin. 1996. *Latin American Nations in World Politics.* Boulder, Colo.: Westview Press.

Newman, Peter C. 1995. "Going Capitalist on the Canbuck." *Maclean's,* February 13.

Nicol, Heather N., ed. 1999. *Canada, the US and Cuba: Helms-Burton and Its Aftermath.* Kingston, Ontario: Centre for International Relations, Queen's University.

Oramas, Joaquín. 1999. "Petroleum: Utopias and Realities." *Granma International,* May 23.

Oramas Léon, Orlando. 1999. "Barbados y Cuba." *Granma International,* June 18.

Pérez, Louis A., Jr. 1988. *Cuba: Between Reform and Revolution.* New York: Oxford University Press.

Pérez-Stable, Marifeli. 1997. "The Invisible Crisis: The Exhaustion of Politics in 1990s Cuba." In *Toward a New Cuba? Legacies of a Revolution,* eds. Miguel Ángel Centeno and Mauricio Font. Boulder, Colo.: Lynne Rienner Publishers.

La Prensa (Mexico City). 2002. "Acusa Cuba a América Latina de ser 'judas,'" April 19.

Richert, Hans-Werner. 1999. "German Industry Wants To Be Number One in Cuba." *Granma International,* May 23.

Riera, Liliam. 1999. "Helms-Burton Act Loses Credibility with Canadian Business." *Granma International,* May 23.

Robbins, Carla Anne. 1993. "Major Crisis in Cuba Possible 'at Any Time,' CIA Warns." *Globe and Mail,* November 23.

Schwab, Peter. 1999. *Cuba: Confronting the U.S. Embargo.* New York: St. Martin's Press.

Selbin, Eric. 1993. *Latin American Revolutions.* Boulder, Colo.: Westview Press.

Serbin, Andrés. 1997. "The Geopolitical Context of the Caribbean Basin in the 1990s: Geoeconomic Reconfigurations and Political Transitions." In *Cuba and the Caribbean: Regional Issues and Trends in the Post Cold-War Era,* eds. Joseph S. Tulchin, Andrés Serbin, and Rafael Hernández. Wilmington, Del.: Scholarly Resources, Inc.

Simons, Geoff. 1996. *Cuba: From Conquistador to Castro.* New York: St. Martin's Press.

Steele, Jonathan. 1997. "Havana Good Time." *Guardian Weekly,* October 26.

Symmes, Patrick. 1996. "Taking the Measure of Castro, Ounce by Ounce." *Harper's Magazine,* January.

Symonds, William C. 1997. "Castro's Capitalist: Canada's Sherritt Cleans Up in Cuba." *Business Week,* March 17.

Thomas, Hugh. 1971. *The Pursuit of Freedom.* New York: Harper & Row.

Toronto Star. 1976. "Money's Back in Style," May 25.

Trabajadores. 1999. "Exitosa culminación de la celebración evangélica cubana," June 21.

Tulchin, Joseph S., Andrés Serbin, and Rafael Hernández, eds. 1997. *Cuba and the Caribbean: Regional Issues and Trends in the Post-Cold War Era.* Wilmington, Del.: Scholarly Resources, Inc.

United Nations Development Programme. "Human Development Report 2001: Addendum, Human Development Index for 12 Countries Not Included in the Main Indicator Tables." See <http://www.undp.org/hdr2001/Addendum4.pdf>.

United Nations High Commissioner for Human Rights. 2002. "Situation of Human Rights in Cuba." Commission on Human Rights Resolution 2002/18, April 19. See <http://www.unhchr.ch/huridocda/huridoca.nsf/(Symbol)/E.CN.4.RES.2002.18.EN?Opendocument>.

Valdés, Julio Carranza. 1997. "Economic Changes in Cuba: Problems and Challenges." In *Cuba and the Caribbean: Regional Issues and Trends in the Post Cold-War Era*, eds. Joseph S. Tulchin, Andrés Serbin, and Rafael Hernández. Wilmington, Del.: Scholarly Resources, Inc.

Wallace, Bruce. 1998. "Connecting with Castro." *Maclean's* 111: 19 (May 11).

Wallace, Bruce. 1999. "Canada's Accidental Tourist." *Maclean's* 113: 17 (April 24).

Washington Post. 1977. "Young Prostitutes Back in Havana," December 13.

Part IV.
Conclusion

CHAPTER SEVEN

(Re)Imagining Cuba in a Global World: The Changing Geopolitical Discourse of Canada-Cuba and United States-Cuba Relations After Helms-Burton

HEATHER N. NICOL

INTRODUCTION

That Cuba is the focus of a disproportionate share of political and media attention in North America cannot be disputed. For example, since 1996, Canadian newspapers alone have carried more than 20,000 articles that touch on the subject of Cuba or Castro — and these represent only a fraction of the number published in the United States. In addition, discussions concerning foreign policy toward Cuba and events involving Cuba, Canada, and the United States have been routine in the Canadian Parliament, Senate, and Cabinet, as well as in the U.S. Congress, Senate, and various governmental committees and subcommittees. Indeed, at times, for example, during the passage of the Cuban Liberty and Democratic Solidarity Act (Helms-Burton); the continuing waiver of some parts of its provisions; and the explosive events surrounding the return of young Elián González to his father in Cuba, these U.S. institutions were intensely preoccupied with policies and protocols regarding Cuba.

While both Canadian and U.S. policies are concerned with Cuba, the two governments do not regard it in the same ways. In fact, Canadian and U.S. citizens historically have built very different types of ties with Cuba, and they hold very different attitudes toward events on the island. These fundamental differences are influenced by and legitimized through unique geopolitical discourses concerning Cuba and its place in the so-called new world order.[1] To Canadians, the concept of a new world order, which emerged in the early 1990s, is taken to mean a new opportunity for global interdependence, stability, and security.[2] To many in the United States, however, the new world order means something different: a global outlook consistent with the new strategic and domestic interests of the United States in the post-Cold War era.[3]

While more than three U.S. administrations have come and gone since the term "new world order" first was coined, the idea that a "new global order" exists and the United States is at its center remains remarkably resilient. Even as the George W. Bush administration made its own tentative moves toward internationalism by signaling its renewed desire to "be friends" with former archenemy Russia, its brand of new world order still managed to exclude Cuba and avoid any critical reassessment of the Cuban situation.[4] Recent attempts to modify the economic embargo in Cuba, allow the shipment of food and medicine to the island, and open a dialogue on the possibility of new types of interaction may continue to take a back seat to concerted U.S. efforts to bring Cuba "into line," as the Bush administration sends somewhat ambivalent signals about its intent to play hardball with the Castro regime.

The essays in this volume have explored this trend very clearly, raising the question of why the Cold War persists in Cuban-U.S. relations. One response to this question is that the burden of history is a powerful force. Indeed, both Stephen J. Randall and Daniel W. Fisk demonstrate in Part 3 of this volume that, until very recently, the U.S. relationship with Cuba was constructed almost exclusively on the basis of concerns and information filtered through the Cuban-American community. Since the Cuban-American community has been in a dispute with the Castro regime since 1959, reliance on its perspective has only served to encourage a hard-line approach in Congress and the Senate, as well as openness to one segment of the Cuban-American community holding reactionary viewpoints regarding U.S. relations with Cuba. This dialogue, while remaining politically expedient even after the end of the Cold War, became even more entrenched after the mid-1990s, when Cuban authorities shot down two civilian planes belonging to Brothers to the Rescue.[5] The result was that rather than softening their position, U.S. policymakers, the U.S. media, and the U.S. public in general expressed support for the continuation and extension of punitive economic and political measures by the United States to weaken the Castro government. This resulted in the passage of the Helms-Burton Act in 1996 and the reaffirmation of a popular and political narrative that justified, indeed required, punitive action long after the so-called Soviet threat was over.

If the United States was moved to drastic action by the plane shoot-down, the same events provoked less political response north of the border. Again, history played a role. Canada chastised Cuba for its actions but did not adopt punitive measures. Indeed, the decision *not to* support an economic embargo against Cuba found agreement at all levels. In general, Canadians agreed with the decision of Prime Minister Jean Chrétien's administration to reject the Helms-Burton Act and support the position of Mexico and the European Union in their protest against it. This response, as many of the essays in this volume have discussed, was constructed officially through parliamentary debate.[6] Equally important, the response gained tremendous popular support. Media accounts from the late 1990s reveal the depth of Canadian nationalism and support for Canada's position vis-à-vis the United States and the Helms-Burton Act. A survey of Canadian newspapers dated between 1996 and 1998 indicates, for example, that the press reinforced Canada's formal opposition to Helms-Burton and the U.S. embargo of Cuba. Some 4,000-5,000 newspaper articles, letters to the editor, and editorials supporting the government's position were generated across Canada in the wake of Helms-Burton — considerably more than the handful of articles that supported the U.S. position.[7] In fact, the idea of conciliatory Canada-Cuba relations, pitted against the United States' uncompromising policies, comprised a story line that remained mainstream and uncontested by most Canadians, who have for decades seen themselves as friends of Cuba.

However, as many of the chapters in this volume indicate, the Canadian political landscape and, consequently, ideas about Canada-Cuban relations are changing, as policymakers adopt a more critical approach and as opinions become diversified. The remarkable consensus about Cuba is no longer quite so universal or monolithic. New viewpoints, multiple discourses, and new modes of analysis arrive on the scene and struggle with the challenge of making sense of Canada's role in a global world.

This chapter looks more carefully at diversification in the evolution of Canada-United States-Cuba relations. It argues that diversity in approach to Cuba and diversity in perceptions of Cuba are noticeable developments of the late twentieth century, not only in Canada but in the United States as well. Neither country now has only a single "story line." In the United States, new challenges to old stories have arisen, sweeping them away and making room for the new. In both countries, both popular and formal texts, including newspaper accounts, the rhetoric of politicians, and the musings of newscasters, all have begun to demonstrate remarkable diversity of opinion and to construct new ways of understanding Cuba. Typical of these narratives is their ability to consider the possibility of a post-Helms-Burton Cuba that is not necessarily post-Castro.

This push to "(re)imagine" and reconsider Cuba — in both Canada and the United States — seems closely related to two major contemporary forces of the late twentieth and early twenty-first centuries. The first is the changing domestic political terrain, under tremendous pressure exerted by globalizing economic trends and neoliberal agendas. The late twentieth century saw tremendous changes in thinking about international relations, in keeping with what has been described as an "economic flurry of interactions" and the rise of "acute interdependence" in information and economic sectors. The shrinking world is now seen by many, notwithstanding the protests at the 2001 World Trade Organization (WTO) Conference in Genoa, as economically beneficial and politically rewarding. This understanding of the world, in turn, requires a new story line, a "(re)imagining" of political space and international relations — drastically different from the old "evil empire" metaphor that dominated the Cold War era and divided the world between two superpowers.

The second major challenge or influence has been the new or heightened degree of interaction between North Americans and Cubans, propelled by popularized media accounts of Cuba during and after the visit of Pope John Paul II. Although the visit occurred in Cuba, that event had symbolic repercussions at the hemispheric level, if not beyond. Taking a critical look at the texts, words, and rhetoric deployed by late twentieth and early twenty-first century decisionmakers, the media, and other popular accounts, the following discussion reexamines the evolving relationships among Canada, the United States, and Cuba in relation to the influence of globalization and increasing interaction with Cuba.

TALKING ABOUT CUBA

L et us begin by defining more clearly what is meant by the "changing story line" and why the examination of such constructions might be useful, particularly in light of discussions in this volume. A story line is a discourse or narrative that organizes how an idea is presented and how, in turn, it will be received. Exploring how Cuba is talked about in Canada and the United States — that is, the words, metaphors, and descriptions employed — is useful in understanding how policies with respect to Cuba have been constructed and implemented over time.[8]

Initially, our ideas about Cuba were framed in reference to a Cold War narrative. Indeed, in looking back at political and diplomatic documents, as well as scholarship, fiction, film, and media accounts, such as newsreels, newspapers, and documentaries, one thing is now very clear. In all of these contexts, the "bipolar world," or "old world order," was described by a series of geopolitical referents that had become symbols for how people should live, think, and imagine how the world worked.[9] *The Atomic Cafe* (a well-known post-modern nonfiction film that spoofs the Cold War through its presentation of disconnected film clippings) is found under "comedy" in video rental stores, attesting to the fact that deconstruction is not only possible but also entertaining. This is because the story line, or the built-in set of assumptions and biases that were essential to make the Cold War narrative work 30 years ago, is not only obvious but also appears ridiculous to contemporary observers. This film demonstrates first-hand how all aspects of popular and institutional culture combined to produce a widely understood narrative, which in turn helped us visualize the world as a strategically "loaded" place where contrasting political ideologies were inherently threatening.[10] In other words, the Cold War was a story line, a way of understanding, seeing, and telling — truly a geopolitical discourse. As such, it organized, oriented, and described political events and geographical locations in ways that had near-universal currency among countries of the developed world and beyond. Almost everyone understood its meanings.

The same is true of historical narratives and discussion regarding Cuba. The texts that record these discussions provide a discourse, story line, or specific "take" on Cuba that builds upon certain common assumptions and collective consensus. These texts are selective, but they play a crucial role in the construction of policy. Not only do they articulate imaginings about Cuba and offer "world pictures" in which Cuba is given a place and a meaning, but, more importantly, they reinforce and confirm certain perceptions and therefore authorize certain actions. They espouse ways of seeing and interpreting Cuba that are highly selective and imbued with meaning, grounded in specific sets of geographical referents and symbolic terrains.[11]

Thus, what is important in the process of evolving international relations goes beyond just formal discussions of policymakers. As this chapter will show, the media and popular forms of culture also play an important role, not only by reacting to foreign policy debates, but also by influencing them. Indeed, it has been suggested that the circulation of images in the media has led to the media's ever-increasing importance in our everyday understandings and conceptualizations of global geopolitics.[12] Moreover, even popular culture, in the format of films like

Patriot Games and *A Clear and Present Danger,* which deal with U.S. security issues at the imaginative level, also exerts influence because the films construct visual reference points for geopolitical frameworks. As Evan Potter has argued from the perspective of political science, "How the debate over Cuba is framed goes right to the heart of explaining the differences between the United States and its allies."[13]

Just how is the debate over Cuba framed? How has it changed in the post-Helms-Burton period? What are the essential differences between Canadian and U.S. narrative discourses at the practical and popular levels? A critical look at the nature of popular and formal narratives deployed by both countries helps to answer these questions.

Changing Canadian Discourses: Moving beyond Constructive Engagement

As many of the chapters herein have shown and as I have discussed elsewhere,[14] in the early 1990s, the Canadian position regarding Cuba was distinct. It had been forged with reference to Canada's historical relationship with the United States and decades of Canadian friendship with the Cuban people. Perhaps because of their country's position as a "middle power" rather than a super power or perhaps because of Canada's proximity to the political and economic colossus to the south, Canadian decisionmakers seemed less concerned with power brokerage than their U.S. counterparts and more concerned with conciliatory international relations and peacekeeping as well as promotion of interdependence among world powers.[15]

These attitudes were instrumental in forging Canadian responses to the Helms-Burton Act in the mid-1990s. Canadians feared the extraterritorial nature of Helms-Burton, the challenge it posed to Canadian sovereignty, and its erosion of a "rules-based" international order.[16] Some analysts have suggested that the virulent Canadian reaction to Helms-Burton was less concerned with its impact on Cuba and more concerned with its impact on Canadian sovereignty.[17] In fact, some key personnel in Canada's Department of Foreign Affairs and International Trade have suggested that this was a deliberate strategy designed to defuse the situation by deflecting it away from Cuba per se and building consensus on safer ground.

Regardless of whether this deflection was intentional, many of the essays in this volume indicate that Canada responded to Helms-Burton with the claim that it had developed a "special relationship" or policy framework with Cuba known as "constructive engagement." To Canadians, constructive engagement meant a working relationship between the two nations in order to foster democratic reform, as well as a history linking the two nations. As Peter McKenna, John Kirk, and Christine Climenhage observe in Chapter Three of this volume, Canada's policies toward Cuba generally have been cordial and supportive, and the fact that Canada can claim a special relationship holds symbolic importance. These policies demonstrate Canada's interdependence in its external relations.[18]

Although Cuba-Canada relations have had a long history that goes back well before the Chrétien administration, constructive engagement generally is associated with that administration's approach to Cuba and its response to the politics of Helms-Burton. Indeed, much of the geopolitical discourse of the Chrétien administration in the mid-1990s reveals a concern with building interdependence and hemispheric (if not global) webs of interaction under conditions of globalization.[19] Its approach to Cuba, in this sense, is part of a larger approach to international relations.

The concept of constructive engagement deployed by the Chrétien administration immediately following U.S. passage of the Helms-Burton Act was, therefore, not only a nationalist narrative, but also part of a more comprehensive late twentieth century political and economic agenda. The concept was consistent with a new emphasis upon global trade and neoliberal trade policies as well as new ideas about hemispheric security. Indeed, the importance of these influences cannot be overstated. James Rochlin has even suggested that in a post-Cold War period, "Inter-American security is more important than ever, but Ottawa's political commitment to the hemisphere, as manifested in its full membership in the OAS, means that Canada has a new responsibility for defining and resolving inter-American security issues."[20] This meant that Canada's response to Helms-Burton was colored by considerations of security and global trade and connectivity in the context of its newfound relationship with the Americas and the world.[21]

The infamous case of the "Wal-Mart pajamas" is illustrative of the tight weave between political and economic agendas that has come into play with respect to Canada's relationship with Cuba and the United States during and after Helms-Burton. In 1997, when Wal-Mart refused to sell Cuban-made pajamas in Canadian stores, Minister of Foreign Affairs Lloyd Axworthy commented that he expected Canadian companies to abide by Canadian law. "That was the intention of our amendments under the Foreign Exchange Measures Act.... We are continuing our opposition to the Helms-Burton law and its extraterritorial application of U.S. law. We believe that it is fundamentally wrong *in terms of trading law*" [emphasis mine].[22]

Sahadeo Basdeo and Ian Hesketh remind us in Chapter Two that the hallmarks of the Chrétien approach, reflected in the statement by Axworthy, always have been trade and diplomacy combined with dialogue on human rights, with the expectation that Cuba would slowly conform with the rules of the hemisphere. This pragmatism clearly spilled over into the construction of traditional narratives regarding Cuban-Canadian relations, particularly the narrative or story line about constructive engagement. The latter relied, ostensibly, upon a specific geopolitical discourse in which Cuba was seen not as a threat but as a symbol of global interdependence.

Analysis of formal political debates supports such interpretation. The parliamentary debates that arose over Helms-Burton and its application are replete with geographical references that support the constructive engagement narrative. For example, Canadian policies with respect to Cuba are framed with numerous references to "Cuba's special relationship" with Canada.[23] At least one member of Parliament also has observed that these similarities between Canada and Cuba are all the more potent because Cuba, like Canada, is in the so-called U.S. sphere of influence.[24] Canada is supposed to act "like a good little neighbor"; size, in this case, is a geopolitical descriptor that describes power relations, rather than mass. Indeed, in the months immediately following the passage of the Helms-Burton Act, Canada's relationship to Cuba constantly was described by Canadian policymakers against the backdrop of Cuban relations with friendly trading nations within the Caribbean Basin, thus exposing the U.S. assertion that Canada's position was unique within the Western Hemisphere.

In defending their relationship with Cuba, then, Canadians evoked the symbolism of hemispheric integration to promote engagement, interdependence, and cooperation. Engagement was to be a tool of Canadian politicians and diplomats, while their goals were to promote neoliberal trade regimes.[25] Such goals were not possible, obviously, without new images and metaphors and new means of legitimizing the interests of the Canadian state within the Western Hemisphere. Thus, constructive engagement became an ideal phrase to describe the process; it was a realistic description of the new goal of the conciliatory relationship between Canada and Cuba.

Clearly, this particular Canadian geopolitical discourse had been framed at the parliamentary and professional level, that is to say, by Canadian politicians and decisionmakers whose job it was to instrumentalize the actions of state in the arena of international relations. However, as we have seen, such discourses are also supported, even constructed, at the popular or informal level,[26] raising the question of whether Canadians, in general, supported the formal decisions and policies of constructive engagement.

The short answer is yes, many ordinary Canadians agreed with their government. Like their decisionmakers, they supported Cuba and opposed the U.S. embargo and the Helm-Burton Act. Indeed, the formal reaction of the Canadian government to Helms-Burton merely articulated what most Canadians sensed — that when it came to foreign relations, something was inherently different between the approaches of Canada and the United States. While academics understood the deep-rooted differences in the international relations agendas of the two nations and could explain them in historical and philosophical terms, it was enough for most Canadians that their country had chosen a different position from that of the United States.

The media contributed to this sensibility, at least initially. In the wake of Helms-Burton, Canadian newspaper coverage was sympathetic to Cuba and to the Chrétien administration's position. Canadian newspapers proclaimed "Cuba's poor, the real victims of U.S. policy," noting that "by heightening tensions and further restricting Cuba's access to the world, the Helms-Burton law will disrupt the work of a growing number of Canadian non-governmental organizations [which], with the support of the Canadian government, provide Cubans with badly needed humanitarian assistance."[27] Canada as a state and Canadians as a people approached Cuba in abstract terms and in the context of their own political culture, which stressed the goals of peacekeeping, goodwill, and interdependence.

The supportive tone of newspaper reportage is consistent throughout the period from approximately 1996 to the spring of 1998. More than ever, a popularized geopolitical dialogue developed, which intensified a distinctive Canadian

position — strongly opposed to Helms-Burton and rooted in thinly veiled senti-
ments of Canadian nationalism.

In this media discourse, goals of Canadian civil society became equated with
the statesmanship used by Canadian decisionmakers in their dialogue with Cuba, so
that even such mundane issues as investment in Cuba were equated with humane
goals and resistance to U.S. political bullying. Canadian business, for example, was
to be protected from U.S. reprisals, prompting some journalists to crow that Helms-
Burton was a "tempest in a teapot" in which Canada had prevailed. Said one
journalist, "Just when we thought we might be going to war with the United States
over Cuba, Uncle Sam blinks...."[28]

With few exceptions, the extremely anti-Castro rhetoric of U.S. discourse was
absent in Canadian newspaper accounts, editorials, and letters to the editor. Indeed,
where Cuba was referred to directly or described within Canadian newspapers,
images of rural agricultural landscapes or urban poverty were evoked, rather than
images of death squads and dictators. Cubans were described as well-educated and
capable, although impoverished people, rather than as passive victims waiting to be
set free.[29]

This popularized narrative concerning Canada's position with respect to
Cuba continued throughout the mid- to late 1990s. Its support for constructive
engagement was consistent with the overall approach of the Chrétien administration
and remained in place well after the immediate crisis of Helms-Burton had passed.
Evident in the media reportage was the emphasis upon an interdependent approach
to foreign affairs based upon dialogue, bilateral agreement, and development
assistance, all of which were metaphors for Canada's role in the new world order.
Clearly, both formal and informal discourses were mutually constitutive and
supportive of a distinctive Canadian approach toward Cuba and toward Canada's
forging of a new political and economic space for itself within the Americas.

While Cuba was always in the news throughout the 1990s, the news was
generally political, but when Canadian newspapers enthusiastically covered the
pope's visit in January 1998, something different took place. The media used the
opportunity not only to report on the pontiff's tour, but also to interpret and explain
Cuban society to Canadian readers. This popular engagement with Cuba carried into
the spring of 1998, when the media continued to report on all things Cuban —
including ongoing analysis of religious freedom, economic conditions, political
dissidents, and the sex trade. Speculation concerning the spiritual and ideological
significance of religious tolerance in Cuba consumed the Canadian public, as did
analysis of the impact of the Helms-Burton Act and its impact upon Cuban society.
During and after the pope's visit, coverage broadened to include discussion of
Canadian businesses in Cuba and the nature of these enterprises, Cuban resorts,
Havana's Chinese community, Cuba's spy museum, the return of Ché Guevara's
remains to Havana, the fortieth anniversary of Castro's New Year's Day victory
over Batista, censorship in Cuba, tobacco marketing, and Cuban-Mexican relations.
Indeed, articles on these topics were almost commonplace in Canadian newspapers
from coast to coast.

In the months that followed, however, this more comprehensive treatment of
Cuba — a Cuba seen in its own right, rather than in abstract terms related to its

symbolic relationship to Canada or the implications for U.S.-Canadian relations —
was not always benign, particularly when it became clear that the euphoric
expectation that the pope would bring real change to Cuba was overly optimistic.
Headlines like "Pope Unhappy Castro Dragging Heels" were common in the
summer of 1998 throughout the Canadian press. There were reports on the pope's
unease with the lack of progress in religious freedom and human rights in the island
nation.[30] Charges began to emerge asserting that Canadian support for Cuba was
misplaced and that Canada had not upheld the lofty ambition of encouraging human
rights in Cuba. The *Calgary Herald* and the *Vancouver Sun*, two major Canadian
newspapers, both noted in November 1998 that although Axworthy's foreign
agenda was responding to the need to fill a vacuum, to take leadership in cooperative
multilateralism, it was not supported by his humanitarian or military-aid budget and
as such was intuitively irksome to the United States, as indeed was Canada's
position on Cuba in general. In contrast to the tone of articles in the wake of Helms-
Burton, however, these newspapers reflected no pride in Canada's position.[31]
Indeed, the *Edmonton Journal* reported on comments made late in December 1998
by Canadian human rights activist Paul Marshall, who noted, "Canada must be
willing to cut off trade and foreign aid to any nation guilty of murdering its own
citizens.... Prime Minister Jean Chrétien and other government leaders have a weak
record when it comes to speaking out on human rights, and particularly on the lack
of religious freedom in countries like China, Cuba, and others."[32] Coverage of the
arrival of author Cecilio Ismael Sambra Habar in Toronto (Sambra was the jailed
dissident released in the wake of the pope's visit and Canadian political pressure)
was big news in Canada's newspapers from coast to coast. Comparisons between
Chile's Augusto Pinochet Ugarte and Fidel Castro were also common, suggesting
that both were evil dictators who should be punished.

In this context, Canada's Prime Minister Chrétien visited Cuba. At that time,
popularized geopolitical discourse on Cuba was undergoing significant change.
Prior to 1998, Cuba was considered an abstract or symbolic geopolitical location
signifying Canada's independence from the United States; it was a tropical island
paradise for Canadians, not for U.S. citizens. These imaginings about Cuba were,
however, idealized and reductionist views of the island's political, social, and
economic situation. Not surprisingly, under increasingly globalizing conditions,
these concepts gave ground. After 1998, for example, while some popularized
geopolitical texts still promoted this discourse, others began to describe Cuba as a
landscape of people. The narratives became multiple, the interpretations more
diverse.

Not all discourses about Cuba were flattering. Indeed, one of the new ones that
gained strength was quite reactionary, complementing the aggressive political
agendas of Canada's more right-wing parties. They argued that Cuba was a place
of repression because of the failure of the Canadian political agenda to secure human
rights concessions that would make Canadians proud and legitimize their ideological leanings toward neoliberal agendas, multilateralism, and economic interdependence. Indeed, the two goals, economic multilateralism and development of human
rights, became counterpoised as mutually exclusive goals. Consequently, although
the Canadian press had begun to challenge the traditional story line and to introduce

a new diversity, a significant proportion of the press coverage became critical and reminiscent of the worst excesses of the U.S. anti-Castro discourse.

Quite apart from media accounts, other elements contributed to the reassessment of Cuba as a geopolitical space. A most significant factor was that Canadians were visiting the island in increasing numbers, expecting to find idyllic tropical landscapes. Increasing mobility meant that in confronting Cuba, Canadians began to discover that the island was neither a paradise nor a communist prison; it was a complex society with significant development problems.

Still, while experience may have tempered many Canadians' imaginings about Cuba and thus led to new elements in geopolitical discourse, even more important in the changing political discourse was the changing domestic political terrain in Canadian federal politics. As has been shown elsewhere in this volume, Chrétien's official visit to Cuba in the spring of 1998 was a critical turning point in the construction of a formal geopolitical discourse regarding Cuba. Indeed, optimistic over the pope's reception earlier that year and mindful of the U.S. charge that Canada should do more to promote human rights in Cuba if its constructive engagement agenda was to succeed, Chrétien went to Cuba ostensibly to raise human rights awareness and to move Cuba more quickly toward the goal of liberalization and democratic freedom. As Basdeo and Hesketh observe in Chapter Two, "Buoyed by a supportive climate in the afterglow of the pope's visit, Canada continued its activist role in the field of human rights in Cuba."

The euphoria was short-lived. Chrétien's visit was not welcomed by his political critics in Canada, who argued:

> The Prime Minister seems to be all over the map when it comes to human rights. On his trip to Cuba, he refuses to raise the issue of human rights abuse publicly. Now, even though the red book says that foreign aid should be linked to human rights abuses, his Canadian International Development Agency (CIDA) minister is talking about going to Burma.[33]

In response, the House of Commons was told by members of the Chrétien administration in May 1998, "Coming fast on the heels of the Prime Minister's ground-breaking visit to Cuba last week, a visit which the Reform [Party] so adamantly protested, it is obvious that the Prime Minister's policy in constructive engagement works." Further, it was said, "In his meetings with [President] Fidel Castro, the Prime Minister tackled many human rights issues and pushed for the release of prisoners."[34]

The intensive scrutiny of Chrétien's ability to gain human rights concessions in Cuba was a response to the political machinations of the Canadian Parliament's opposition Reform Party, a party considered reactionary in relation to the Chrétien administration's multilateral political policies and global trade agenda. Still, the new so-called human rights agenda offered by the Reform Party was constructed not so much with a vision of foreign policy in mind as in response to a desire to carve out a distinctive niche and curry political favor in certain domestic circles. Consequently, in taking aim against Chrétien, the Reform Party argued against constructive engagement with Castro and for a sharper human rights agenda. The process was reminiscent of what Benjamin Barber once called "Jihad" versus

"McWorld": "In Reform's view, soft diplomacy with Castro should give way to political and diplomatic rigidity."[35]

Initially, many Canadians who witnessed the Reform Party's attack dismissed it as a riposte of partisan politics, a smokescreen for a political agenda that represented a sectionalist and minority viewpoint. The argument was increasingly seductive, however, because of its self-assurance and relatively simplistic solutions. While the Chrétien government was involved in internationalism, expressed through a complex series of long-range discussions and negotiations with Cuba, the Reform Party called for "concrete proposals" and for public demonstrations of a "hard line."[36]

As Basdeo and Hesketh argue in Chapter Two, by April 1998, it was apparent that this "(re)visioning" of Canada's international agenda and Cuba's situation with respect to Canada was gathering force. Indeed, at the same time that Chrétien responded to the pope's plea for engagement with Cuba, the Chrétien administration's discourse was labeled by many as "too soft."

As the Reform Party gained credibility, letters and editorials in Canadian newspapers moved to the right. One observed, "Earlier this year Prime Minister Jean Chrétien came under strong pressure to raise human rights issues with Cuban President Fidel Castro during a visit to Havana but did not succeed in getting a public comment from him...."[37] Others asked why only Pinochet, and not Castro and his ilk, was being singled out for punishment, while reprinted articles with Washington and Miami datelines reported on the continuing human rights carnage in the waters off Florida or the rising crime rates in Havana, described by one editorial as "this dilapidated communist capital filled with derelict automobiles."[38] Marcus Gee, noted columnist for *The Globe and Mail*, who held U.S. sympathies to the point of arguing for the United States to play "global cop," also stoked the fires of the new geopolitical discourse. His comments had a familiar ring, resonating with the language of Helms-Burton.[39]

By the fall of 1998, even elements of Canada's Cuban community, which often had supported humanitarian aid efforts in Cuba and had previously complained about the U.S. embargo, were portrayed by the media (perhaps falsely) as opposed to Canadian business ventures on the island. Cuban-born activists supposedly argued that Canada was propping up a tyrant and should support the Helms-Burton Act.[40] Support for constructive engagement appeared under attack from all sides.

What are we to make of these dramatic departures? As Basdeo and Hesketh argue, "Since the visit by Pope John Paul II to Cuba, Canada has displayed an element of unnecessary impatience by pushing for quick change in the human rights sector in Cuba in hopes of winning political kudos at home for its policy of constructive engagement." Moreover, they suggest, "The rush to push Castro failed. Canada's style was both uncharacteristic and not in conformity with constructive engagement. It contradicted what Canadians themselves had been saying."[41] Kirk, McKenna, and Climenhage agree, in Chapter Three, suggesting that a major change has occurred in the tenor of Canadian-Cuban relations, due largely to the changing terrain of domestic politics. Human rights became a rallying point and, as such, stood counterpoised to Chrétien's constructive engagement approach.

While this assertion contains real elements of truth, the process may have been a bit more complicated than simply the fact that the political right successfully seized the moment on behalf of human rights. Numerous accounts, such as that of Barber, suggest that, in the wake of global interconnectivity and fast capitalism, conservative political reactions like those of the Reform Party (now the deeply divided Canadian Alliance Party) have become commonplace.[42] Indeed, Timothy W. Luke and Gearoid Ó. Tuathail, both scholars who address political responses to the new world order, have argued that the process of globalization encourages multiple interpretations of events, some of which are fundamentalist resistance to the friction-free dynamics of the global economy.[43] In this sense, the anti-Cuban geopolitical discourse that has emerged only recently at the popular and political level in Canada becomes one of several new and alternative narratives that attempt to "instrumentalize" the Canadian state with regard to changing conditions. In keeping with this tendency, it would seem that discursive elements of Canadian-Cuban relations also have become contradictory, revealing some of the structural tensions within this not-so-seamless new world order.[44]

THE UNITED STATES AND CUBA: NEW DISCOURSES EMERGE IN THE UNITED STATES

S imilar events have taken place in the United States and also may be explained with reference to the diversifying impact of a theory of globalization on geopolitical discourse.[45] Indeed, the U.S. government has long displayed an innate hostility toward the Castro regime. In some ways, this hostility has been exacerbated since the end of the Cold War, possibly because the collapse of the Soviet Union did not see "the end of history" or the end of the Castro regime, as predicted. Instead, it saw the Cuban government respond to the loss of cheap oil markets, machinery, imports, and aid with increases in foreign investment,[46] at the same time as the Cuban-American community in the United States gathered force in terms of its political influence on domestic policies (see Randall and Fisk in this volume). Cuba and Cuban-Americans have been on a collision course for over four decades.

If the end of history was not about to occur in Cuba, neither was the end of the Cold War, as far as Cuban-U.S. relations were concerned. Geopolitical discourses concerning Cuba constructed both by U.S. decisionmakers and the public at large remained ideologically based and strongly nationalistic well past the period that saw the collapse of the Soviet Union, Cuba's staunchest ally. U.S. decisionmakers continued to use highly inflammatory rhetoric when referring to Cuba and Cuban issues. The result was a political discourse or story line that referred to the island as "Castro's Cuba" and explained its continuing existence as a threat to democratic freedom in the Western Hemisphere. The picture of Cuba as an island trapped by an evil dictator whose goal is nothing short of worldwide domination remained — and indeed still remains — in force with many groups, even as the United States enters a new era of internationalism and a new world order.

This situation raises many questions concerning why and how the anti-Castro narrative remains viable and how it has been reinvented to accommodate changing political times. For example, why is the narrative that describes an evil dictator and oppressed people still cogent, and how has it been modified to retain its viability under new circumstances? Why has the Cold War witnessed the refocusing of attention upon Cuba as the main event rather than the journalistic sidebar?

I have argued elsewhere that the new Cuba narrative in the United States — that is to say, the normative post-Cold War discourse constructed in the United States over the past decade — has relied upon an inherent symbolism that mimics the Cold War yet is not the same as the Cold War discourse. The narrative has been driven by considerations of domestic politics with the coming of age of the Cuban-American political community rather than by a foreign affairs agenda in the traditional sense. This discourse is grounded in a series of words and images that have reduced Cuba, a nation of 11 million people, to a tiny island with only one significant citizen — its "evil dictator."[47] This kind of language is as true of formal debates and discussions about Cuba, that is to say, official government texts, as it is of popularized and media accounts. All of these sources have tended to be highly charged with selective imagery and symbolic referents that make Cuba look bad, and, as in Canada, all these accounts have been mutually constitutive.

Until a few years ago, it might have been possible to leave matters there and to argue that the U.S. viewpoint concerning Cuba was monolithic, reactionary, and virulently anti-Castro, insofar as the construction of geopolitical discourse at the institutional level is concerned. For example, Cuba was described within the pages of texts accompanying the passage of the Helms-Burton Act as a "hell hole," a "dreary communist outpost," and a "nation of potato tillers." None of these descriptors engender a sense of the legitimacy of the people or the validity of life on the island. Now, however, it can no longer be said that Americans construct only pejorative, universal narratives describing Cuba. The growing influence of the right in U.S. domestic politics has been offset by the new global economic agenda. The latter is reflected in a growing acceptance of diversity of viewpoints concerning Cuba, as well as the recognition that Cuba is a legitimate place.

As a result, several diametrically opposed points of view or geopolitical discourses about Cuba have emerged, each championed by different aspects of the political system. For example, elements of the Cuban-American community retain a militantly anti-Castro agenda, citing human rights abuses and arguing for maintenance of the U.S. embargo on Cuba. In contrast, the U.S. business community, which has long objected to the Cuban embargo, now has had its voice heard over the clamor of anti-Castro rhetoric, even, as Randall demonstrates (in this volume), in the accounts promulgated by Radio Martí and later by TV Martí. Moreover, more moderate sectors of the Cuban-American community have been able to express their points of view and to be heard in various congressional and Senate hearings or conference boards dealing with U.S.-Cuban policy. These other groups have also expressed themselves informally on websites, in the media, and in publications that challenge the more conservative points of view of the traditional Cuban American National Foundation (CANF). Meanwhile, the pope's 1998 visit became a turning point, acting as a trigger for new imaginings of Cuba and a new diversity in geopolitical discourse regarding Cuban relations. In this sense, U.S. and Canadian experiences display great similarity, suggesting that common processes have influenced them. In order to assess this similarity, let us look in more detail at the construction of and change in the U.S.-Cuban narrative.

CHANGING OF THE GUARD?

Nothing is more typical of the type of narrative constructed about Cuba than the one that surrounds the Cuban Missile Crisis. All the elements are in this story. High drama surrounds the near-attack by the communists and eventual victory of the democratic forces of the United States. The story portrays good and evil, threat and counterthreat, and the eventual success of U.S. "morality." While elements of this narrative or discourse still are found in contemporary discussions about Cuba, the decade of the 1990s has seen a clear shift in how U.S. citizens talk about Cuba. Part of the reason, as Fisk has indicated, is that the U.S. political terrain has undergone tremendous change, resulting in the heightened saliency of domestic issues within the foreign policy-making arena.

William Hyland suggests that this shift began with the Clinton administration's strategic goal of developing new levels of engagement with economic globalization, beginning with the North American Free Trade Agreement (NAFTA), in which neoliberalism and transnational corporate flows took precedence in foreign policymaking.[48] The impact upon international relations was immediate and tangible, with real repercussions on how — and where — foreign affairs were conducted. Regarding policy toward Cuba, the desire for new levels of engagement saw the development of new fault lines between the traditional or state position on Cuban-American relations and the new demands for integration and engagement. This was primarily because neoliberalism of the type envisioned by former President Clinton required openness to international trade and a definition of national interest consistent with the domestic economy. Economic embargoes were inconsistent with this approach, as were general statements about strategic and moral issues. Indeed, Fisk has suggested that to many politicians and policymakers of the period, Clinton's approach departed so much from the traditional path that it seemed to indicate a policy and leadership vacuum at the highest levels. Consequently, a more hard-line approach to Cuba was engineered successfully by elements of the opposition in the United States.

Although he toed the traditional line more closely at the beginning of his tenure, Clinton, in his second term, raised objections to a hard-line approach to Cuba. He supported the Helms-Burton Act only reluctantly, when the plane shootdown made it politically expedient. His veto of Title III of the Helms-Burton Act (which would allow Cuban-Americans to sue those companies doing business on or with confiscated properties) was consistent with his earlier reservations as well as those of the U.S. State Department. In the long run, the ideological foundations of neoliberalism, as practiced by the Clinton administration, and its particular approach to Cuba were at odds with the ideological basis of anti-Castro geopolitical discourse. While internal politics complicated this fact, leading to complex political compromises in many areas, the basic ideological and political inconsistencies between the president's policies and the Cuban embargo grew over time. Indeed, as many of the essays in this volume suggest, by the end of the Clinton administration, it seemed as if the United States might really be ready to end the embargo and enter a post-Helms-Burton era.

As in Canada, the change or diversification of discursive elements did not occur in a vacuum in the United States. The U.S. business lobby, the agricultural community, and elements of the academic and religious communities pushed hard for reconsideration of the embargo. For those groups, reorientation of U.S. international relations was necessary in a changing world order. Clearly, however, while opportunities existed for new points of view and for new voices to be heard, other voices that were increasingly opposed to the continuing isolation of Cuba and that can only be termed anti-Castro or ideology-based geopolitical discourse — those other voices were not about to go away. Indeed, Fisk has suggested that, although embargo supporters felt under fire toward the end of the Clinton administration, the election of George W. Bush in the fall of 2001 changed the landscape and staved off any death throes for Cold War, anti-Castro rhetoric.[49] Indeed, this narrative has been newly reassessed and is gaining ground in some areas.

Why is this so? As stated previously, part of the reason has been the success with which the Cuban-American community has reorganized the anti-Castro narrative, moving its focus from Cold War communism to human rights issues. The growth of the Cuban-American community in the United States, along with its success in dominating geopolitical discourse concerning Cuba, have pushed U.S. policies regarding Cuba and forced reorganization of domestic issues to reflect the growing concerns of Cuban-American ethnic groups in Florida, New Jersey, New York, California, and Illinois. As both Fisk and Randall observe (in Chapters Five and Four), U.S. decisionmakers no longer see Cuba as a security threat in the same way as they did during the Cold War. Rather, the pressure for punitive measures emanates from politics and political cultures situated within the United States. Indeed, rather than being an idiosyncratic throwback, the Cuban-American position is strong evidence of how traditional beliefs retain their currency by adapting themselves to new circumstances. The survival of this position and its currency in popularized geopolitical discourse provide powerful proof not only of the ability of multiple narratives to flourish under contemporary conditions of globalization, but also of the fact that fundamentalism and conservatism often are not throwbacks but responses to contemporary global processes. Indeed, Randall suggests that, if anything, the more conservative elements of the Cuban-American community have hardened their position in recent years.

However, with the George W. Bush administration, change clearly is once more on the horizon, although the nature of the change remains speculative. Preoccupied with other international issues, the Bush government has had little time to rethink its Cuba policies. Fisk suggests that despite the election rhetoric of Bush, which was clearly in support of economic embargo, the new government might temper its tone and policies because of the realities imposed by pressure from both domestic and international constituencies. Yet, the discourse on Cuba, as Fisk demonstrates, remains truculent, with Bush arguing that the calculus of U.S. relations with Cuba is based on moral considerations, thus reducing the island, once again, to a caricature of people and places that have no legitimacy on their own terms. Fisk suggests that the real struggle over Cuba now will be, in many respects, one of competing story lines, and the question of which story line will dominate is not as clear in 2002 as it was in 2000.

POPULARIZED NARRATIVES

Does evidence elsewhere support the theory that the same processes that have led to hardening of the conservative position on Cuba have also resulted in the development of new narratives, authorizing new policies and approaches toward the island? If so, how are popular accounts and the media important in contributing to these new narratives?

The obvious example is the media coverage that surrounded the Elián González affair. Prior to Elián's arrival, newspaper and media accounts of Cuba remained focused squarely upon the shortcomings of the Castro regime. The U.S. press was not known for covering Cuban events in comprehensive or sympathetic terms but rather for focusing upon crises, human rights abuses, and political scandals. Putting it bluntly, Canadian author Arnold August suggests that U.S. media coverage of Cuba, at least until recently, consisted of "bits and pieces...from the Associated [Press wire service], [which] obscures everything with comments [that] confuse the issues."[50] Moreover, the media contribute to the construction of specific narratives as much by what is not said as by what is said. For example, by giving cursory coverage to the Cuban elections, August charges, U.S. newspapers promulgated a simplistic view of Cuban political process and contributed to a wrongly constructed but popularized view of democratic abuses. U.S. newspapers observed that "elections have single candidates"[51] in Cuba, a pronouncement that August suggests is misleading and misrepresentative of nomination processes preceding the ballot box. Moreover, he says, "On the election day itself and during the period of vigorous debate following the publication of results, one U.S. wire service... carried 69 items on Cuba, but only two of which dealt with the elections.... There was a virtual blackout even against these items by the main U.S. newspapers."[52]

August also notes that even the *Washington Post*, "one of the most important consumers of the Associated Press wire service, did not carry either of these two new dispatches from the Associated Press on the Cuban elections. Instead, mention was made of the political system in Cuba only in context of a January 14 editorial on the pope's visit."[53] In the Washington newspaper, complex community-based political processes within Cuba were reduced to discussions of "a dictator experiencing 39 insecure years in power" and "a crumbling dictatorial rule."[54]

After the visit of Pope John Paul II, a watershed in Cuban-American relations, a June 1998 column in *The Miami Herald* by Juan O. Tamayo presages more openly stated views within Cuba and perhaps more complex, thoughtful views within Cuban-American communities:

> There's a twisted logic to the argument that Cuba's future looks so bright right now that President Fidel Castro is about to detonate a crisis. Castro has done this before, provoking the Mariel crisis in 1980 just when President Carter was

moving to improve relations with Cuba, and shooting down two Miami-based planes in 1996 when President Clinton seemed to be following suit.

I am not completely persuaded, but there are many Castro watchers in and out of Cuba who believe he does this on purpose — he torpedoes hopes for major progress so that he's not forced to relax his grip on the island.

Pope John Paul II and Cuba's Roman Catholic bishops are disillusioned with the lack of change inside the island since the Pope was there in January and called for the world to open itself to Cuba and Cuba to open itself to the world. . . .

'A lack of enthusiasm for change' is how Archbishop Pedro Meurice of Santiago de Cuba described the government's position for reporters Tuesday in the Vatican. John Paul called Meurice, Cardinal Jaime Ortega and 11 other Cuban bishops to Rome this week to discuss that very topic.

And two weeks ago the Cuban bishops issued a pastoral letter urging the government to respect all human rights and offering their support for any reforms.[55]

Recently, though anti-Castro discourse remains a force in contemporary popularized geopolitical imaginings, fissures have begun to develop.

Clues to the nature of this changing discourse are revealed only too clearly in the wake of the Elián González affair, an event that saw mutual interactions between formal and popular geopolitical discourse and caused tremendous cracks to appear in what had been a monolithic narrative interpreting Cuba's place. Even policymakers themselves attest to this: For example, Senator Charles Rangel (Democrat, New York), when interviewed on CNN in June 2000, remarked that the González affair was all about having voices other than those of the Cuban-American community determine Washington's Cuban policy. It marked a turning point when the interpretation of one sector of society was no longer hegemonic, thus legitimizing alternate views and authorizing alternate policies. Indeed, the story, which dominated media broadcasts throughout North America for nearly a year, was indicative of both the potency of geopolitical discourse and its socially constructed nature. The González incident was not to be a rallying point for anti-Castro fervor and the re-entrenchment of monolithic narratives concerning Cuba; instead, the incident caused the anti-Castro stance and narratives to weaken, by exposing the shaky legal foundations of such ideological leanings when applied to international situations and "other realities." The failure to have González declared a legal refugee and his return to his native Cuba signaled that the "evil island" mythology was losing its authority at the official level, fading in the light of a more multifaceted rather than unidimensional understanding of Cuba in a geopolitical context.

The Elián González affair may have polarized U.S. domestic politics, yet in doing so it allowed breathing room, authorizing a different way of responding to imperatives of international relations than those dictated by more conservative elements and their openly anti-Castro discourse. The latter was discordant with the internationalism of the Clinton administration, whose agenda appeared more flexible and economically contingent than those of previous administrations. As such, the new geopolitical discourse of Cuban-American relations assumed a remarkable multiplicity over which conservative elements have lost some of their hegemonic control.

Finally, although the Elián González affair proved to be major rallying point for a new geopolitical imagining of Cuba, this reassessment also was influenced by popular and political reaction to the pope's visit in 1998. Political analyst Gillian Gunn Clissold urges us, as follows, to appreciate the importance of the pontiff's presence on the island:

> Imagine a picture of the Pope, standing in the middle of the Florida Straits, opening a very large umbrella that covers a portion of the U.S. and Cuban territory. The umbrella provides protection for the elements of civil society in both countries, permitting people to say things that have long been on their minds, but which they were previously hesitant to state openly.[56]

Gunn Clissold argues that until then, "Domestic politics in Washington made it possible to propose dialogue with Cuba only if the proposal [was] dressed-up with sufficient anti-Castro language to make it acceptable to the conservative sector."[57] In the wake of the pope's visit, however, considerable response answered the call for humanitarian treatment of the island and its population. Realizing that the political terrain in the United States had somehow shifted and that new geopolitical imaginings had been prompted, even CANF began to reconsider the language and purpose of the Cuban embargo, while a "crescendo of newspaper articles" called for "reassessment of U.S. policy towards Cuba" and politicians responsible for the embargo legislation began to reassess the situation.[58]

This reassessment, in the early twenty-first century, led to the return of Elián González by U.S. authorities to Cuba. It also led to reassessment of the need to prohibit the shipment of food and medicine to Cuba, and it led to the possibility that, increasingly, U.S. citizens would openly support opening trade relations with the island nation. What contributed to the shifting landscape was not only the freedom to say things openly but also the mutually constitutive role played by popularized and formal geopolitical discourses. These discourses were subject to (re)imagination as the new political metaphors governing the analysis of spatial relations were constructed because Cuba was now legitimized (if only symbolically) by the pope's visit. Moreover, in the wake of the interest created in Cuba by the pope's visit, people in the United States were exposed to descriptions of Cuba that were not constructed for political purposes nor filtered exclusively through the Cuban-American community.

CONCLUSION

Karl B. Koth began Chapter Six with a discussion of the impact of neoliberalism on political stability in Cuba, recognizing that globalizing economies demand a political, economic, and ideological response by Cuban authorities as well by as civil society. The ongoing dynamic of adjusted expectation in response to global events is felt not only within Cuba but also in other Western Hemisphere countries in terms of their relationships with Cuba. Consequently, beginning with the pope's visit and culminating in the Elián González affair, a reexamination of the legitimacy of normative post-Cold War thinking about Cuba has been evident in both Canada and the United States. The result has been considerable diversification of monolithic geopolitical discourse in both countries. These events were turning points, allowing what can be described as a postmodern multiplicity of meaning to creep into previously monolithic, ideological visualizations held by both nations and allowing new possibilities to emerge. These new possibilities have become embedded within both formal and popularized geopolitical discourse — that is to say, within popularized media and news accounts as well as in the deliberations of political decisionmakers, so that these discourses have become mutually constitutive. Indeed, one of the most significant changes associated with formal geopolitical discourses, in both Canada and the United States, is the emergence of multiple narratives or discourses that authorize different imaginings and treatments of Cuba, which affect policies toward Cuba. These formal geopolitical discourses, one moving to the right in a reactionary process and the other becoming less and less conservative, are supported by changing popularized discourses in which Cuba and things Cuban are represented in new ways.

The immediate reasons for the shift are not always clear, but partisan domestic politics and increasing flows of media information that promulgate new images of Cuba seem to have contributed to the multiplicity of visions. Equally important is the legitimacy given to Cuba in a humanitarian context by the pope, who emphasized that the island was not one man's home but home to many. The pope's plea for more humanitarian treatment of Cubans resonated in an international climate that professes itself in favor of global interdependence and flows of capital, goods, and people and in favor of a singular style of democratic politics.

In the final analysis, although the most recent round of diversification of geopolitical discourse has had different consequences in the United States than in Canada, real similarities in the process of diversification speak to the need to understand Cuban relations in cultural as well as political and economic contexts. The formal construction of Cuba-U.S. and Cuba-Canada relations is intimately connected to popularized geopolitical accounts that reflect globalized "material conditions, social forces, and intellectual discourses that work to produce state action."[59] Analyses of the various geopolitical discourses surrounding Cuba, Canada, and the United States shed light on ways in which international relations are socially and intellectually constructed with each new round of change in global political and economic organization.[60]

In his analysis of contemporary geopolitical discourse, Tuathail asked if geopolitics can be postmodern and, if so, in what sense.[61] Based on our study, it would seem that the answer is yes — the result is a set of constructed discourses in which formal and popularized geopolitical narratives reinforce each other. Moreover, as the essays in this volume demonstrate, not only one, but several discourses represent a range of world pictures, possible under an increasingly globalizing, post-Cold War sense of internationalism. Therefore, even more is at stake than the history of a set of relations among a group of specific countries. Larger processes are revealed, and the evidence of changing political relationships also reveals changing ground rules at an international level. A slow shift toward Cuba is already occurring among policymakers and politicians and, ultimately, among the public in general. These groups — on a formal level, policymakers and politicians and, on a practical or popular level, the public — contribute to the construction of geopolitical discourse. This shift is a response to the exigencies of new geopolitical realities compatible with the new global order, although it may not be clear what the new global order ultimately will mean for the international community.

Notes

1. For full discussions, see Heather Nicol, 1999b, "The Geopolitical Discourse of Helms-Burton," in *Canada, the United States and Cuba: Helms-Burton and Its Aftermath,* ed. Heather N. Nicol (Kingston, Ontario: Centre for International Relations, Queen's University), 93-111.

2. For full discussions, see Nicol 1999b, 93-111.

3. Nicol 1999b. See also Gearoid Ó. Tuathail, 1993, "Japan as Threat: Geoeconomic Discourses on the USA-Japan Relationship in U.S. Civil Society," in *The Political Geography of the New World Order,* ed. Colin H. Williams (London: Bellhaven), 183.

4. This was the message reported by several U.S. newspapers after President Bush's first trip to Europe in the summer of 2001. Pictures of George W. Bush and Vladimir Putin were shown in many newspapers as front-page news under the caption "Let's Be Friends."

5. Originally founded in 1991, Brothers to the Rescue is an aerial rescue mission that purportedly has assisted in the rescue of some 4,200 rafters (as of May 2002) from the waters of the Gulf of Mexico and the Florida Straits. The group's small fleet of Cessna aircraft, piloted by leader José Basulto and about 20 other individuals, has coordinated many of its rescue missions with U.S. Coast Guard authorities. On February 24, 1996, two planes carrying three U.S citizens and one resident of Florida were shot down in international airspace by Cuban MiGs as they flew their civilian aircraft for one of their missions.

6. See Nicol 1999b, 93-111.

7. See *Canadian News Disc* for the years 1996-1998. This bibliographic tool is used for newspaper research.

8. Gearoid Ó. Tuathail has observed, "Geopolitical discourse is itself comprised of multiple sets of discursive elements at various levels. Practical, formal, or official geopolitical discourse refers to the activities and discourse of practitioners, foreign policymakers, and government bureaucracy, while popular geopolitical discourse is promoted through mass media, entertainment, print, and film." He suggests that geopolitics saturates everyday life and that its sites of production are "multiple and pervasive, both high (like a national security memorandum) and low (like the headline of a tabloid newspaper), visual (like the images that move states to act) and discursive (like the speeches that justify military actions)." The sites also can be "traditional (like religious motifs in foreign policy discourse) and postmodern (like information management and cyberwar)." See Gearoid Ó. Tuathail, 1998, "Postmodern Geopolitics? The Modern Geopolitical Imagination and Beyond," in *Rethinking Geopolitics,* ed. Gearoid Ó. Tuathail (London: Routledge), 5.

9. For further discussion, see John Agnew and Stuart Corbridge, 1995, *Mastering Space: Hegemony, Territory, and International Political Economy* (London: Routledge), as well as Tuathail 1998.

10. Tuathail 1998.

11. Nicol 1999b, 93-111.

12. Joanne P. Sharpe, 1998, "Reel Geographies of the New World Order: Patriotism, Masculinity, and Geopolitics in Post-Cold War American Movies," in *Rethinking Geopolitics*, ed. Gearoid Ó. Tuathail (London: Routledge), 154.

13. See Evan Potter, 1999, "Canada and Helms-Burton: Perils of Coalition Building," in *Canada, the United States, and Cuba: Helms-Burton and Its Aftermath*, ed. Heather N. Nicol (Kingston, Ontario: Centre for International Relations, Queen's University), 82.

14. Nicol 1999b, 107-109.

15. Nicol 1999b, 107-109.

16. Nicol 1999b, 107.

17. Analysis of Canada's response to Helms-Burton supports such a viewpoint. At both practical and popular levels, Canadian media, newspaper accounts, and formal political debates and discussions of Cuba in the wake of Helms-Burton were not as replete with pejorative descriptions of the island (or reductionist statements about its people) as their U.S. counterparts. In fact, Canadians had relatively little to say about Cuba itself. They focused instead on Canada-Cuba relations. Consequently, descriptors of Cuba used in popular and institutional Canadian descriptions of Cuba were overtly political and symbolic. For example, Cuba often was described as "David against Goliath." The latter, a popular biblical metaphor in which sympathy for the "little guy " (Cuba) is implicit, is used both in parliamentary debates on Cuba and in media accounts. The other implicit assumption — that the United States is Goliath — resonates with Canadians, who perceive Cuba as an ally holding out against U.S. domination.

18. Peter McKenna and John Kirk, 1999, "Canadian-Cuban Relations: Principled Pragmatism in Action?" in *Canada, the United States, and Cuba: Helms-Burton and Its Aftermath*, ed. Heather N. Nicol (Kingston, Ontario: Center for International Relations, Queen's University).

19. For discussion, see Canada, 1996, *Parliamentary Debates*, Ref. 09-20-1996 4488-English. As one member of Parliament notes in these debates, "The dispute between Cuba and the United States provides a patent example of the complexities in the relationship among the countries of the three Americas.... This conflict also reveals the close weave of political, economic, and commercial ties among the various trading partners."

20. James Rochlin, 1994, *Discovering the Americas: The Evolution of Canadian Foreign Policy toward Latin America* (Vancouver: University of British Columbia Press), 103.

21. For example, in 1997, when queried about Canada's ongoing response to Helms-Burton, Minister of Foreign Affairs Lloyd Axworthy replied that "the idea was to get it into a new forum, away from the World Trade Organization in which the [United States] said it would not participate, to the Organisation for Economic Cooperation and Development (OECD), where it will participate. I think it is a useful move because Canada has hit the table in those discussions on the multilateral agreement on investment. In fact, Canada has just raised the issue with respect to extra-territoriality and the Helms-Burton law. We will continue to pressure it." Canada, *1997 House of Commons Debates* 134 (138) March 5.

22. Canada, *1997 House of Commons Debates* 134 (156), April 15.

23. Nicol 1999b, 107.

24. Nicol 1999b, 107.

25. Nicol 1999b, 107.

26. See Tuathail 1998, 5.

27. *Calgary Herald,* July 10, 1996.

28. *Toronto Sun,* December 31, 1996; see also the *Hamilton Spectator*, July 20, 1996, and the *Halifax Daily News*, July 21, 1996.

29. *Calgary Herald*, July 10, 1996. See also the *Canadian News Disc*, 1996-2000, for listings of all Canadian newspaper articles that contain references to Cuba.

30. See, for example, the *Calgary Herald*, June 11-12, 1998.

31. See the *Vancouver Sun*, November 21, 1998, or the *Calgary Herald,* November 23, 1998.

32. *Edmonton Journal,* December 27, 1998.

33. Canada, *1998 House of Commons Debates* 135 (90), April 22.

34. Canada, *1998 House of Commons Debates* 135 (98), May 4.

35. Benjamin R. Barber, 1994, *Jihad vs. McWorld* (New York: Random House), and Basdeo and Hesketh, Part 2 of this volume.

36. Canada, *1998 House of Commons Debates* 135 (90), April 22.

37. *Vancouver Province*, December 24, 1998.

38. *Vancouver Sun*, December 9, 1998.

39. See the *Canadian News Disc*, 1996-2000, for listing of all Canadian newspaper articles that contain references to Cuba.

40. *Toronto Sun*, October 8, 1998.

41. See Barber 1994; also Basdeo and Hesketh, in Part 2 of this volume.

42. Barber 1994.

43. Timothy W. Luke and Gearoid Ó. Tuathail, 1998, "Global Flowmations, Local Fundamentalisms, and Fast Geopolitics," in *An Unruly World? Globalization, Governance, and Geography*, eds. Andrew Herod, Gearoid Ó. Tuathail, and Susan M. Roberts (London: Routledge), 23.

44. Williams 1993b.

45. Luke and Tuathail 1998, 74.

46. Brian Blout and Olwyn M. Blout, 1997, *Latin America and the Caribbean: A Systematic and Regional Survey* (New York: John Wiley and Sons), 307.

47. Nicol 1999b.

48. William G. Hyland, 1999, *Clinton's World: Remaking American Foreign Policy* (Westport, Conn.: Praeger).

49. Nicol 1999b, 101-102.

50. Arnold August, 1999, *Democracy in Cuba and the 1997-1998 Elections* (Havana: Instituto Cubano del Libro), 33.

51. *Miami Herald*, 1998, "In the Americas," January 11.

52. August, 1999, 32-33.

53. August, 1999, 33.

54. August, 1999, 33. Arnold August notes that even as late as January 1997, *The Miami Herald*, perhaps the most openly anti-Castro English-language newspaper in the United States, reported, "Fact-finding is one thing. Quite another is asking Fidel Castro whether he is torturing political prisoners and taking his 'No' to suggest that Americans need not be concerned about human-rights abuses in Cuba."

55. Juan O. Tamayo, 1998, "Will Castro Spark Crisis Once Again?" *Miami Herald*, June 11, 20A.

56. Gillian Gunn Clissold, 1998, "The Pope's Umbrella and the Door with the Rusty Hinge: The Scene in Washington and the Impact on Cuban Civil Society," in *Cuba Today: The Events Taking Place in Cuba and the Ensuing Issues for Canadian Policy*, a collection of background papers presented on March 6, 1998, at a roundtable of the Canadian Foundation for the Americas (Ottawa: FOCAL), 34.

57. Gunn Clissold 1998, 34.

58. Gunn Clissold 1998, 34.

59. Tuathail 1993.

60. For a discussion of what this might mean, see Agnew and Corbridge 1995.

61. Tuathail 1998.

References

Agnew, John, and Stuart Corbridge. 1995. *Mastering Space: Hegemony, Territory, and International Political Economy.* London: Routledge.

August, Arnold. 1999. *Democracy in Cuba and the 1997-1998 Elections.* Havana: Instituto Cubano del Libro.

Barber, Benjamin R. 1994. *Jihad vs. McWorld.* New York: Random House.

Blout, Brian, and Olwyn M. Blout. 1997. *Latin America and the Caribbean: A Systematic and Regional Survey.* New York: John Wiley and Sons.

Calgary Herald. 1996. July 10.

Calgary Herald. 1998. June 11-12.

Calgary Herald. 1998. November 21, November 23.

Canada. 1996. *Parliamentary Debates.* Ref. 09-20-1996 4488-English.

Canada. *1997 House of Commons Debates* 134: 138 and 156, March 5 and April 15.

Canada. *1998 House of Commons Debates* 135: 90 and 98, April 22 and May 4.

Canadian News Disc. 1996-2000. Electronic Resources.

Centeno, Miguel Ángel, and Mauricio Font, eds. 1997. *Toward a New Cuba? Legacies of a Revolution.* Boulder, Colo.: Lynne Rienner Publishers.

Edmonton Journal. 1998. December 27.

Fukuyama, Francis. 1992. *The End of History and the Last Man.* New York: Free Press.

Gunn Clissold, Gillian. 1997. "Cuban-U.S. Relations and the Process of Transition: Possible Consequences of Covert Agendas." In *Toward a New Cuba? Legacies of a Revolution,* eds. Miguel Ángel Centeno and Mauricio Font. Boulder, Colo.: Lynne Rienner Publishers.

Gunn Clissold, Gillian. 1998. "The Pope's Umbrella and the Door with the Rusty Hinge: The Scene in Washington and the Impact on Cuban Civil Society." In *Cuba Today: The Events Taking Place in Cuba and the Ensuing Issues for Canadian Policy.* Background papers presented on March 6, 1998, at a roundtable of the Canadian Foundation for the Americas. Ottawa: FOCAL.

Halifax Daily News. 1996. July 21.

Hamilton Spectator. 1996. July 20.

Herod, Andrew, Gearoid Ó. Tuathail, and Susan M. Roberts, eds. 1998. *An Unruly World? Globalization, Governance, and Geography.* London: Routledge.

Hyland, William G. 1999. *Clinton's World: Remaking American Foreign Policy.* Westport, Conn.: Praeger.

Kirk, John M. 1990. "Cuba at the Crossroads." *International Perspectives* 19 (8): 91-99.

Kirk, John M., and Peter McKenna. 1998. *Canada-Cuba Relations: The Other Good Neighbor Policy.* Gainesville, Fla.: University Press of Florida.

Kirk, John M., and Peter McKenna. 1999. "Canada, Cuba, and 'Constructive Engagement' in the 1990s." In *Canada, the United States, and Cuba: Helms-Burton and Its Aftermath,* ed. Heather N. Nicol. Kingston, Ontario: Centre for International Relations, Queen's University.

Luke, Timothy W., and Gearoid Ó. Tuathail. 1998. "Global Flowmations, Local Fundamentalisms, and Fast Geopolitics." In *An Unruly World? Globalization, Governance, and Geography,* eds. Andrew Herod, Gearoid Ó. Tuathail, and Susan M. Roberts. London: Routledge.

McKenna, Peter, and John Kirk. 1999. "Canadian-Cuban Relations: Principled Pragmatism in Action?" In *Canada, the United States, and Cuba: Helms-Burton and Its Aftermath,* ed. Heather N. Nicol. Kingston, Ontario: Centre for International Relations, Queen's University.

Miami Herald. 1998. "In the Americas." January 11.

Nicol, Heather, N., ed. 1999a. *Canada, the United States, and Cuba: Helms-Burton and Its Aftermath,* Kingston, Ontario: Centre for International Relations, Queen's University.

Nicol, Heather N. 1999b. "The Geopolitical Discourse of Helms-Burton." In *Canada, the United States, and Cuba: Helms Burton and Its Aftermath,* ed. Heather N. Nicol. Kingston, Ontario: Centre for International Relations, Queen's University.

Potter, Evan. 1999. "Canada and Helms-Burton: Perils of Coalition Building." In *Canada, the United States, and Cuba: Helms-Burton and Its Aftermath,* ed. Heather N. Nicol. Kingston, Ontario: Centre for International Relations, Queen's University.

Rochlin, James. 1994. *Discovering the Americas: The Evolution of Canadian Foreign Policy toward Latin America.* Vancouver: University of British Columbia Press.

Sharpe, Joanne P. 1998. "Reel Geographies of the New World Order: Patriotism, Masculinity, and Geopolitics in Post-Cold War American Movies." In *Rethinking Geopolitics,* ed. Gearoid Ó. Tuathail. London: Routledge.

Tamayo, Juan O. 1998. "Will Castro Spark Crisis Once Again?" *Miami Herald,* June 11, 20A.

Toronto Sun. 1996. December 31.

Toronto Sun. 1998. October 8.

Tuathail, Gearoid Ó. 1993. "Japan as Threat: Geoeconomic Discourses on the USA-Japan Relationship in U.S. Civil Society." In *The Political Geography of the New World Order,* ed. Colin H. Williams. London: Bellhaven.

Tuathail, Gearoid Ó. 1998. "Postmodern Geopolitics? The Modern Geopolitical Imagination and Beyond." In *Rethinking Geopolitics,* ed. Gearoid Ó.Tuathail. London: Routledge.

Tuathail, Gearoid Ó., ed. 1998. *Rethinking Geopolitics.* London: Routledge.

Vancouver Sun. 1998. November 21.

Vancouver Sun. 1998. December 9.

Vancouver Province. 1998. December 24.

Williams, Colin H., ed. 1993a. *The Political Geography of the New World Order.* London: Bellhaven.

Williams, Colin H. 1993b. "Towards a New World Order: European and American Perspectives." In *The Political Geography of the New World Order,* ed. Colin H. Williams. London: Bellhaven.

Abbreviations and Acronyms

AI	Amnesty International
BCNI	Business Council on National Issues
CALACS	Canadian Association for Latin American and Caribbean Studies
CANF	Cuban American National Foundation
CBI	Caribbean Basin Initiative
CDA	Cuban Democracy Act
CDR	Committees for the Defense of the Revolution (Comités de Defensa de la Revolución)
CIA	U.S. Central Intelligence Agency
CIDA	Canadian International Development Agency
CLC	Canadian Labour Congress
CMEA	Council for Mutual Economic Assistance
CNN	Cable News Network
COMECON	Council for Mutual Economic Aid
CTC	Confederation of Cuban Workers (Central de Trabajadores Cubanos)
CUSO	Canadian University Students Overseas
DEA	U.S. Drug Enforcement Agency
DOD	U.S. Department of Defense
EU	European Union
FAR	Revolutionary Armed Forces (Fuerzas Armadas Revolucionarias)
FMLN	Farabundo Martí National Liberation Front (Frente Farabundo Martí para la Liberación Nacional)
FOCAL	Canadian Foundation for the Americas (Fundación Canadiense para las Américas)
FTAA	Free Trade Area of the Americas
G-7	Group of Seven
G-8	Group of Eight
GST	Goods and Services Tax
ISLA	Iran-Libya Sanctions Act
LIBERTAD	Cuban Liberty and Democratic Solidarity (LIBERTAD) Act (Helms-Burton Act)
MINFAR	Revolutionary Armed Forces Ministry (Ministerio de las Fuerzas Armadas Revolucionarias)

MININT	Ministry of the Interior (Ministerio del Interior)
MTT	Territorial Militia Troops (Milicias de Tropas Territoriales)
NAFTA	North American Free Trade Agreement
NATO	North Atlantic Treaty Organization
NGO	Non-governmental organization
OAS	Organization of American States
OECD	Organisation for Economic Cooperation and Development
PAHO	Pan American Health Organization
PM	Prime Minister (Canada)
PRC	People's Republic of China
SOLIDARIDAD	Cuban Solidarity Act of 1998
UN	United Nations
UNITA	National Union for the Total Independence of Angola (União Nacional para a Independência Total de Angola)
WTO	World Trade Organization

Contributors

Sahadeo Basdeo teaches at Okanagan University College in Kelowna, British Columbia. Formerly Trinidad and Tobago's minister of external affairs and international trade and professor of history at the University of the West Indies, he has written extensively on Caribbean issues, including definitive works on labor and Caribbean foreign affairs. His most recent book, coauthored with Graeme S. Mount, is *The Foreign Relations of Trinidad and Tobago 1962-2000: The Case of a Small State in the Global Arena.*

Christine Climenhage earned her Ph.D. from Cambridge University in the Faculty of Social and Political Sciences. She holds a Bachelor of Honours degree from the University of Western Ontario as well as masters' degrees in international political economy from the Norman Paterson School of International Affairs at Carleton University and in administration and politics from the College of Europe. The author of numerous studies on various Latin American topics, Dr. Climenhage is an economic policy analyst at the Canadian Embassy in Havana, Cuba.

Daniel W. Fisk is deputy director of the Kathryn and Shelby Cullom Davis Institute for International Studies at the Heritage Foundation, Washington, D.C. He is a member of the Council on Foreign Relations and was a member of its 1998 and 2000 independent task forces on U.S.-Cuba relations. Mr. Fisk is also an adjunct fellow of the Americas Program of the Center for Strategic and International Studies (CSIS) and a member of the board of directors of the Institute for U.S.-Cuba Relations. During the 2000 term, he was chairman of the Foreign Claims Committee of the American Bar Association's Section of International Law and Practice. Mr. Fisk has served on the staffs of the U.S. Senate Foreign Relations Committee and U.S. House of Representatives Foreign Affairs Committee, where he was responsible for Western Hemisphere issues.

Ian Hesketh is a graduate student in the history department of York University, Toronto, Ontario. A graduate of Okanagan University College, he is currently pursuing his doctoral degree in political theory and philosophy of history.

John M. Kirk teaches in the Department of Spanish at Dalhousie University in Halifax, Nova Scotia, and is one of Canada's foremost Cuba experts. Professor Kirk has written numerous books and articles on Canada-Cuba relations, including, with Peter McKenna, *Canada-Cuba Relations: The Other Good Neighbor Policy.*

Hal Klepak is professor of history at the Royal Military College in Kingston, Ontario. A well-known specialist on Cuban and Latin American history and war studies, he has spent considerable time in the region and has written extensively on its strategic and political issues.

Karl B. Koth teaches Latin American history at Okanagan University College in Kelowna, British Columbia, where he also serves as associate dean in the Faculty of Arts. Originally from the Caribbean, he spends considerable time traveling in the region. He is the author of *Waking the Dictator: Veracruz, the Struggle for Federalism and the Mexican Revolution, 1824-1927.*

Peter McKenna is assistant professor in the Department of Political and Canadian Studies at Mount Saint Vincent University in Halifax, Nova Scotia. He has published widely on Canada-Cuba relations, Canada-OAS affairs, and Canada-Latin America relations.

Heather N. Nicol is assistant professor in the Department of Geosciences at the State University of West Georgia, in Carrollton, where she teaches economic, political, and cultural geography. Her research focuses upon the emerging political geography of the Caribbean Basin under conditions of globalization.

Stephen J. Randall is professor of history and dean of the Faculty of Social Sciences at the University of Calgary in Calgary, Alberta. He is the author or editor of many books on aspects of inter-American relations, most recently, *The Caribbean Basin: An International History,* coauthored with Graeme S. Mount and David Bright.

Index